The Manly Modern

Sexuality Studies Series

This series focuses on original, provocative, scholarly research examining from a range of perspectives the complexity of human sexual practice, identity, community, and desire. Books in the series explore how sexuality interacts with other aspects of society, such as law, education, feminism, racial diversity, the family, policing, sport, government, religion, mass media, medicine, and employment. The series provides a broad public venue for nurturing debate, cultivating talent, and expanding knowledge of human sexual expression, past and present.

Members of the editorial board are:
Barry Adam, Sociology and Anthropology, University of Windsor
Blye Frank, Medical Education, Dalhousie University
Didi Khayatt, Education, York University
Philinda Masters, Resources for Feminist Research, OISE/University of Toronto
Janice Ristock, Women's Studies, University of Manitoba
Becki Ross, Sociology and Anthropology, University of British Columbia
Gamal Abdel-Shehid, Physical Education and Recreation, University of Alberta
Tom Waugh, Mel Hoppenheim School of Cinema, Concordia University

Other volumes in the series are:
Masculinities without Men? Female Masculinity in Twentieth-Century Fictions, by Jean Bobby Noble
Every Inch a Woman: Phallic Possession, Femininity, and the Text, by Carellin Brooks
Queer Youth in the Province of the "Severely Normal," by Gloria Filax
Sexing the Teacher: School Sex Scandals and Queer Pedagogies, by Sheila L. Cavanagh

Christopher Dummitt

The Manly Modern
Masculinity in Postwar Canada

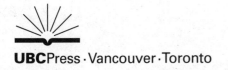

UBCPress · Vancouver · Toronto

16 15 14 13 12 11 10 09 08 07   5 4 3 2 1

Printed in Canada on ancient-forest-free paper (100% post-consumer recycled) that is processed chlorine- and acid-free, with vegetable-based inks.

Library and Archives Canada Cataloguing in Publication

Dummitt, Chris, 1973-
    The manly modern : masculinity in postwar Canada / Christopher Dummitt.

(Sexuality studies series)
Includes bibliographical references and index.
ISBN-13: 978-0-7748-1274-0

    1. Men – Canada – Social conditions – 20th century. 2. Masculinity – Social aspects – Canada – History – 20th century. 3. Canada – Civilization – 20th century. 4. Men – British Columbia – Vancouver – Social conditions – 20th century – Case studies. 5. Masculinity – Social aspects – British Columbia – Vancouver – History – 20th century – Case studies. I. Title. II. Series.

HQ1090.7.C2D845 2007   305.31'097109045   C2006-906249-8

Canadä

UBC Press gratefully acknowledges the financial support for our publishing program of the Government of Canada through the Book Publishing Industry Development Program (BPIDP), and of the Canada Council for the Arts, and the British Columbia Arts Council.

This book has been published with the help of a grant from the Canadian Federation for the Humanities and Social Sciences, through the Aid to Scholarly Publications Programme, using funds provided by the Social Sciences and Humanities Research Council of Canada, and with the help of the K.D. Srivastava Fund.

Printed and bound in Canada by Friesens
Set in Stone by Artegraphica Design Co. Ltd.
Copy editor: Robert Lewis
Proofreader and indexer: Dianne Tiefensee

The photograph of the Fraser Wilson mural that appears on p. 1 was kindly provided by Shannon Solby of the Maritime Labour Centre in Vancouver.

UBC Press
The University of British Columbia
2029 West Mall
Vancouver, BC V6T 1Z2
604-822-5959 / Fax: 604-822-6083
www.ubcpress.ca

Contents

Acknowledgments / vi

1 Introduction: The Manly Modern / 1

2 Coming Home / 29

3 At Work / 53

4 In the Mountains / 77

5 Before the Courts and on the Couch / 101

6 On the Road / 125

7 Conclusion: Manly Modernism in Hindsight / 151

Notes / 163

Bibliography / 197

Index / 213

Acknowledgments

Brevity may be the soul of wit but it appears, in recent years, to be the antithesis of academic thanks. At the risk of appearing outlandishly out of date, I would like to thank those who had a direct and important role in getting this book to press. This includes two efficient and amiable editors at UBC Press, Jean Wilson and Ann Macklem; the anonymous reviewers of the manuscript; and several inspiring academics who helped at the dissertation stage, including Karen Ferguson, Jack Little, my advisor Tina Loo, Bob McDonald, and Keith Walden. It also includes some institutions – Simon Fraser University and the University of Manitoba – whose financial support was key to the whole process of researching, writing, and eating. The Aid to Scholarly Publications Program provided a grant to support publication, for which I am thankful. And most importantly I want to thank – despite the utter inadequacy of the word in this context – my wife Juliet Sutcliffe and my family. I hope they know why; I certainly do.

The Manly Modern

1
Introduction: The Manly Modern

If you wanted a postcard image of mid-twentieth-century high modernism, you could do a lot worse than Fraser Wilson's majestic mural of an imagined British Columbia. Painted in 1947, it is clearly looking over its shoulder at the realist murals of the 1930s with a great relief that times have changed, work and industry have returned, depression and war are ended, and progress is finally possible. The colours are brighter, the drudgery reduced, and the signs of progress more pronounced. It is all there: the triumphant and thorough control of the natural world, nature turned into bounty, cleanly, efficiently, through work that is tough and rugged but completely manageable. Everything is connected, from mines and forests to harbours and factories. There is no danger here, only risk, well planned for and skilfully supervised. Of course, this mural is a working man's modernism. The skyscrapers are in the background, and the managers, scientists, entrepreneurs, and engineers are absent. Instead, we see mine and machine, logger and welder, hard-working men cutting, drilling, and driving forward progress. Middle-class men had their own murals in these years: newspaper stories, radio broadcasts, celebratory books that told of their role in making possible this brave, new, and expertly planned world. But whether they told of scientists or lumberjacks, threshing machines or social surveys, images of postwar high modernism, Wilson's mural included, had one thing in common: men.

In the mural, this is fairly easy to see because there is no alternative: there are no women. All of the movers and makers of progress – miners, lumberjacks, welders, and fishers – are men. But the plot goes much further than the people in central casting. The mural's real stars are its ideas: the belief in the rational control of nature, in the possibilities of planned progress, and in the skilful transformation of dangers into manageable risks. And it is these ideas that are gendered. For much of the history of technocratic modernity, many of its key values – expertise, instrumental reason, stoical self-control – have been understood to be masculine. Between the end of the Second World War and the late 1960s, the importance of these gendered ideas grew substantially. The two terms – masculinity and modernity – could have been used almost synonymously in many incantations. In taking up his high-modernist vision, then, Wilson's mural not only extolled workers and the idea of progress, but also pushed into the limelight a particular style of masculinity that shared the modernist traits of reasoned and expert control. This book is an exploration of this profoundly important, yet often overlooked, historical link between masculinity and modernity in postwar Canada.

The timing is key. The ideal of the manly modern came into prominence in these years because of a set of historically specific circumstances with two major components: first, the success of the technocratic structures and values of industrial modernity in establishing themselves as the status quo in Canadian living; and second, the desire to reaffirm gender divisions after the flux of depression and war and in light of the relative lessening importance of other patriarchal controls in the family and economy. In other words, the manly modern ideal fitted nicely into an increasingly modernized Canada in which patriarchal privilege had been shorn of some of its more traditional supports. In this context, those who linked ideal masculinity with the benefits of modern technology and progress provided contemporary justifications for gender hierarchies that were under threat. They updated patriarchy.

Manly modernism took on a renewed significance in these years, but it was not new. The belief in men's greater rationality goes back at least to the Greeks, and as Robert Connell notes, it "is a deep-seated assumption of European philosophy."[1] From this perspective, men's alleged ability to objectively assess situations and themselves and to coolly make decisions has made them everything from great leaders to brilliant scientists. The always assumed counterpoint, even if unspoken, is the illogical and potentially hysterical woman, or in more positive renditions, the intuitive and emotional but ultimately less rational woman. While this relationship is sometimes presented as being complementary, it has nonetheless frequently been invoked to justify gender inequality. The importance of reason and rational efficiency to post-Enlightenment and especially industrial societies has meant that this patriarchal notion has become increasingly important since at least the eighteenth century. There is, however, something particularly important about how the idea of rational man came to be invoked in postwar Canada.

For those eager to bolster the power of masculinity in the postwar years, this connection between the manly and the modern could not have been more propitious. The postwar years represented the high point of the modernist project in Canada, the time when affluence, scientific development, and the emerging welfare state combined to make it seem as though Canadians could manipulate the environment for the ever greater social good. A slew of experts took on more and more significant roles in shaping the economy and society. Undoubtedly, the process had begun much earlier,[2] but it reached its apex with the Second World War and its aftermath. By this time, governments had thoroughly integrated experts into the public service and the political decision-making process. Wartime exigencies accentuated the reliance on experts. As with the Great War, but this time with more rigour, the values of efficiency and planning became watchwords for success. And even after the war, these ideas continued in civilian guises, shaping an expanded welfare state and a Keynesian-tinged economic policy whose backbone was a belief that experts should, and could, shape social processes that only several years earlier had been considered beyond control. In the personal realm, a range of experts, including psychologists, psychiatrists, and social workers, took on an even more important role in influencing the mental and cultural processes of the postwar generations.[3] Some Canadians fretted about the excesses of rationality and warned against a too heavy reliance on science at the expense of human values, but their pleas for caution only confirmed the extent to which modern values had become the new normal.[4] When some postwar Canadians linked modern values with masculinity, then, this had the effect of privileging certain kinds of men by linking them with the dominant spirit of the times. At a moment when the modern represented the promise of ultimately controlling risks – whether social, psychological, or economic – masculinity's connection with the modern simultaneously established the social significance of risk management for men.

The connection between men, modernity, and risk was not new, but given the challenge to other bastions of male authority, these ideas were increasingly drawn upon to boost a flagging set of gender relations. The years after the Second World War saw a backlash against the threat of gender uncertainty and ambiguity that had been brought on by depression and war. The main facts of this story are fairly well known, but they do bear repeating, as they have not before been connected with changing ideas of gender and modernity. The Great Depression had cast doubt on a number of longstanding beliefs about the natural divisions between the sexes, perhaps the most important being that men were the natural breadwinners in a family. By throwing many Canadian men out of work, the Depression had simultaneously created the conditions for gender anxiety as men and women wondered how – or whether – the "normal" set of family economic roles could be re-established. No sooner had the Depression ended than wartime conditions created new worries. Wartime industry demanded women workers in paid employment, much of it the kind of work that had previously been performed by men. Although every effort went into insisting that such work was feminine, this cultural whitewashing could not completely hide the fact of increased womanly independence and the breakdown of gendered workplace categories previously considered sacrosanct. This social, and gender, tumult was the backdrop to many Canadians' desire, immediately after the war, that everything should return to normal.[5] It was hoped that Canadians' pent-up desires to marry and start families could now be realized and that the idealized type of family life, with a male breadwinner and female homemaker, could be re-established.[6] This response was the backlash of a generation too familiar with turbulence. But it was also, on a social and political level, a large-scale re-emphasis on a set of patriarchal values whose force had been diminished.

In this context, the idea of the manly modern provided an explanation of men's and women's differences and a powerful justification for inequality. It contained a neat logic of gender distinctions, presenting men's leading roles in the public sphere as a natural outgrowth of basic proclivities, which was not to say that women could not work but simply that men were better suited by reason of their ingrown capabilities to do many of the most valuable kinds of work. In an age ostensibly devoted to democratic family life and when many of the public signposts of gender difference such as voting restrictions had been removed, the manly modern ideal was appropriately contemporary. Postwar Canadians could look askance at the backward Victorians and their patriarchal families even as they continued to support a quite similar structure of family life. Manly modernism operated on a similar type of logic as the earlier ideal of the Christian gentleman, with its emphasis on manly virtue and stoical repression, but it did so without religious overtones.

The renunciation of the manly modern was mental and secular, not spiritual.[7] In other words, manly modernism was significant in the post-war years because it seemed to provide a convincing and up-to-date justification for a gender system under attack.

In teasing out how manly modernism worked in the postwar years, this book takes a new approach. Previous historians have spent a great deal of time explaining the changing position of men and women in the home and workplace. We know much about how the breadwinner-homemaker family has been both challenged and supported from the 1940s to the present day.[8] What remain to be explored are the other constellations of cultural values that influenced Canadians' thoughts about gender and how people put these thoughts into practice. In particular, men's position as family breadwinner – an issue well covered in the historiography – was an important part of postwar masculinity, but the basis for its justification reached far outside the family to cultural beliefs that need much more enquiry. Ironically, in an attempt to compensate for the prejudices of the age, scholarly work on men in the postwar years focuses mainly on men in the home. This book certainly takes men's position as breadwinner into account, but it also delves into a related but separate gender ideal: that of the manly modern. This book is an attempt to show what happened when manly modernism came into greater prominence – the cultural logic that it embodied, its role in reasserting men's privileged social position, and ultimately, its unanticipated consequences.

This final issue of manly modernism's unintended consequences provides the basis for this book's second main theme and argument. Although the ideal of the reasonable man became ever more important in shoring up patriarchy in these years, the consequences of this support were not always straightforward. Far from being clear-cut sources of power and authority, modernist values and institutions created a sense of alienation in many men. As often as postwar Canadians equated masculinity with modernity, they also, paradoxically, suggested that being modern was antithetical to being masculine. Many critics argued that various features of modern life – from bureaucratic rationality to suburban living – harmed an allegedly primal masculinity; they suggested that men *suffered* by becoming modern, that they were hard-done-by and thus deserved special treatment. Popular culture represented these concerns in a variety of ways, ranging from the fascination with such anti-responsibility figures as the playboy and the young rebel to the victimization of such stock figures as the beleaguered breadwinner, the mistreated veteran, and the potentially emasculated "Organization

Man."[9] This approach represented men as modernity's victims, stretched out upon the altar of progress, baring their chests for the mechanical sacrificial knife.

Where did these attitudes come from? How could modernity be inherently masculine and, at the same time, hurtful to men? The answer lies in two areas: first, in the processes of alienation that are integral to the modernist project; and second, in how this alienation was mapped onto other social hierarchies such as class and race. That modernity creates alienation is widely recognized. The modernist celebration of rationality, efficiency, and control represents an unbalanced selection of human traits and values. When this unbalanced mix came to be ever more thoroughly established in the institutions and processes that affected individual lives, the result was a widespread social disciplining, a shutting off of alternative ways of being human, with the attendant widespread feeling that something primal, some integral part of life, was missing. Marxists capture this well in their discussion of the effects of capitalism on workers. Under capitalism, workers are estranged both from the process of their labour – how it is done, its timing, pace, and quality – and from the end product of their labour, as they have little control over what it achieves. Ultimately, this leads to an estrangement from something essential both in themselves and in their relations with others.[10] While some Marxist scholars claim that alienation needs to be understood as a product primarily of capitalism, this type of alienation is in fact a feature of the modernist project more generally. Everything from large-scale bureaucracy and systems of expertise to rationally planned cities and living spaces has had the unintended consequence of creating a sense of alienation in those moderns who otherwise benefited from these attempts to better plan and control the environment. Alienation was integral to high modernism.

The sense of an alienated modern masculinity grew directly out of this connection between modernity and manhood. As modernist beliefs and practices came to be ever more closely associated with an idealized masculinity, the effect on individual men was contradictory. On the one hand, they benefited en masse by their association with a dominant cultural symbol and by the continued insistence on gender differences. Yet on the other hand, the mechanisms for supporting these gender differences created their own hardships. Manly modernism produced a widespread sense of alienation. It is this alienation that lay at the heart of the postwar ambivalence about the effect of modernity on men.[11]

Alienation was also a kind of resistance. The consequences of modernist alienation were meted out more severely to men already set aside because of differences of race and class.[12] By defining masculinity's interests as analogous to those of technology and progress, manly modernism involved a regulation of individual men and groups of men who failed to match up to these standards. Manly modernism privileged rational and expert masculinity even as it sought to control other forms of manly aggression, passion, and the working-class or racial "other."[13] Middle-class men may have felt some unease about the constrained nature of white-collar work, but working-class men were usually more thoroughly disciplined by workplace regulations that threatened their control over their work and the feelings of competence with which that work was associated. In other words, manly modernism did not uniformly benefit all men, and its side effects were more keenly felt by working-class men and racial minorities.

We need, however, to be careful to see these complaints in their larger context. There is something more to these complaints about modernity than simply resistance or antimodernism. Yes, working-class men – and veterans specifically, to take one example – suffered alienation because of the liberal bias of corporate capitalism that was built into the bureaucratic processes that they were made to navigate. But it was not a universal human alienation. It was an estrangement from the prerogatives of male power. It was an estrangement from the full benefits of male citizenship that would have then placed them above women and other men. The essential point to notice here is that the presumed wholeness that was seen to be lacking implied the possible existence of a more thorough and appropriate gendered society in which men's worth and competence were adequately rewarded. Manly modernism's "others" cannot simply be seen as victims – whether of capitalism, the state, or some other modern process – because their complaints arose from their being excluded from power, not from the problems of power in its own right.

Making Sense of Modernity

This book explores both sides of manly modernism – its role in rejuvenating postwar patriarchy and its ambiguous effects on individual men and groups of men – in a series of case studies centred on one city, Vancouver, in the years between 1945 and the late 1960s. In focusing exclusively on Vancouver, this book looks to one of the most important Canadian cities in a period that was increasingly both urban and suburban. In this sense, the experience of those in Vancouver was characteristic of social and economic changes occurring throughout Canada in these years. I do not make an argument for the uniqueness of the Vancouver experience of manly modernism (such an assessment would need more studies with which to compare the Vancouver experience). Instead, my focus is on a modern culture that was rooted in urban centres like Vancouver and that was increasingly the norm. The earlier twentieth-century dream of a rural Canada based on small independent farmsteads increasingly came to be seen as moribund in these years. Indeed, the transformation to an increasingly urbanized life could not have been clearer: the main source of new migrants to Vancouver in the war years and after was the Prairies. As mechanized and corporate agriculture took over on the Prairies, more and more Prairie residents moved to the cities, particularly to Vancouver.[14] Such trends continued in myriad other areas of life. The power of mass consumer culture in this era – everything from commercialized music to television – meant that new technologies and the corporate messages with which they were imbued needed to be negotiated at an accelerated rate. All of these trends predated the postwar years, but the era's economic and political stability meant that the process of modernization itself came to be more of a dominant concern. The ideal of the manly modern had a home in this modern urbanized Canada, where large corporations and institutions were increasingly the norm, where individuals' daily lives were more bound up in corporate and government structures of management, entertainment, and expertise, and where these trends were both celebrated and fretted over.[15]

What did it mean to be modern in postwar Vancouver? In the first instance, the discussion of modernity must be more description than definition.[16] The most obvious beginning is with the war, with the emphasis on planning and efficiency, with centralized controls on labour, production, prices, and myriad other aspects of daily life. Here, the possibilities of, and belief in, control were essential. But the call to action did not merely come from the exigencies of wartime, although the urgency of national peril made the desire for modernist schemes that much more pressing. As other historians have shown, the culture of planning that flowered in the war years had been tended through the early years of the twentieth century. It took root with the progressive impulse of the social gospel before and during the Great War; it sprouted in the growing role of the practical sciences in both public life and the universities in the 1920s; and it grew to adolescence dealing with the seemingly insoluble problems of the Depression in the following decade.[17] Before this, capitalists added their own contribution, improving techniques of workplace control and efficiency through the schemes of Frederick Winslow Taylor's scientific management and carefully formulated systems of corporate paternalism meant to create a more pliable workforce.[18] And we must not forget the many attempts to create order out of the social chaos wrought by industrial capitalism. In this sense, the ancestors of wartime planning and efficiency were many and included the industrial exhibitions of the nineteenth century that sought to assure Canadians of the ultimate beneficence of capital; they were the urban planners who attempted to create more rational and rule-bound cities; and they included Depression-era leftists who saw the answers to economic problems in comprehensive state planning.[19]

The high modernism of the postwar years clearly did not emerge out of a vacuum; its singularity lay in the longstanding period of economic boom that allowed the promises of previous years to become the realities of the present. After the war, Canadians retreated from much of the emphasis on hyper-efficiency that had characterized the war years, but a widespread belief in the possibilities and benefits of control remained. This was reflected in a variety of ways. Partly, it meant managing economic and social life through the welfare state, and a host of new programs came into place, including the Veterans Charter, family allowances (1944), a new old-age pension (1951), and hospital insurance (1957). This was all part of what might be called a "new liberalism," one that had been forced to give up slightly on its laissez-faire values in the face of political challenges from the left. It subsequently found a home in modest calls for some kinds of social and economic controls, if only to prevent an even more radical alternative. The preventive nature of the new liberalism can clearly be seen in the way that control figured in another area of the period's political culture: Cold War politics. Here, dominant elements in the political culture stressed the need to contain the alleged communist menace both abroad and at home. The rationality of the manly modern was often in this way a statement of capitalist liberal values, a presumed difference from the irrational and authoritarian communist.[20] In the realm of technology, efforts to tame the natural environment were evident in the completion of several megaprojects, most notably the deepening of the St. Lawrence Seaway and Newfoundland's Churchill Falls hydroelectric project. When these diverse strands were combined with such developments as the democratization of car ownership and technological transformations in the workplace, there was seemingly good reason to believe that the social and natural environment could be continuously manipulated as a matter of course. Although high modernism predated these years, the postwar era saw its consolidation as the nation's dominant ideology.[21]

The postwar modernist project in British Columbia mirrored national trends, albeit in a radicalized fashion. The still frontier-like conditions in much of the province in 1945 gave British Columbia's version of high modernism a revolutionary shine. It was not so much that modernization occurred differently in British Columbia as it was that there was such a short distance between the premodern and the modern, between the absence and the shocking presence of industry, urbanization, and technological development. Building on the strength of wartime prosperity and continuing from the same conditions after the war, the province's population grew from just over 800,000 in 1941 to more than 2 million in 1971. Economically, governments, corporations, and unions emphasized planned and sustained growth. In a province so broken up by mountains and water, governments considered transportation initiatives to be the main impetus to development. Earlier governments had placed great importance on transportation, but the postwar governments of John Hart (1941-47), Byron Johnson (1947-52), and especially W.A.C. Bennett and the Social Credit Party (1952-72) expanded resources devoted to such projects to unprecedented levels. A Ministry of Highways was created in 1955 and quickly became one of the most important government portfolios. Commenting on the dominant ethic of the time, political historian Martin Robin characterizes Social Credit's highways minister, Philip Gaglardi, as "the high priest of a secular religion long practised in a province fragmented into isolated regional and cultural entities ... [whose inhabitants] worshipped the highways, by-ways, and thru-ways, things of brick, mortar and asphalt, which brought them into closer communion."[22]

Aside from highways, governments took on a great many other projects, including expanding the provincial railway, the Pacific Great Eastern, and building new bridges. Devotees of what Robin calls "the ideology of raw growth," the Social Credit party felt no compunction about using the state to shape the economic life of the province. As the provincial historian Jean Barman notes, "a strong verbal commitment to free enterprise cheerfully coexisted with a willingness to use the power of the state to set capitalism's direction."[23] In 1958 the Social Credit government took over Black Ball, the private company that ran the province's ferries, and created the BC Ferry Corporation. In an even more dramatic move, Bennett provincialized BC Electric in 1961 and then joined it with BC Power to create the BC Hydro and Power Authority in 1962 to develop hydroelectric energy on the Peace River. Such state initiatives went hand-in-hand with the continuing private development of forestry, mining, fishing, and other provincial resources. These years saw great expansion in these industries but also consolidation of corporate ownership and increased use of technology to manipulate the natural world in order to feed what Bennett and others liked to call "the good life."

Vancouver's history is replete with the same moments of sudden disjuncture between what used to be and what is. Although the city was not favoured by the provincial government for most of these years, it remained the centre of provincial economic and cultural life. The population of Greater Vancouver almost tripled between 1941 and 1971, going from 374,000 in the early 1940s to more than 1 million inhabitants in the early 1970s. And although this growth occurred in all areas, suburban growth far outpaced that of the city centre. Whereas the City of Vancouver had made up almost 80 percent of the total Greater Vancouver population in 1941, this number shrank to just under 40 percent thirty years later. North and West Vancouver on the north shore of Burrard Inlet became, along with Burnaby, Surrey, Richmond, New Westminster, Coquitlam, and Port Moody, large suburban centres of social and economic activity that changed the nature of urban life and drastically reduced the region's amount of undeveloped land. Early baby boomers who grew up in Vancouver might still remember milk delivery by horse-drawn cart, iceboxes, and furnaces fed with sawdust, but these rustic aspects of Vancouver's past quickly disappeared as the city became a much more regulated, automobile-centred, and densely populated place to live. Growing up in Vancouver in these years meant viscerally experiencing the capacity of governments, corporations, and individuals to radically alter the environment with the hope of creating a modern city.[24]

Indeed, this may be what helped to make Vancouver such a leading light in modernist architecture in the postwar years. The University of British Columbia established a School of Architecture in 1946 and named Fred Lasserre, modernist fan of Le Corbusier, as its first director. The Modernist architecture of Lasserre and others (like the young Arthur Erikson, who designed Simon Fraser University) prided itself on its totalizing vision, which did away with previous traditions and histories for the sake of the architect's own authority. Although it did try to accommodate itself to the local region and landscape, such natural elements merely acted as one more ingredient through which the architect could design his total vision. Lasserre claimed that, in British Columbia, "we can build the best school of architecture in the country [because] we have no old wood to clear away."[25]

All of this gives us a thick description of modern life in postwar Canada, British Columba, and Vancouver, but the theoretical underpinnings of modern existence still need further explanation. In one sense, of course, modernity refers to the historical process of tumultuous and ongoing transformation that resulted from the revolutions in science, governance, and economy in seventeenth-century Europe and that has since spread to encompass the globe.[26] It encapsulates all those features of the historical record – the development of nation states, industrialization, the spread of worldwide capitalism, massive urbanization – that are usually studied individually but that are in fact part of a larger process that we can refer to as modernity. To truly understand modernity, however, we need much more than this. Marshall Berman has given us one of the most evocative (and often quoted) descriptions of modernity. "To be modern," Berman argues, "is to find ourselves in an environment that promises us adventure, power, joy, growth, transformation of ourselves and the world – and, at the same time, that threatens to destroy everything we have, everything we know, everything we are ... It pours us all into a maelstrom of perpetual disintegration and renewal, of struggle and contradiction, of ambiguity and anguish."[27] Ultimately, modernity is an ambiguous and dichotomous process. The contradictory ideas that surrounded modern manhood in the postwar years were, in this sense, to be expected, as they merely reflected the more general ambiguities of the modern.

But where do these contradictions come from? There are two central dynamics at work. The first is what John Jervis calls the "modernist project." What binds the modernist project together is a shared belief among modernizers in the inherent value of progress and in the general means of achieving it. The modernist project was both a desire for development as well as a faith that its means – "the rational and purposive control of the environment"[28] – were beneficent and aesthetically valuable in themselves. The modernist project reified regularity and discipline; it cherished instrumental reason for its ability to make progress possible. James Scott defines high modernism as "a strong, one might even say muscle-bound, version of the self-confidence about scientific and technical progress, the expansion of production, the growing satisfaction of human needs, the mastery of nature (including human nature), and, above all, the rational design of social order commensurate with the scientific understanding of natural laws."[29] The modernist project included figures on both the left and the right politically. In the twentieth century, capitalist and communist came together in this one respect to walk in parallel (if tensely arranged) lines toward a vision of progress and the ultimate possibility that nature, society, and the self could be tamed by the application of instrumental reason and sound expertise.[30]

In this book, most of the modernist dreams of control that I examine have to do with situations of risk. Risk itself is a modern concept. It is not to be confused with the somewhat similar concept of danger. Dangers are troubles that have always existed, such as the danger of combat or accident. The emergence of risk as a significant social category is something else altogether. To call something a risk means that one is trying to control it, that one assesses it, calculates the probabilities of harm, establishes mechanisms and routines to minimize difficulty, and thoroughly examines anything that goes wrong in order to learn from mistakes and improve safety in the future. To take one example that will be pertinent later in the book, while bridge builders in early times no doubt faced many dangers, they did not create the large bureaucracies of workplace safety and compensation that emerged in the late nineteenth and early twentieth centuries. To do this was to reimagine the dangers faced in the workplace as risks whose social and economic effects could and should be planned for. In this case and others, the modern focus on risk led to the establishment of whole systems and professions of expertise to assess and manage risk. Such risk management expertise – whether in managing the economy, workplace accidents, or public safety – was integral to the modernist belief in the possibility of control and progress.[31]

Because the dictates of modernist planning and risk management required constant change and modification, their ironic effect was to create a great sense of uncertainty. The one-dimensionality of the modernist project, with its excessive promise of control, radicalizes the potential for its opposite. The incongruous effect of an increased emphasis on managing risks was that the mechanisms of progress often created risks in their own right. The postwar years saw the rise of many such modern risks both from the spread of car accidents in the wake of rising car ownership and from the threat of nuclear holocaust that followed from nuclear technology. Although the main goal of the modernist project is to create ever greater trust in the possibilities of progress, such trust can and did become undermined, for it became apparent that although progress eliminated some risks, it also created entirely new ones.

The same process worked at the social and psychological level, where high modernism's faith in systems of rationalistic knowledge and organization creates the kinds of restrictions that need to be escaped. The responses to this continual process of transformation have taken a variety of forms, from antimodernist nostalgia to a hyper-celebration of the immediacy of the present. Collectively, these responses make up the second main dynamic of modernity, what John Jervis calls the modern "experience."[32] Modernist experience was, in a sense, a continual revolt against the one-dimensional dictates of the modernist project. As Jackson Lears has put it, by creating such a limiting "culture of control," modernity created, in its very wake, the "allure of accident."[33] The modern period is replete with such moments when modernist values have turned back on themselves, from the celebration of the noble savage in the eighteenth century to the heroism of the gambler in the mid-twentieth. Such figures came to represent those features of life – chance, wildness, nature – most obscured by the modernist project in any one period.[34] They were its ghosts. There was always a sense in which the very best features of the modern, when taken to the extreme, came back as a form of haunting. Modernity's ghosts did not, as good ghosts should, wait until after death to begin their haunting but were already a spectral presence in the here and now, a mocking shadow of the modern promise of eternal possibility.

During the postwar years, modernity's ghosts popped up in many places. On the national level, a number of intellectuals made the most serious and consistent criticism of modernity's ill effects. A variety of figures, including Harold Innis, Arthur Lower, and George Grant, publicly voiced their fears about the increasing role of science and technology in educational institutions and public life more generally. They worried about the loss of community values, traditional forms of social organization, the value of deference, and, in the face of growing Americanization, the loss of Canada's connection to Britain.[35] The Massey Commission into the arts and cultural life of Canada (1949-51) reflected these fears, and the creation of such institutions as the Canada Council originated, in part, from fears about encroaching Americanization and its "crass" popular culture. Antimodernism in Canada during the 1950s often doubled as anti-Americanism. Although a certain amount of snobbery undoubtedly fed this criticism, it would be wrong to see postwar antimodernism as solely an elite intellectual concern.[36] Indeed, Len Kuffert argues that Canadian cultural critics openly embraced a more populist common culture as a "corollary of unmasking the conformity and false democracy of the cultural marketplace." Far from unstinting acceptance, then, many Canadians' response to high modernism was one of deep ambivalence.[37]

The same kind of ambivalence could be found in British Columbia, particularly in Vancouver. Robert McDonald and Arn Keeling have shown how the popular nature writer Roderick Haig-Brown presented his own criticism of the era's dominant development ethic. Although Haig-Brown still accepted many features of the modernist project (as do most antimodernists), he nonetheless "sought to forestall the creation of an ultra-modernist social and natural order in BC in order to protect the non-material, non-capitalist values of nature and community."[38] Many Vancouverites expressed their own anxiety in a variety of ways that, while less publicized, reveal the tensions that underlay the modernist project in this Canadian city. Mothers complained to the city about the speed limit on residential streets, questioning the dominance of the car in an area used for childhood play. Vancouverites who liked to hike in the mountains formed organizations to promote wilderness leisure and to protect some forest areas from the axes of industry. Veterans complained about the excessive bureaucracy of the institutions set up to re-establish them in civilian life. They criticized the way that new forms of expert knowledge and rationalized forms of governance mediated their entitlement and its fulfilment. In all of these situations and more, high modernism's unanticipated consequences caused Vancouverites to become aware of the double-edged nature of that seemingly positive phenomenon called progress.

This book is an exploration of the fundamentally gendered nature of this mediated existence, for as much as postwar Vancouverites saw modern life as contradictory, they also saw the same sorts of contradictions in modern manhood. Men were associated both with the great modernist postwar projects of risk control, namely, managing the economy and welfare state and regulating social life via expertise, and with the adverse side effects of this regulation: emasculation by such trends as complacency and suburban civilization. This book explores the significance of this mirroring. The great irony of this period was not just that of modernity more generally, but also that the idea of the "modern man" could be so frequently invoked in contradictory ways. This leads us to a second notion in need of explanation: masculinity.

Gender and the Politics of Masculinity
Gender, as Joan Scott famously argues, "is the social organization of sexual difference." It is a historically changing set of concepts and relations that gives meaning to differences between men and women. "This does not mean that gender reflects or implements fixed and natural physical differences between women and men," Scott claims; "rather gender is the knowledge that establishes meanings for bodily differences." Contrary to popular wisdom, there are no ahistorical foundations for sexual difference rooted in biological or some other solid foundation that exists prior to being understood culturally. We do not have only bodies (sex) upon which gender (culture) is set. Bodies are

not just coat racks upon which genders can be hung, changing colour and style but always remaining the same shape. Instead, the cultural and the bodily come into existence together in the social process of knowing and determining differences between the sexes. It is not a matter of figuring out which came first – the chicken (gender/culture) or the egg (sex/body). Such a linear conception misses the point. Our knowledge of gender is created *simultaneously* with our ideas of the body. This is why, in part, so many scholars use the term gender, not sex: it offers a better sense of how differences between men and women are, and have been, modifiable. For historians, this is an important insight. We have the task of exploring the different ways that conceptions of gender have come into being and changed historically. The task is to scrutinize our ideas about gender and how they are part of larger processes of social organization, cultural values, and individual psyches. "Sexual difference is not," Scott argues, "the originary cause from which social organization ultimately can be derived. It is instead a variable social organization that itself must be explained."[39]

Gender is also about power. Historically, gender is one of the main categories of identity (along with race, class, religion, age, and others) through which and by which societies organize themselves and their knowledge. The apparent solidity of gender – its supposed naturalness – makes it a good concept upon which other differences can be mapped. Saying that the differences between such concepts as public and private, passive and aggressive, and so forth are akin to those between masculinity and femininity is a way of saying that they too are natural and comprehensible. Similarly, these and other differences can then be mapped back onto gender in reverse, reinforcing the notion that historically contingent distinctions between the sexes are natural and normal. Because they are so enmeshed in the broader network of social organization, providing support and being supported, claims about differences between the sexes are never apolitical, never mere description. To refer to two concepts in a way that codes one as masculine and the other as feminine is to set up a hierarchy between the two and to contribute to a political knowledge. When postwar childrearing experts emphasized women's motherly instincts and men's greater powers of reasoning, implying that women would be most satisfied in the home and men at the drafting table, they did not simply make benign observations, but also made political statements.[40]

Seeing gender in this way – as a social construction and as a way of signifying relations of power – allows us to historicize the ideas of masculinity current in the postwar years. In many different contexts, masculinity came to be defined as that which was powerful. In part, this can be seen in the tolerance and even celebration of certain forms of men's violence, and even more prominently, it can be seen in the matching up of manly and modern risk-management ideals. Our task is to understand why masculinity came to be defined in this way. How did this process of gender construction work? What was excluded or denied in order to make the contradictory ideas that went into the ideology of manly modernism seem coherent and stable? To historicize masculinity is to ask both traditional historical questions – such as "Why did it happen?" "Who benefited?" "What was at stake?" – and questions more attuned to gender history and poststructuralism, including "How was the ideal constructed?" and "What was hidden, denied, or overlooked in the quest for the appearance of cultural permanence?" The postwar ideology of manly modernism was not simply prescription or description; instead, it was a particular conception of manliness created (and recreated) in specific contexts, for political purposes, that depended upon a historically specific logic of creation. Common sense is rarely so common or so sensible in hindsight; it is always partial, situated, and interested. Under the scrutiny of gender history in this book, we will see that postwar ideals of manliness also lose their façade of false universality.

To historicize masculinity is a radical endeavour. Until recently, historians had not seriously considered men's gendered identities. The omission was not a minor one; it was not as though the profession had simply forgotten about hair colour or shoe size. The omission meant that historians had neglected one of the primary ways that power operates and is symbolized. Some conservative historians have lamented the loss of unity brought on by the proliferation of historical topics in the turn to social and cultural history since the 1970s.[41] Yet the comforting national historical narratives that they lament were part of (and not incidental to) a broader process of making men's power seem natural by making the historical process of its creation invisible. Women had gender: they were the different sex; they were those who possessed (or were possessed by and thus diminished by) a sex. Men were politicians, union leaders, citizens, and most important, humans. That historical traits of good citizenship conveniently mirrored good manly characteristics and, even more conveniently, matched ideals of normal human behaviour was not (according to this line of thinking) part of gender. It just was. To challenge this whitewashing of the historical narrative, to show the contingency of ahistorical pretensions about men's nongendered being, and to show that men have had a gender and that this identity has often been constructed in a way that leads to exploitation and domination are worthwhile and long-overdue tasks.[42]

Any tale of manhood's "modernization" presents historians with a dilemma. The two terms do not seem to fit together well. Historians are more accustomed to discussing gender and modernity in reference to women. A number of excellent monographs over the past twenty years have shown how single women in the city, whether the middle-class New Woman or the working-class factory hand, became key symbols of modern fears and aspirations. Such women's apparent (although often not actual) freedom from parental regulation, their sexual practices, and their presence on street corners and in workplaces drew the ire of critics of modern life. The "woman adrift" came to symbolize the often contradictory nature of changes in the emergent industrial capitalist societies of North America and Europe that sought to ensure a patriarchal separation of spheres, on the one hand, while supporting the value of young women's cheap wage labour, on the other, all the while opening up the possibility for new and unanticipated liberating cultures in the city. This important figure of the modern past has come to dominate our discussion of gender and modernity.[43]

The frequency with which women have been invoked as symbols of the modern in contemporary historiography tends to obscure that women were usually seen as problematic moderns. As a number of feminist scholars have pointed out, the very meaning of modernity (the modern "canon" as one puts it) is understood in ways culturally understood to be masculine. Marshall Berman's account of modern experience highlights male philosophers, engineers, and architects; it is about the massive reordering of nature and society so often associated with masculine endeavour.(The world of women that could be seen as modern – new domestic arrangements, the independence of the New Woman – either is not a part of this canon or is a part of it, but only as a challenge to the older order.)This sharply contrasts with the very central place given to certain types of men and masculinity. While there is value in rewriting women into the history of modernity, as others have done, it is also worthwhile to point out how and why modernity was defined as masculine.[44] This is one of the purposes of this book.

In Canadian history, when masculinity has arisen in discussions of modernity, the two terms have frequently been presented as antagonistic. The gendered anxieties of men dominated much antimodernist thought throughout the nineteenth and twentieth centuries. While women figure in antimodernist fears because of their activity (their presence on the streets and in workplaces), men have become the subject of antimodern anxieties more often because of their passivity (because of the way that institutions and organizations dampened competition and action). Those in the postwar years who decried the effect of modern life on manhood had many predecessors. Turn-of-the-century Ontario doctors prescribed wilderness holidays so that men suffering from the disease of overcivilization, or neurasthenia, could get in touch with their rugged, manly sides and (presumably) get better. Canada's most famous painters, the Group of Seven, owed much of their popularity not only to their skill with the brush, but also to the way that their wilderness paintings spoke to a culture that feared the effect of overcivilization on men. Such gendered antimodernist fears also inspired the popularity of big-game hunting in British Columbia. We can also see them at work in the beliefs of many early-twentieth-century Protestants who advocated a more muscular Christianity, notably one of Canada's most popular writers, Ralph Connor. South of the border, Teddy Roosevelt drew upon the same ideas to foster his own cult of popularity. All of these writers, thinkers, politicians, hunters, ministers, and others collectively saw a disjuncture between the manly and the modern. They looked to a time in the past when men were men, a time that, according to these renditions, was ending.[45]

Many recent works on manhood continue in this formulation, presenting men (and the ideals of masculinity that they proffer and try to emulate) as reactive to modernity. Masculinity is a defensive category, the voice of tradition: it is what is being changed and never what is active, new, and modern.[46] Several prominent examples should help to demonstrate my point. In *Manhood in America*, Michael Kimmel argues that an ideal he calls "the Self-Made Man" arose in the early nineteenth century. Most of *Manhood in America* recounts how generations of middle-class white American men strove to live up to this ideal, never feeling the power that it promised, and blaming various others (women, blacks, homosexuals) for men's failure to *be* this kind of man. The problem of masculinity, in this historical account, is that the ideal can never be met, that power is a promise rarely fulfilled, and that masculinity is therefore continually challenged, threatened, and in crisis. In her recent account of the contemporary "crisis" of American manhood, *Stiffed*, Susan Faludi adopts a similar approach, although with less historical range. Oddly for a feminist, Faludi looks back fondly on the immediate postwar years, arguing that contemporary gender troubles including high rates of sexual violence and the crisis of masculinity result from the rise of an ornamental culture that destroyed socially utilitarian values of masculinity that had been so prominent during the Second World War and immediately thereafter. Echoing 1950s social critics of the "Organization Man," she laments the loss of male stoicism and competitiveness and yearns for a time when being a man really mattered. Manhood had once been full of promise, but recent events had led to what she refers to in her subtitle as "the betrayal of the American man." A more sophisticated version of the threatened manhood thesis is evident in British feminist Lynne Segal's *Slow Motion*. Segal shows how the popular culture of 1950s Britain celebrated a defensive masculinity in which men railed against the multiple threats of domesticity, unmanliness, and overbearing mothers. All of these developments, she argues, prefigured more radical divisions to emerge in the 1960s and 1970s. Men were changing but not quickly enough. As with Kimmel and Faludi, Segal presents masculinity as something that happens *to* men. The recent history of masculinity is one of retreat and backlash, of too much or not enough change. Masculinity, presumably, is a single entity that can be threatened. Like a tough child on the top of a hill, it keeps its place by kicking and punching those who try to get to the top even while the dirt is being dug out from beneath its feet.[47]

In this book, I want to suggest that we historicize the threatened manhood thesis. Instead of taking the threats at face value, we need to see how the notion of threatened manhood is itself a historical construction. We should not be particularly surprised that there has often been a disjuncture between the ideal and the experience of manhood. Gender is an intrinsically unstable category of personal and social existence. At the psychological level, to fully occupy a coherent and purely masculine identity is to repress many other alternatives; to be masculine is to wholly deny femininity. And if the Freudian century has taught us anything, it should be that the repressed never truly stays repressed, that it can bubble over in all kinds of troublesome and contradictory ways. The same can be said for gender on the social level. Coding certain practices, institutions, and cultural symbols as masculine and others as feminine depends upon denying alternate readings and the reality of complex experiences in which, to take but one example, women can be aggressive and men passive. Differences between ideals and realities are to be expected. To say that masculinity is "in crisis" in any one historical era is to say very little.[48]

In the postwar years, the idea of a threatened manhood was part of a process of consolidating some men's social power. Just as modernity was itself doubled, creating anxiety as well as optimism, so too were the ideas of masculinity with which it was associated. Far from being a reflection of a reality in which men and ideas of masculinity were endangered, the discourse on threatened manhood represented one response to a cultural process of re-establishing men's authority. One of the most significant new outfits of postwar masculinity was the ideal of manly modernism. In a variety of contexts, Canadians put men at the centre of the modernist project. Modern life created new risks and demanded a great deal of trust in the engine of progress. One of the ways that this trust was consolidated was by coding as masculine the expertise needed to ensure successful risk taking and risk management. That this process worked unevenly, sometimes bringing unintended consequences, should be seen not as a sign of male disenfranchisement but as exactly what it was: the unplanned side effects of an imperfect strategy of male authority.

The Essays
This book is a series of essays, each of which explores different facets of the doubled nature of manly modernism. Each chapter shows an instance where modern risk management and risk taking were discussed in connection with manhood. In each case study, modern expertise was brought to bear on some aspect of postwar life that came to be seen as needing risk management – whether this was the reintroduction of veterans into the economy and society after the war or evaluating the dreadful deeds of murderers. Moreover, each case shows a different way that modern expertise was gendered as masculine and, equally, where the effects of this expertise on other men was seen to be troublesome. As in all such projects, the choice of case studies is ultimately not exhaustive.[49] However, the sheer range of situations covered in this book – the incredible variety of situations in which manly modernism reared its head – should go some way toward showing just how extensive, and how ambivalent for some men, were the workings of manly modernism.

Chapter 2 begins in the most logical place to begin any study of postwar masculinity and modernity, with the experience of veterans, who occupied a privileged place in the culture and politics of the postwar years because of their service in war. This special place was inherently gendered, based as it was on men's willingness to serve. (Although women could and did serve in the armed forces, men's wartime sacrifices were understood to be at the heart of the war.) Because of their service in the war, they had earned special entitlements, represented in the federal government's swath of legislated benefits, collectively called the Veterans Charter. Aside from rewarding manly sacrifice, the other driving force behind the Veterans Charter was an attempt to manage the social, political, and economic risks associated with the return of soldiers. In other words, the Veterans Charter represented the coming together of both the manly and the modern, the risk taking of war and the risk management of the modern bureaucratic state. This chapter explores how exactly they meshed, which emerges through the records of a small Royal Commission convened when a group of Vancouver veterans of both the Great War and the Second World War complained that they had not been treated properly by government officials. The ideology of manly modernism permeated the language of those on the commission and those appearing before it. The commission upheld the notion that male veterans had a special entitlement and that the state had a key role to play in re-establishing a certain kind of masculinity after the war. The challenge thus became how to best manage and organize the rights of this manly entitlement. This is where most of the complaints arose, pitting veterans against the expertise of psychiatrists and the bureaucratic logic of the Department of Veterans' Affairs and the Canadian Pension Commission. Masculinity occupied both sides of the modernist project in this interaction between men and the state: it provided the reason for the creation of a huge state apparatus to provide compensation and benefits for wartime service; and at the same time, masculinity seemed to be threatened when this bureaucracy created its own unanticipated problems.

In Chapter 3, we move directly into the heart of postwar mythology: the notions of economic progress and development, myths that were especially important in Vancouver and British Columbia. This chapter looks at how Vancouverites responded to a bridge collapse in 1958. On 17 June of that year, the Second Narrows Bridge collapsed during construction, killing eighteen workers. The bridge was one part of a broader process of economic modernization in British Columbia and Vancouver, meant to facilitate suburban growth on the north shore and to boost shipping trade in Burrard Inlet. The response of many Vancouverites to the bridge's collapse demonstrated how they associated the risks that made this economic development possible (building and engineering the bridge) with idealized conceptions of masculinity. As in war, contemporaries defined the ability to handle and manage risk as masculine traits, those that also just happened to be essential to the postwar vision of economic growth. Within this broader consensus, however, hierarchies of men and masculinities emerged. While newspapers and politicians praised working-class men's risk taking, they ultimately valued the rational, expert knowledge of middle-class engineers, using this knowledge (and these types of men) as arbiters of the collapse's official truth. In this case, the tensions within postwar ideas of masculinity – between the bodily and the rational, or risk taking and risk managing – worked along class lines.

Clearly, then, many middle-class men benefited from their privileged place as experts within the postwar modernist project, with the tendency of Vancouverites to identify middle-class masculinity with all that was progressive about postwar modernization. Some of these men, however, found the bureaucratic, rational, and suburban world of postwar affluence to be more stifling than inspiring. For these men, the risk taking of bridge workers and veterans served as a kind of romantic fantasy, something that they could try to live out through their leisure activities. Chapter 4 looks at the history of the British Columbia Mountaineering Club and at a group of postwar Vancouverites who took to climbing mountains as a way to find a more meaningful connection to their surroundings. While both men and women belonged to the club, mountaineering was a distinctly gendered activity in which men dominated the riskiest ventures and in which the traits of the ideal mountaineer matched the traits of the ideal man. Yet here, too, the ironies of manly modernism persisted. Mountaineers took up their sport in part because it offered them an escape from the seemingly emasculating effects of the urban and suburban experience of postwar Vancouver. They went to the mountains in order to find a more primal experience. However, their choice of mountaineering as an escape belied their claims to truly leave behind the values of postwar modernity. Mountaineering was a blend of risk taking and risk management that mimicked the modern expertise of engineers, scientists, and bureaucrats. Mountaineers ended up advocating a balance between the twin possibilities of manly modernism: the daring risk taker and the cautious risk manager.

This ambiguous collaboration between expertise and definitions of masculinity also figured prominently in another major way in which postwar Vancouverites turned to modern expertise to manage social risks: the interpretation of the actions of murderers. In the postwar years, a variety of experts (especially psychiatrists and psychologists) increasingly entered into the criminal justice system, acting as a main source of knowledge about men and their violence. Contemporaries picked up the language of these mental health experts and, in the process, contributed to the medicalization of masculinity, which is the focus of Chapter 5. Between 1945 and the late 1960s, Vancouver courts convicted twenty-four people (all men) of capital murder, a crime punishable by hanging. Within these trials, and especially in the discussions leading up to the decision over whether to commute the death sentence, a murderer's manhood mattered a great deal in how he was treated. As in earlier periods, Vancouverites judged the severity of murder not just by the details of the crime itself, but also by the gendered identity of the murderer. The subject of this chapter is the relation between evaluations of masculinity and medical expertise. Although convicted men often turned to experts to help explain their actions, the experts could end up alienating the men from their actions and potentially also from their identity. The men could not define themselves on their own; instead, both they and their actions required expert interpretation. As in the case of veterans and that of the bridge collapse, these murder cases show the growing collaboration with (and tension between) ideas of masculinity and the institutions and practices of (often middle-class) modern expertise.

In Chapter 6, we deal with the link between manhood and what is perhaps the most everyday form of risk in the postwar years: driving a car. The postwar years saw a dramatic rise in car ownership in Vancouver, and this "Golden Age" of the automobile also brought an increase in the number of traffic accidents. The safety expertise that grew up alongside the postwar car culture responded to this increased risk in a characteristically modern way. Eschewing any criticism of the technology itself, they called upon drivers to become rational, calculating experts, assessing all dangers before they arose. The best way to deal with the risks created by the automobile age, they argued, was to balance the desire for speed and power against the necessity of careful risk management. In this appeal to a uniquely modernist expertise, the ideal driver looked much like the ideal mountaineer and bridge worker: all invoked a discourse of risk management that mirrored the ideology of manly modernism. From the perspective of traffic safety discourse, the process of becoming a safe driver closely resembled the process of becoming a modern man. In the mid-1960s, however, a growing number of critics emerged to challenge the safety consensus and the idealized manly driver that it advocated. Building on the impetus provided by American critics of car culture, Jane Jacobs and Ralph Nader, a group of Vancouverites argued against and defeated plans to build a freeway through, and to redevelop part of, the eastern end of the city's downtown. These critics found fault with many of the same features of the modernist project that earlier Vancouver men found to be troublesome: the authoritarian nature of modern expertise and the negative unanticipated consequences of unfettered rational and instrumental reason. In taking this stand, they represented a broader challenge to the modernist project and to its accompanying celebration of manly modern ideals. Ironically, these 1960s radicals also, for different purposes and to different effect, picked up on a criticism of modernity that had been a central feature of discussions of masculinity throughout the postwar years.

Each of the essays examines a moment when the contradictions of modernity were laid bare; they highlight the disjuncture between promises of control and the possibilities of chaos, between the terror and the beauty of rationalization and organization. Collectively, the essays show the development of an ideology of manly modernism at just these moments of modernist crisis. In these instances, the modernist project showed itself to be ultimately about controlling and manipulating bodies and environments through the rationalistic practices of expertise and risk management. In these contexts, a range of Vancouverites defined modernist expertise and masculinity in nearly identical terms, providing a cultural foundation that backed up the reality that most such experts were in fact men.[50] However, like the modernist project more generally, this process was inconsistent, disciplining some men and some traits of masculinity even as it upheld the manly modern ideal. So while the case studies show manly modernism at work, they also show it in decay: we see its inadequacies, its fault lines, and the possible reasons why some men would increasingly come to look for other ways to define manhood. The celebration of the rational risk manager coexisted uneasily with other traits previously associated with masculinity; and while contemporaries coded modern expertise as masculine in a general sense, such expertise also had the effect of disciplining men themselves, often based upon lines of race, sexuality, and class. This tension continued throughout the postwar years, providing a persistent sense of doubt about the benefits of modernity and a previously unexplored (and certainly unintended) legacy for the more sustained criticism of the modernist project that emerged in the later 1960s.

This book is an itinerary of my trip through past understandings of masculinity and, like any such document, reflects my own particular sense of the places that I knew to visit. I have been most interested in stretching the boundaries of what we think of as masculine and in the ways that we might see masculinity as being constructed. A few absences are worth regretfully mentioning. My desire to show how masculinity and men's power has operated in all-male encounters has meant that I focus less on relations between the sexes than a fuller account of postwar gender relations warrants. And in an effort to see the main attractions of a dominant form of masculinity, I sometimes do not spend time searching out the very important places where subordinate and alternate masculinities were formed. This is also not a history of *Vancouver* modernity and masculinity but a history of manly modernism as it took shape *in* Vancouver; it is not a work of local history, with that genre's emphasis upon specifically regional particularities. I hope, however, that these absences will be taken as the logical outcome of a still useful endeavour. From the very beginning, the project always seemed too large and in need of restraint. To discuss either masculinity or modernity is a great deal of work. To take on both together has meant more years of struggle than I care to remember, only toward the end of which have I truly been able to see and explain the connections that my instincts had told me were there from the beginning.

When he painted the giant mural for the Marine Workers' and Boiler Makers' Industrial Union Hall, Fraser Wilson knew all about the contradictions of manly modernism. He came to paint the mural only after he had been blacklisted from his regular work. Wilson had been a prominent political cartoonist on the Canadian left, most notably for the Cooperative Commonwealth Federation. But after he took a lead role in a 1947 newspaper strike, the main Vancouver dailies blacklisted him, forcing him to find other work. The mural was one of the jobs he found that year. In the Cold War climate, the beneficence of capitalist modernity was likely lost on Wilson. Yet it is striking that he still took up and celebrated the modernist spirit of control, rationality, and efficiency in the mural. In his version, of course, it is the workers who are in control. Manly modernism was clearly not to be abandoned. It was a source of inequality, frustration, and difficulty yet at the same time also clearly a symbol of potential authority and status. Despite the inequalities and contradictions, symbols of manly modernism moved across social boundaries, touching a wide variety of men in postwar Vancouver.

In an age when so many discussions of gender difference rely on biological, evolutionary, and "caveman" explanations, the category of the modern man may seem a quixotic digression.[51] Yet, in the uneven balance that postwar Canadians tried to achieve in their definitions of what made one a man, we may find the very unexpected roots of our current gender fixations. The postwar struggle between notions of man as ideal modern and man as modern victim was not just an interesting sidebar to the era's cultural history. Instead, it was part of a broader ideology of manly modernism that pervaded the postwar years, providing a source of gendered power and authority in a variety of contexts from mountaineering expeditions to workplaces. Manly modernism identified as masculine the very traits that were considered normal and appropriate to being modern even as it invented a history of primitive manhood to bolster this association and to retreat into when necessary. That such an ideology mattered, that it was not simply an ideal against which men struggled, that it helped to provide men like Fraser Wilson with greater authority in concrete situations, and that it had important repercussions for the era that followed are what, in the following chapters, I shall endeavour to prove.

2
Coming Home

It is often said that the end of the Second World War evinced from Canadians a long collective sigh. Finally, it was over. Maybe, just maybe, everything would return to normal. The historian Doug Owram goes so far as to say that the trauma of depression and war led to the conservatism so often associated with the late 1940s and 1950s. This is the version of postwar history that sees the quest for normality as a generational security blanket. Postwar Canadians valued home life, traditional gender relations, and the idea of security because such things had been so endangered by international economic and political events in their youth. "The generation that came of age in the late 1930s and early 1940s," Owram notes, "could scarcely remember a time when home life had not been threatened."[1]

This evocation of a shared identity and experience, a collective seeking of security, is deceptively compelling. The desire for wholeness, for certainty, is hardly something to criticize or interrogate. Yet societies, no less than individuals, achieve security (i.e., a stable sense of identity) only by denying alternatives that may lead to uncertainty. Whether we understand this in a Freudian sense, in which a secure ego is a result of the successful disciplining of the id and the super ego, or in the social sense, in which stability comes by establishing the dominance of one form of political authority over others, creating security is a political process of excision and expurgation. The Depression and war had not only disturbed individual lives, but had also threatened economic and political relations and the notions of gender through which they had been sustained. The crisis years of the 1930s and 1940s challenged the ideology of male breadwinning: first, by putting so many men out of work; and second, by drawing so many women into the workforce. As the historian Nancy Christie has argued, state planners during these years saw re-establishing the role of the male breadwinner as one of the main goals of social-welfare policy.[3] The postwar emphasis on returning to normal, then, needs to be seen in this context – that is, as an attempt to re-establish dominant notions of masculinity. As is so often the case in the history of masculinity, men's gendered identities were equated not with themselves as men but with a larger, seemingly ungendered category – in this case, the nation. Canadians may have suffered during the war, but this universalized national subject hid specific and unequal ideas about *who* had sacrificed and what they deserved in return. The meanings of entitlement were gendered.[4]

One figure in particular stood out as deserving more than all the others: the male veteran. The postwar desire to return to normal often coalesced around this figure, his needs and wants, what he deserved, and the indignities that he had to suffer. While the Depression and war were said to have hurt everyone, the veteran occupied a special place in this discourse of deservedness. It was he who had fought and suffered, who had left his job and family to go abroad for his country. Women had served both on the home front and, in small numbers, in the armed forces. Yet a hierarchy of sacrifice and entitlement pervaded both popular culture and state policy that put the male combat veteran at the very top. In returning home, the soldier became the veteran, and his relation to the state switched from one of sacrifice to one of entitlement.[5] And these entitlements drew forth the largest set of social programs that Canada had ever seen in the form of the Veterans Charter.[6] The emergence of this key plank in the postwar welfare state was, in other words, intimately connected with heavily gendered ideas of entitlement. The effect of this on the welfare state has recently been studied by a number of historians.[7] This chapter takes up the subject of its effect on masculinity.

In postwar Vancouver, the figure of the deserving veteran and his relation to the state came under scrutiny in a 1947-48 Royal Commission. The federal government established the commission to deal with a group of veterans from Vancouver who had complained that the government and its agencies had not treated them properly. These veterans argued that the state had not offered just compensation for military service and its repercussions. In a political context sympathetic to such complaints, the federal Liberal government took the significant step of establishing the Royal Commission to hear the men's grievances. On its own, the commission was not particularly momentous. It sat for only a short time, its mandate was limited, and its report was modest. Yet the issues with which it dealt could not have been more central to social life in postwar Canada. The commission records offer first-hand accounts of individual Canadians struggling to interpret the physical and financial impact of war upon both the lives of veterans and political culture more broadly. The commission offers a neat packaging of diverse viewpoints on the meanings given to masculinity and entitlement. Participants included veterans and their organizations, politicians, doctors, and officials of the Department of Veterans' Affairs (DVA) and of the Canadian Pension Commission (CPC). Although all involved spoke of particular cases, they drew on a broader language of gendered entitlement.

In this chapter, we examine what came of this unprecedented connection between masculine deservedness and the high-modernist state. Although men's deservedness from their militarism was nothing new, the extent of state reconstruction plans, combined with the era's general faith in planning and expertise, was significantly novel. What happened when this modernist emphasis on managing the risks of social and economic turmoil became bound up with the traditional manly imperatives of war? What did manly modernism look like in practice?

The Commission
The 1947-48 Royal Commission into the complaints of disabled and injured veterans resulted from twin pillars of traditional political history: personality and timing (or as Donald Creighton might have said, character and circumstance). It is hard to imagine how such a commission could have come about were it not for the favourable postwar political climate and the dogged efforts of one man, Walter H. Kirchner. Of the sixty-six veterans whose cases the commission examined, almost half were veterans of the First World War. They had sought compensation before this time, but only in the years after the Second World War did the government agree to set up a special forum to hear their complaints. And much of the credit for this must go to Walter H. Kirchner. In the 1930s and 1940s, as secretary of the Canadian Combat Veterans' Association (CCVA) and as a representative of the Veterans' Bureau, Kirchner struggled incessantly on behalf of veterans' pension entitlements. He took up individual cases before the CPC, DVA, and anyone else who would listen. His letters on behalf of veterans and on pension issues appeared in newspapers in British Columbia and across the country.[8] When the federal government established the Royal Commission, they sought to deal with Kirchner's complaints exclusively; indeed, the official title of the commission was the Royal Commission to Investigate Complaints Made by Walter H. Kirchner.

What did Kirchner want? Quite broadly, he represented a group of veterans who sought better compensation from the state for the effects of war upon their lives. The complaints stemmed from inadequate material reward and from the more nebulous but still important issue of status, the idea that because of who they were and what they had done, they deserved a better kind of treatment. Kirchner and the CCVA took a more radical stance than did larger veterans' organizations such as the Legion and the Army and Navy Veterans' Association, but his argument and actions appear to differ in tone rather than in kind. Like other officials in veterans' organizations, Kirchner regularly acted on behalf of individual veterans in their appeals for pension entitlement. Most of those whom he represented received treatment in Vancouver's veterans' hospital, Shaughnessy Hospital. Through this advocacy work, Kirchner became increasingly dissatisfied with the DVA's and CPC's handling of pension cases. He felt that these organizations regularly and unfairly denied pensions to veterans either in whole or in part. Throughout the early to mid-1940s, Kirchner's complaints became louder and more public.[9]

The immediate postwar context provided a favourable climate in which to argue that the government needed to do right by veterans. The experience of war had changed the relation between Canadians and the state. The heavy involvement of the state in the everyday lives of Canadians during wartime heightened expectations that governments could and should take action to regulate social and economic problems. Key figures working within the wartime state ensured that the services offered to veterans of the Second World War would be superior to those offered to Great War veterans. Plans for reconstruction and the re-establishment of veterans began early, and the number and extent of programs expanded. The Veterans Charter sought to ensure that veterans enjoyed a safe return to "civvy street." Part of the desire to implement these programs came out of fears about the economic consequences of doing too little and risking another postwar recession and labour struggle. However, the Veterans Charter also resulted from widespread beliefs that veterans deserved a better deal.[10] It was in this altered political context that Walter Kirchner finally had some success in getting the government to listen.

In the summer of 1947, after repeated appeals on behalf of Kirchner and his supporters in the House of Commons, Mackenzie King's Liberal government set up an inquiry to investigate the complaints. The commission included four sitting members of Parliament with medical backgrounds: Energy Minister James J. McCann (chair), Dr. M.E. McGarry, Dr. W.G. Blair, and J.O. Probe. Partway through the mandate, McCann became ill, and R.H. Winters stepped in. F.L. Barrow, an official with the DVA, acted as commission secretary. The group first held meetings with government DVA and CPC officials in Ottawa before taking the train across the country to Vancouver. They held sessions both on the train and at various stops along the route, but most of their time was spent in Vancouver, the site of most of Kirchner's problem cases. They reviewed the files of the sixty-six cases that Kirchner had brought to their attention and met with a small number of those whose cases they felt required more explanation. After a week of hearings in Vancouver, the commission retired to Ottawa and published its report two months later.

It is difficult to know exactly why the government decided to take the official step of establishing a Royal Commission. As I noted above, many of Kirchner's complaints involved First World War veterans whose cases dated back to the 1930s and, for some, the 1920s. Yet in 1947 the government nevertheless felt compelled to establish a commission. Most likely, Mackenzie King's government, like other governments before and since, hoped that by establishing a Royal Commission, they could silence critics through paper work and delay.[11] Whatever the precise reason, that they felt the need to publicly address Kirchner's concerns demonstrated the power of veterans' claims in the mid- to late 1940s. As we shall see, such claims depended upon a cultural logic that equated manliness with breadwinning, risk, and entitlement.

The Deserving Veteran
The material and cultural salience accorded veterans' entitlement drew much of its force from the connections between military service and two dominant features of mid-century masculinity: breadwinning and risk taking. All involved in the commission shared a belief that men's involvement in war was a necessary, if unfortunate, part of civilized life. This connection between men and military risk was not new.[12] Part of the willingness of men to volunteer in both world wars came from the popular connection between manhood and militarism. To be a man has, historically, often meant being able and willing to be violent and to risk violence according to the strictures of social regulation and authority. Just as the monopoly of violence by the modern state provided its authority, so too did the granting of the right to be violent only to male citizens during wartime serve to define masculinity as socially powerful. This can partly be seen by the great desire of nonwhite men – Aboriginal, Chinese, and African Canadian – to celebrate their part in the world wars. To claim that they too sacrificed and risked their lives along with white Anglo-Saxon men has been a way of writing themselves into a powerful rendition of modern manhood.[13] Men's service in the military also fitted in with the ideal of the male breadwinner. By joining the service, men had shouldered their responsibility as family

wage earner. Postwar plans to support veterans were predicated upon the notion that the state would do what it could to allow men to resume this role in civilian life. While both of these ideals – breadwinning and soldiering – had long been equated with masculinity, the emergence of a significant set of state assistance plans in the Second World War meant that they were directly built into the functioning of the welfare state as never before.[14]

Combat and military risk played important roles in the celebration of veterans and in the notion that they were especially deserving. While government propaganda referred to war as a collective national effort, soldiers occupied a privileged position. Some veterans became resentful when this privilege was not immediately apparent. In their later recollections, veterans drew boundaries between those who did and did not serve. One veteran explained, "to this day I can't meet a man my age without somehow trying to find out if he was in the war, and if I find out he was, then fine, but if he wasn't, I feel contempt for him." Ruth Roach Pierson notes that "when a man donned a uniform he stood to see his masculinity enhanced" and that men who did not wear the uniform "felt threatened not only by the possible charge of cowardice but by the possible loss of girlfriends to the soldiers, sailors and airmen." Notions of veterans' deservedness pervaded postwar popular culture. Political parties fought the 1945 election over how Canada would change in the postwar years to secure wartime economic progress for its returning veterans. Mackenzie King won re-election on a platform of social change directed at guaranteeing the entitlements earned by war, most notably through family allowances. One of the most significant political controversies of the early postwar years centred on the housing crisis and the need to ensure sufficient housing for returning veterans and their families. Concern for veterans continued on movie screens in 1946's *The Best Years of Our Lives,* Hollywood's most celebrated version of homecoming. The film follows three veterans as they adjust to domestic life, each with their own set of problems. One issue unites them: the unjust actions of civilians who stand between veterans and a fair chance. Such civilians come in varying forms – bankers who refuse loans, unfaithful wives, or children who show too little respect. The film made the message clear: veterans deserved better.[15]

Those who had volunteered for service also came to occupy a more privileged place did than those who were conscripted. Although conscription has been an important topic in military and political history, historians have largely overlooked its gendered aspects. When Mackenzie King introduced conscription, he did so in a piecemeal fashion. Ever the compromise maker (and with the memory of the First World War conscription crisis firmly in his mind), he promised that conscripted troops would serve only at home and not go overseas. The different treatment of volunteers and conscripts led to different gendered meanings being attached to these identities. Soldiers who were conscripted under the National Resources Mobilization Act (NRMA) became known by the derogatory term "zombies." The term had become popular in the 1930s because of a variety of Hollywood films and was generally known as a "resuscitated body without a soul acting mechanically." NRMA conscripts wore different uniforms marked with the letter "A." These uniforms, and the conscripts generally, took on a wider social significance of lesser value and honour based on an unwillingness to face risk. Brigadier W.H.S. Macklin reported on the situation in Vancouver, noting that "it is not too much to say that the volunteer soldier in many cases literally despises the NRMA man ... The volunteer feels himself a man quite apart ... He regards himself as a free man who had the courage to make a decision." When Mackenzie King announced overseas service for NRMA conscripts, the resulting riots by groups of the conscripts in British Columbia were greeted with derision in the press. Critics cast aspersions on the soldiers by claiming that they were of disproportionately French Canadian or foreign, especially German, ancestry. While it is clear that not all looked down upon conscripts, it is equally true that there was a special honour attached to the volunteer.[16]

Kirchner and the veterans whom he represented took up this notion that a willingness to face combat meant something special. They felt that wartime service provided entitlement. Risk and sacrifice lay at the centre of their claims. Kirchner's organization, the CCVA, made combat central to its mandate by restricting membership to those who had seen frontline service. When he first appeared before the commission, Kirchner wanted to know whether the commissioners matched up to his ideals. "I just want to make a few inquiries here regarding the competence or otherwise of the men on this Commission who can rightfully be termed war veterans in the actual meaning of that term," he began. "I mean men who have seen service in an actual theatre of war. It seems to me that there should be on this Commission of enquiry at least one that I would term combatant officer or man ... in view of the fact that the charges are based upon the sworn complaints of men who are actual war veterans ... with service in a theatre of actual war."[17] Military risk underpinned Kirchner's conception of entitlement and authority. If the commissioners had not risked their own lives, how could they judge those who had risked theirs?

Veterans believed that their part in this form of manly risk taking had earned them entitlement. This rights-based approach was typically masculine. As a number of historians have argued, gender shapes claims to state assistance. Historically, rights-based claims such as those put forward by veterans have been seen as masculine and deserving, while claims for charity and handouts such as those put forward by single mothers have been seen as feminine and less deserving. This represented a shift in thinking about masculinity from a view that presented man as self-sufficient and independent to one that translated these claims into those of entitlement.[18] In the 1950s and 1960s a number of women's groups and social-welfare activists sought to break down this traditional division, making claims based upon women's rational citizenship and disavowing the earlier emotive appeal.[19] In the mid-1940s, however, the division held, and veterans clearly placed themselves within the rights-based masculine stream. "I have a clear cut entitlement which I think is coming to me,"[20] is how one veteran put it. Another, John T., distinguished between entitlement and charity even more clearly. At the time of the commission, he was in receipt of the war veterans' allowance (WVA). Canadians also called the WVA the "burnt-out veterans' allowance." It was based on the idea that due to their war experience, veterans aged more quickly than civilians and should therefore be entitled to a pension at an earlier age.[21] The main difference between WVA and a pension from the CPC was that the WVA was means tested. John T. wanted to switch from the WVA to a pension from the CPC. His exchange with commissioner R.H. Winters accentuated the distinction between charity and rights:

> *Winters:* Are you in receipt of War Veterans' Allowance?
> *John T.:* Yes.
> *Winters:* And are you aware, or is it a fact, that if the amount of your pension is increased the amount of your War Veterans' Allowance will be decreased?
> *John T.:* Certainly, I expect to be cut off altogether; I don't want it. I want 100% pension, that's what I want ...
> *Winters:* What difference does it make to you whether you get the money as War Veterans' Allowance or as Pension?
> *John T.:* Because I want justice; I don't want a handout.[22]

The distinction between feminine handouts and masculine justice was key. John T. and other veterans demanded masculine entitlement based on masculine sacrifice.

These claims dovetailed nicely with traditional manly entitlements based on men's role as family breadwinners. The men's claims before the commission moved quickly and softly between these similar cultural foundations. In making this argument for a rights-based entitlement, these veterans were part of a larger movement away from the means-tested programs associated with Canada's (and especially the Depression's) "poorhouse" past. As Nancy Christie has shown, this critique drew much of its force from the notion that such rights were derived from men's status as breadwinners. This theme emerged strongly in the commission.[23] A man's physical condition, so important in wartime, also figured prominently in his civilian work, especially in the climate of 1940s British Columbia, where primary industry reigned and light secondary-industry jobs were few. After having suffered wartime injuries, the working-class veterans who appeared before the commission could no longer perform the kind of tough physical labour that had been routine before the war. Their injuries forced them into less physical and, consequently, less well-paying jobs. The case of John B., a Hong Kong veteran, was typical. John B. emphasized his positive work ethic: "I like to work," he told the commissioners. "I can't sit around the house. I had a few weeks holidays, Christmas and New Years, and that about drove me nuts, sitting around the house." He claimed that war injuries stifled his ability (although not his desire) to earn a living. Before the war, he worked as a grain buyer and physical labourer, but at the time of the commission, he worked as a driver for the DVA, a position that paid less. John B. complained of not being able to do harder and more rewarding work despite wanting to. "I like this job, sure, but there's not much pay to it. I would like to be able to make a little more money. But I can't go up to a man and do a day's work ... If I was A-1, I would go out and get a job."[24] John B. wanted to fulfill his breadwinning responsibilities, but the costs of another manly responsibility – war – prevented him from doing so.

The state accepted this broad-based masculine claim rooted in a gendered nationalism and economics. The Royal Commission sympathetically engaged veterans whose testimony best encapsulated these ideals. In the commission transcripts, the exchanges between many veterans and the commissioners provide an almost palpable feeling of shared compassion between the two groups. This is difficult to demonstrate in a line or paragraph from the text. But it is evident in subtle continuities: a line of questioning cut off when it became too painful, appreciative silences, long pauses, delicate wording around sensitive issues, and offers of personal assistance. The commissioners respected the sacrifices by which Kirchner and his veterans claimed entitlement, even though, as agents of the state, they ultimately refused parts of such claims.

This belief in the value of military service and entitlement shaped the most significant element of the state's reconstruction policy, the Veterans Charter. This legislation created programs that gave the discourse of militaristic nationalism a material reality. It provided, among other things, grants and loans to buy a home, get an education, and start a business. Walter Woods, deputy minister of veterans' affairs, explained the cost of these programs as a necessity. "It is regarded," he claimed, "as a preferred charge on the country's reserve; an obligation that must be fulfilled; part of the cost of freedom." The type of service that a veteran had rendered mattered. The Veterans Charter granted greater entitlement to those who had faced actual combat overseas. The government worked this recognition of service into a number of programs, including the War Service Grants Act, the Veterans' Land Act, the War Veterans' Allowance Act, and the Civilian War Pensions and Allowances Act. According to Don Ives, "the highest value in terms of earned entitlement went to those whose service required them to engage the enemy." Although most historians who study this topic do not explicitly deal with gender, we can certainly read a masculine vision into their celebration of the greater reward given to combat soldiers.[25]

Links between masculinity, entitlement, and combat filled the writing of Robert England, secretary of the General Advisory Committee on Demobilization and Rehabilitation and one of the key architects of the Canadian plan for postwar reconstruction. His book *Discharged* consistently praised the fighting man: "In war, it is the combatant who goes over the top. He it is who attacks the enemy; upon him success rests – all military glory derives from the man ... who fights." For England, the length and intensity of a man's risk as a soldier determined his level of entitlement: "The ultimate risk is that of endangered life ... To be enrolled or commissioned on the understanding of the acceptance of risk is good but surely greater honour attaches to the man who serves at a mortal risk continuously for his fellow-men whether in military or in civil life." England came back to this distinction again and again, arguing that the term veteran should really apply only to men who were "conditioned so thoroughly for war."[26]

This idealization of military service and its entitlement proved a significant legacy for postwar Canada. Veterans came to the state demanding aid in their re-establishment in civilian life. They believed that they had earned it. They set themselves apart from other Canadians based on their service. And the state shared this vision of citizenship. Indeed, it seemed common sense. Soldiers had suffered on behalf of their nation; some, including many of Kirchner's veterans, had been severely injured. They deserved compensation. Veterans' entitlement seemed logical because it fitted so neatly with the discourses of manly heroism, stoicism, and breadwinning, which already dominated Canadian culture and state policy. In the powerful salience granted to veterans' entitlements in the commission records, in other words, we can see that many Vancouverites defined citizenship in a way that coded its prerogatives as masculine.

The Threatened Man: Veterans and the Slippery Slide to Entitlement

Although Kirchner's veterans attributed their suffering to their wartime experience, they did not criticize the military more generally. Indeed, they embraced their identity as soldiers in order to strengthen their claims. Ideals of manly modernism enabled working-class veterans to claim a privileged status next to the middle-class politicians and bureaucrats who had denied their entitlements. The language of gendered military citizenship provided a source of power, a potential equalizer in the tilted political landscape. Yet despite the many issues on which the Royal Commission and veterans agreed, the commission was far from harmonious, for Kirchner and his veterans brought forward serious concerns that went beyond the details of actual cases. What, then, did they criticize? If veterans and the state shared a commitment to masculine military entitlement, where did this collaboration end? What were its fracture points? And what does this tell us about how manly modernism actually functioned in postwar political culture?

The answer to these questions brings us back to the doubled way that men's relation to modernity was understood in these years. Again and again, the commission came back to the notion that men were victimized by the modern processes that their entitlements had set in motion. Kirchner and his veterans targeted the institutions and experts of the modern state as the source of their troubles. In other words, the organizations created as a result of their privileged masculine citizenship became the reason to claim that veterans lacked privilege. The veterans' very closeness to the modern state, the mirroring of interests between masculinity and the modern, made veterans the objects of state action. They were simultaneously the reason for the state to act *and* those who were acted upon. It is this latter status, as those who were acted upon, that drew the ire of Kirchner and his veterans. Three features figured most prominently in this idea of the threatened man: rules-based bureaucracy; the state's limited gaze, which saw all veterans (regardless of class or personal circumstance) as the liberal "everyman"; and competing types of expert knowledge. Bureaucracy, discipline, expertise: these are all subjects regularly associated with the advance of high modernity and the development of the modern state in particular. Yet, as ideals of masculinity in the form of veterans' entitlements became enmeshed in the complicated processes of the emerging welfare state, all of these problems also became the crisis points of a modern masculinity.

The bureaucracy of the institutions set up to facilitate veterans' entitlements – especially that of the DVA and CPC – became one of the major targets of veteran criticism. Many of the veterans who appeared before the commission blamed their problems – denial of pensions mostly – on the overly bureaucratic mentality of the Canadian Pension Commission and the Department of Veterans' Affairs. Stories of post-First World War bureaucratic entanglements were legion. Popular lore called such entanglements the "run-around," meaning the process whereby veterans went from one government office to the next in a continuous cycle as officials at each place sent the veteran off to yet another office, assuring them that the answer lay with someone else.[27] For disabled veterans, the situation could be even worse, as DVA and CPC officials shuffled men back and forth between different doctors and from hospital to home and back again all in the context of uncertain income and personal health. All involved in plans for postwar reconstruction wanted desperately to avoid similar problems. While there is some evidence that more generous measures for veterans of the latter war made the situation slightly better,[28] the stories of veterans both generally and from the Royal Commission that we are examining here show that returning men still faced the dreaded "run-around."

The perception that veterans' legitimate entitlements were being turned aside by a bureaucracy bent on its own concerns lay at the heart of Kirchner's veterans' initial desire for a Royal Commission. Kirchner consistently criticized government bureaucrats. He lamented that "the administration of the department concerned with the well-being of Canada's fighting men ... is inefficient, bureaucratic and archaic." Kirchner and his organization believed that this bureaucracy stood in the way of legitimate pension claims. He particularly disliked the war veterans' allowance, referring to it as a "reactionary regulation" and noting how the "bureaucracy" had used it "to take the place of the Canadian Pension Act, and, in numerous cases, deprived the front-line veteran with long years of combatant service of his proper assessment and remuneration for war disabilities."[29]

Genuine sympathy for the concept of veterans' entitlement often ran up against – and was beaten back by – a bureaucratic mentality. The most consistent problem with establishing the legitimacy of a veteran's pension claim lay in determining the injury's origins. If doctors and the CPC concluded that the veteran had suffered the injury (in whole or in part) before enlistment, they awarded a smaller pension or none at all. This became especially complicated. The CPC stuck by a single policy. If there was any information on record that an injury had some possible precedent, they would rule that the disability was "pre-enlistment" in origin. For example, the commissioners asked Dr. Laing, the Pension Medical Examiner at Shaughnessy Hospital, about the case of John M., who claimed a pension for osteoarthritis. He linked this condition to his service in a tank during the Second World War. The tank had been fired upon, seriously jostling him and his companions. John M. claimed to have been injured, and he linked his later pains to this wartime incident. However, on his pre-enlistment assessment, he had admitted that a heavy weight had fallen on his hip in 1939. No concrete evidence linked the 1939 injury with his later condition, but the possibility of a connection was enough for the CPC. They ruled the injury to be partially based on the pre-enlistment incident, and John M. received a lesser pension amount.[30]

The rules could also work in a veteran's favour. Dr. Laing emphasized the system's consistency. He presented a hypothetical case of a First World War veteran who reported stomach symptoms in 1915 while in the service. Laing explained what would happen if "in 1930, he comes with a duodenal ulcer, and wants us to connect it up with his service. What do we do? We connect it up, because it is on the record ... the Commission is consistent. They'll connect it up because there is some proof, not duodenal ulcer, mind you, but stomach symptoms on service. They'll connect it up and say: 'Yes, that's due to service.' That's what they do ... the system is consistent."[31]

Yet it was this very consistency that so frustrated veterans. Kirchner's veterans made their claims based on notions of character, deservedness, and merit. The system, they thought, ought to recognize and react to individual needs. Yet linking manly entitlements to the normal functioning of the modern state forced veterans to live their entitlements through the dilemmas of high-modernist bureaucracy. And this bureaucracy was inevitably less complex than were the veterans' own diverse realities. The gap between the rules made to manage entitlements and the entitlements themselves, then, became the site of conflict for a modern manliness.

The state's desire to discipline as well as reward its veterans provided another practical barrier to entitlement. When states become involved in organizing their citizenry, they do so with very specific purposes in mind. While the state in postwar Canada sought to provide service and benefits to veterans, it also sought to instil in them the values of liberal individualism as it related to life in a capitalist society. And these conflicting desires of the state – its mutual support of manly modernism and liberal capitalism – led to conflict. The federal government's ability to manage all the programs in the Veterans Charter depended on collecting and organizing information about all veterans. It gathered the information that it felt to be necessary and important. That such information could not reflect the complex reality that it sought to represent is obvious. The information about the veterans was never an accurate representation. More significant, however, is that the state's involvement in veterans' lives based on this inaccurate representation worked to shape and manipulate the veterans. It tried to turn them into what was represented in an attempt to make a complex reality simple. The very power of veterans' claims, that which made them the beneficiaries of government programs, meant that they were also the target of government manipulation.[32]

We can see the state's disciplinary desires in writings on the ideal soldier. According to Major J.S.A. Bois, the successful soldier exhibited physical and moral endurance above all else. "Pride in physical toughness must be cultivated," he wrote in 1943. "Taking risks must be a matter of constant challenge and competition; personal comfort and absolute cleanliness at work must be disregarded; personal safety must become a question of confidence in one's own abilities and not one of watching anxiously for dangers to be avoided." A good soldier, he argued, learned "to keep his personal troubles to himself; to take worries and disappointments as one takes physical discomfort or bad weather conditions."[33] Undue emotionalism and complaining would not be tolerated. Soldiers, like men generally, should be stoic.

Disciplinary desires leaked over into discussions of postwar reestablishment. State propaganda called on soldiers to fit themselves into the mould of active citizenship and to accept rather than criticize traditional institutions. Robert England explained that the soldier's return home was a process fraught with gendered insecurities. He linked going to war with achieving manhood: "the ex-Service man may have gone away a boy, immature, willing to be ordered about a little, falling into line with family standards of living, but he comes back a man who has had experiences about which it is awkward to talk in the home." While at war, claimed England, the soldier "lost touch with the occupations and life of his community ... he may have to readjust his attitudes to the readily available feminine society of civilian life in contrast with the masculinity of his associations while in the Service."[34] And the answer to the feminizing influence of civil re-establishment, according to England, lay in good old masculine discipline. In the melee of instability upon release, England claimed that the soldier may initially forget, but must be made to realize, "that new self-motivating disciplines of significant work, self-respect, and reasoned social attitudes must replace military regulations and order."[35] The tract *The Common-Sense of Re-Establishment* exhorted its soldier/veteran readers to be patient and to adapt to postwar civilian life. No doubt with fears of a recurrence of 1919 in their minds, the writers of this tract told their readers: "While you have been away Canada has changed and perhaps you have changed too. The changes in Canada have been brought about by the war. At first, on your return home, some things may strike you as strange. But you have proved your adaptability in war – there is no reason to believe that you will find it any harder to readapt yourself to home."[36] The ideal of masculinity that emerged from these documents focused on the need for discipline in achieving one's goals as a breadwinner, soldier, and citizen.

The state's commitment to liberal individualism underpinned its emphasis on disciplined manliness. This commitment meant that King's Liberal government provided concrete entitlements only reluctantly, often out of fear of what inaction might bring rather than out of positive social longing. Two fears dominated. First, they desperately wanted to prevent a recurrence of 1919. This meant avoiding – or at least minimizing – economic recession and labour strife. Second, they wanted to retain political power. This meant caving in to pressure from the left, which had grown stronger during the war. The Cooperative Commonwealth Federation victories in several federal by-elections and in the Ontario and Saskatchewan elections, as well as the party's strong support in public opinion polls generally, created a crisis atmosphere for traditional parties across Canada. Seen in this light, the federal government's plans for postwar reconstruction appear not so much as a bold step forward toward a new sense of citizenship entitlements for Canada's soldier citizens as they do a hesitant manoeuvre to ensure a limited welfare state based on a fear of the alternatives.[37]

The Veterans Charter's emphasis on individual self-sufficiency reflected this Liberal (and liberal) hesitancy. While much has been made of the influence of Keynesian economics on the state's willingness to spend its way through reconstruction, this in no way eliminated an emphasis upon traditional liberal values.[38] The state repeated the self-sufficiency theme ad nauseum. Even Ian A. Mackenzie, minister of veterans affairs and the Cabinet member most in favour of extended social welfare in the postwar years, made this link. In the Ministry of Veterans' Affairs pamphlet, *Back to Civil Life,* he declared "Canada's rehabilitation belief is that the answer to civil re-establishment is a job." The same pamphlet went on to claim that "the object of Canada's plan for rehabilitation of her Armed Forces is that every man or woman discharged from the forces shall be in a position to earn a living." The government would not provide handouts. In bold print, the pamphlet stated, "The Canadian program of rehabilitation for ex-service personnel can succeed only to the extent that ex-service personnel are prepared to help themselves and to the extent that employers will provide opportunity. It cannot help those who have no desire to help themselves." The same mix of economic help and self-sufficiency is evident in the Veterans Charter legislation generally and in the government publications meant to explain it in particular. *The Common-Sense of Re-Establishment* put it this way: "The purpose of [Canada's re-establishment policy] is to help you in your return to civil life. It is up to you to use it."[39]

The awkward overlap between the state's emphasis on the ideals of liberal self-sufficiency and manly breadwinning revealed itself most in the state's treatment of disabled and injured veterans. Government programs had the ultimate goal of getting the man back to working condition. If a veteran's emotional state was considered at all, it was only because of a fear that psychological problems would prevent him from returning to work and becoming a competent citizen. As in British Columbia's workmen's compensation scheme, the Veterans Charter provided different amounts of money for different types of injury according to a standard chart – x amount for the loss of one arm, y amount for the loss of both arms, and so forth. Pension amounts depended on the loss of earning capacity. If a man suffered a serious injury that did not hamper his work ability, he was not eligible for a pension. *Back to Civil Life* defined a disability pension as "compensation for the loss or lessening of normal abilities as a result of war service and not for length of service. Entitlement may be conceded for a gunshot wound but if there was no assessable degree of disability there would be no payment of pension."[40] The needs of the capitalist supporting state could – and did – conflict with the prerogatives of manhood.

The class-based assumptions of liberal self-sufficiency made life difficult for some working-class veterans, especially the disabled and seriously injured. The state created its idealized notion of self-sufficiency based on the generalized liberal "everyman" – who, in reality, did not exist. The experiences of many veterans who appeared before the commission clearly exposed the notion's limitations. The economic problems that these men faced did not result from a lack of individual effort – their poverty and disability could not be explained by inadequate "gumption." Instead, each veteran came forward with a case that escaped the ideal's narrow confines. In some cases, it was just a matter of timing. Long delays had kept their pension appeals from being heard, while at the same time, injuries prevented the men from finding suitable employment. In the meantime, the men were left to wonder whether their problems would ever be solved. For others, the structures of the British Columbia economy worked against them. With a strong resource and primary-industry base and little secondary industry, British Columbia had a significant shortage of "light" jobs suitable for disabled veterans. This problem consistently plagued workers who fell under the jurisdiction of the Workmen's Compensation Board, and it was no different for veterans. No amount of individual initiative on the part of disabled men could immediately transform the nature of the provincial economy. Veterans slipped through the cracks. The absence of a universal old-age pension system created similar problems. Veterans could appeal to a patchwork of schemes including the federal government's 1927 old-age security legislation, the war veterans' allowance, and veterans' pensions through the CPC. Some veterans, such as Sholto M., did not fit into any. At the age of seventy-two, Sholto M. did not qualify for a military pension and thus worked as a dishwasher at Vancouver's Hotel Georgia to earn enough money to supplement his other means-tested income.[41]

The state's desire to instil self-sufficiency through its postwar reconstruction schemes did not always account for the real social and economic conditions faced by those to whom, based on strictly military grounds, it granted entitlement. This gap between intention and action, between the limited vision of the state and the more diverse social realities, fed a sense of unease and anger (here expressed by Kircher and other veterans) that the modern state actually worked against manly prerogatives.

For a number of veterans who appeared before the commission, the worst agent of the modern state was the psychiatrist. The commission spent a disproportionate amount of time on the psychiatrist's role in determining veterans' treatment and pension entitlements. Injured veterans felt that they owned a clear and straight entitlement; psychiatrists had different priorities. The increasing reliance on psychiatrists within the DVA represented a more general trend (as seen in later chapters) in which the dictates of masculinity were medicalized. Determining just how one could or should, for example, fulfill one's breadwinning duties or deal with risk, violence, and trauma became not just a matter of individual or even social decision, but also the subject of scientific knowledge. The group of doctors responsible for this medicalization were themselves going through an expansive period of professionalization, pushing forward the boundaries of how and when they could speak as experts. While doctors emphasized their desire to help (and it seems that in many cases this is exactly what they did), the medicalization of manhood implicit in their assistance meant that masculinity was once again being acted upon.

Canadian psychiatrists who worked for the DVA had very particular ideas about the causes of wartime mental illness. They believed that it stemmed from background personal characteristics, not from the immediate environment (i.e., battle and/or service). By the Second World War, psychiatrists had replaced the old term "shell shock" (with its connection to battle) with the more ambiguous term "battle exhaustion." The condition of battle exhaustion was, they thought, fairly common. However, they noted that most soldiers could recover quickly. As Terry Copp has stated, this official belief went against the actual experience of wartime psychiatrists, who reluctantly came to realize that the policy of treating soldiers early and sending them back into combat simply did not work; too many cases recurred. The general trend in psychiatric and psychological expertise, however, ran in the opposite direction in the 1940s, emphasizing the importance of behavioural explanations. Officials in the DVA's Division of Treatment Services continued to argue after the war that the real cause of battle exhaustion lay in the individual soldier's own troubled background.[42]

This individualistic perspective led them to advocate treatment over compensation. A concern with economic matters and the allegedly disturbing effect of the dole on manly responsibility (ideas no doubt shaped by the Depression) clearly influenced some psychiatrists as well as government policy. In contrast to those in the United States, few Canadian veterans who suffered psycho-neurotic injuries received pensions, and those who did earned very little. The Canadian policy was based on a belief that monetary compensation could hurt the recovery process. Instead of providing compensation, the Canadians emphasized treatment.[43] Travis Dancey, head of the DVA's Division of Treatment Services, best summarized the Canadian policy in a 1950 article in *The American Journal of Psychiatry*. Dancey reiterated the standard Canadian line on the importance of a soldier's/veteran's childhood in explaining battle exhaustion. He linked this to ideas of personal responsibility, so important to notions of manhood at mid-century.[44] Long-term sufferers of battle exhaustion often used the disorder, he wrote, "to avoid painful experiences and to escape certain responsibilities." Awarding these men pensions would be an "encouragement toward the acceptance of his illness as a means of escaping his responsibilities [and] is therefore dangerous ... The subject, under such conditions, is apt to feel more and more disabled and to demand repeated increases in his income from a state that has already assumed a certain responsibility for his illness."[45] From this perspective, psychiatrists and the CPC had the best interests of veterans at heart when they limited financial compensation.

In the mid-1940s, the psychiatric profession's ability to claim expertise was still new enough to be reasonably and seriously questioned. The use of psychiatrists and psychologists in the Second World War had contributed to the growing reputation of both professions. The Canadian Psychological Association was founded in 1941, while the Canadian Psychiatric Association was not founded until 1951. Until that time, Canadian psychiatrists belonged to the American Psychiatric Association. Within psychiatry, Freudian notions of psychoanalysis were beginning to challenge earlier medical models of mental illness. Indeed, it was during the postwar years that Freudian ideas entered into Canadian psychiatry and into the popular lexicon. Government psychiatrists during and after the war, including those connected to Shaughnessy Hospital, were largely anti-Freudian, relying instead mostly on biological/medical models.[46]

Kirchner and other veterans challenged the right of this newly important profession to decide the fate of a veteran's claim. They saw a much more direct link between injury, service, and compensation. They served, they suffered, and they deserved. Much of the heat and vitriol of the Royal Commission arose in discussions over psychiatrists and their interruption of this basic equation. Veterans resented the implication that they would fake their injury or attempt to malinger in any way. They presented themselves as respectable and hard-working men who suffered loss through no fault of their own. Indeed, in their personal narratives, they presented themselves as going above and beyond the arduous life struggles of the ordinary man.[47] Kirchner targeted "the pseudo-psychiatrists whose subversive, anti-social theories have been superimposed, in practice, over the findings of the legitimate medical profession of Canada."[48] J.H. Blackmore, member of Parliament for Lethbridge, also lashed out at "pestilential psychiatrists" for their role in harming veterans' pension claims.[49] Blackmore could not believe that any sane man would tell a veteran suffering physical injury that he had made it up. He stated before the House of Commons: "I would stop here to advise the veterans affairs department to clear out these people [psychiatrists] as one would clear vermin out of a house ... If we should have another war, and if any of us should have a boy going to that war, I think we should offer a silent prayer that they will never fall into the hands of a psychiatrist."[50]

The case of John B., discussed earlier, provides an instructive example of this conflict between veterans and psychiatrists, of how the psychiatric expertise impinged upon notions of manly independence. John B., a veteran and former prisoner of war of the Japanese in Hong Kong, complained of his treatment by a psychiatrist at Shaughnessy Hospital: "He [the psychiatrist] says 'we know you were a prisoner in Hong Kong, and you had a pretty rough go of it, sure we'll admit that, but you've been back eighteen months, you look good' he says 'we have done all we could do for you, but the trouble with you fellows from Hong Kong is from here up. You sit at home and you brood, and you worry about yourself,' and he said 'that's your trouble – you sit and worry about yourself and you think you have got [sic] ailments, pains, sickness and disease.'" John B. resented the implication that he had invented his injuries. The psychiatrist sent him to be examined at "South-4," the psychiatric wing of Shaughnessy Hospital. This brought on a host of worries, both material and emotional. He worried about what this would do to his pension claim. And he also worried about his self-image. "I had no visitors while I was here," he told the commissioners. "I wouldn't tell them [his friends] where I was at. I would be liable to tell them I would be over at the Physiotherapy or something or down swimming – that's the attitude, South 4 attitude."[51] When psychiatrists diagnosed and prescribed upon veterans, they trod on the territory of manliness, secreting negative attitudes toward mental illness into this domain that the veterans considered sacrosanct.

The methods of "assisting" veterans who potentially suffered psychiatric injuries created new tensions and sources of unease. Yet the psychiatrists' expertise gave them a privileged place within the DVA and

CPC bureaucracy. Even when the commissioners found the treatment of individual veterans to be quite odd, the profession itself could close ranks and explain unorthodox techniques within a scientific language that gave it credence. This is what happened when the commissioners questioned John B.'s treatment by one psychiatrist, Dr. Margetts. Margetts ordered pentothal testing. Psychiatrists used pentothal, popularly referred to as "truth-serum," to facilitate their questioning of reticent patients. To John B., this type of test challenged his character. "I heard that they give it to jailbirds – murderers," he recalled. "I'm not a jailbird, am I?" John B. also objected to the sexual nature of the questioning. "They start off with a normal conversation, and the first damn thing it ends up in sex. All they discuss is sex, nothing but sex." Even though John B.'s condition included sexual problems, he felt awkward during the questioning, particularly considering the tone and ordering of questions.

> *John B.:* I was asked by Dr. Margetts how many times I pulled my wire in Hong Kong and Japan. A man's pretty bad when he gets down so low that [he] refuse[s] to get a woman. You don't bother with women.
> *Dr. Blair:* That's about the last thing you have got in your head.
> *John B.:* Your [sic] thinking of food.
> *Winters:* Of course, I guess he was just trying to find out the start of – when the thing started over there.
> *John B.:* Oh yes, that's it. But if they would explain for me what they want. Anything he asked me – I answered every question to my ability, you know ... and still I got so I just couldn't tell about it.

The unequal relation between psychiatrist and patient as well as the significant effect that the psychiatrist's judgment could have on his pension, let alone his own personal life, made the questioning painful and traumatic. John B. wanted to give his interpretation of events but was consistently worried that the psychiatrist's knowledge would win out. And it did. Although the commissioners had problems with the type of questioning that John B. described, the medical staff rallied around Margetts and explained his questioning within the framework of expertise.[52] Ironically, and unfortunately for John B., it was the very support for his entitlement as a veteran that had impressed upon the state the need to call forth this expertise in the first place.

A Legacy for the Postwar Years?
After hearing from the witnesses in Vancouver, the commissioners retired to Ottawa to draft their report. They sought to balance their support

for the work of the DVA and the CPC against the desire to improve the treatment of a few individual veterans. The commission found no cause for complaint in the majority of cases that Kirchner had put before it. However, it did single out two groups of veterans as deserving a better deal. The commissioners expressed sympathy for the former Hong Kong prisoners of war and found some of the psychiatric questioning to be problematic, blaming this on the "lack of experience on the part of a junior psychiatrist and the inability of these patients to understand the reasons for psychiatric methods." In addition, a few individual veterans who had complained about poor treatment by the CPC had their criticisms upheld. The report emphasized that it believed the CPC to be a generally very good organization but found that it had, in these cases, forgotten its mandate to give the benefit of the doubt to veterans. Overall, no major shocks or recommendations for systematic change came from this Royal Commission. It had been created to deal with the concerns of individual veterans, and it had responded by doing just that. Kirchner seemed satisfied with his involvement. Despite being hostile at the very beginning, questioning the ability of the commissioners to hear the cases, he ultimately praised them for their even-handed guidance.[53]

The image of masculinity and entitlement that emerged from the commission, as with manly modernism more generally, was doubled. On the one hand, the ideal of the manly modern risking his body on behalf of the state infused contemporary notions of entitlement. When veterans appeared before the commission, they emphasized their status as male breadwinners who had given up their positions in the civilian economy and had offered to join the military. One of the reasons that this commission could end with less acrimony than it began with was that all involved in the process intimately connected ideas of what it meant to be a man with the process of postwar reconstruction.

On the other hand, this connection between masculinity and the state's reconstruction policies also led to a new series of gendered anxieties and complaints. The veterans who appeared before the commission found their experience with the state to be anything but empowering. They complained of inefficient (or too efficient) bureaucracy, of the inability of the system to see individuals as people with specific life histories, and of the methods used by the experts, particularly psychiatrists and doctors, who had so much control over how a veteran's entitlement was understood. Veterans had become the main clients of the burgeoning Canadian welfare state at mid-century, with all the promises and frustrations that this entailed. The great task of the modernist project in Canada during the 1940s lay in ensuring a successful transition to peace. For state planners, this meant avoiding (or at least managing) a postwar recession, dampening wartime radicalism, especially among returning veterans, and ensuring the successful transition to a postwar period in which the breadwinner-homemaker family resumed its normative status. These veterans were experiencing the common deficiencies in high-modernist schemes for social organization and human improvement. Postwar plans for veterans' re-establishment reflected other similar modernist plans to assist, help, and improve people in that they often sought to manipulate, alter, and control those whom they were ostensibly trying to help. While much of this was perhaps inevitable, simply reflecting how schemes for social regulation typically work, they nonetheless helped to cement the other key element of manly modernism: the notion that manhood was threatened by modernity.[54] Although it was the very strength of the veterans' gendered entitlement that made them the clients of the state in the first place, masculinity nevertheless emerged from the commission as something that was threatened, that needed protection. The logic of veterans' entitlement rested on these two contradictory premises: that men were the ideal moderns because of their risk taking; and that they were simultaneously the victims of modern bureaucracy and expertise.

The experience of veterans has been a good place from which to begin. In the switch from soldier to veteran, Vancouverites moved from war to peace, from the sacrifices of the past to the alleged promises of the future. With the figure of the mistreated and deserving veteran, we have been introduced to the gendered logic of manly modernism that predominated in the postwar years. We have seen that state planners established reconstruction policies with the twin goals of re-establishing men as breadwinners and fulfilling the entitlements of veterans to the "good life." But what happened in the later 1940s and 1950s? Did these same notions of manly sacrifice and deservedness persist in the way that Vancouverites interpreted the modernist project? And if so, how and to what effect?

3
At Work

The fearful projections of state planners about the postwar economy largely did not come to pass. The economy bounced out of the Second World War and into the late 1940s and 1950s in good shape. Indeed, the period between the end of the war and the late 1960s saw the single largest period of economic expansion in Canadian history, greater even than the era of the Laurier Boom, which saw the opening of the Canadian West. In the global context, the historian Eric Hobsbawm refers to these years as a "Golden Age," noting that the period's economic growth, certainly in retrospect, marked it off as a unique moment in history. While such large economic measures do not always translate into improved quality of life for individuals, the relative advance over wartime and depression provided a genuine indicator of improvement for many. The promises made to returning soldiers had found a favourable climate in which to bear fruit.[1]

The postwar "good life," however, brought its own worries: progress had many risks to be managed, not least of which were the accidents caused by industry. This chapter looks at the collapse of Vancouver's Second Narrows Bridge in 1958 to explore the ways that Vancouverites thought about progress and its risks. When all goes well, much is assumed and left unsaid. But when disaster strikes, when the unexpected happens, much is said that is usually left unspoken. This was the case in June 1958, when the Second Narrows Bridge collapsed, killing eighteen workers. The collapse riveted public attention on the risks of modernization and the dangers of economic development. Newspaper headlines and pictures brought the disaster into Vancouver homes. Unlike other incidents of workplace danger, which usually occurred in remote areas in the logging and mining industry, this accident occurred within the city, within the known space of those who assumed that such events would not (and should not) occur.

The response to the collapse – on the part of the public, the provincial government, the local media, as well as the companies and workers involved – revealed a great deal about how popular notions of progress and risk were gendered. During the war, the masculinity of risk had been constructed through discussions of winning the war and ensuring the successful re-establishment of the postwar economy. After the war, the masculinity of risk still featured prominently in ideas about the modernist project. In the response to the collapse, we see how these ideas persisted, centring on men's ability to control the environment through engineering and everyday personal feats of daring in order to build the infrastructure of the economic boom. Building the bridge demanded that risks be taken, that they be assessed and calculated. In the commentary upon the collapse, such basic features of the modernist project emerged as aspects not only of modernity more generally, but also of manliness. But as with the veterans, the manly modernism of bridge building was anything but straightforward. The mechanisms of safety, administration, and control again emerged as frustrations. With the bridge collapse, the class-based nature of such complaints became even more apparent.

Bridges, Modernity, and the Discipline of Safety

Accident stories typically begin just before disaster. Everything is as usual. Men concentrate on their jobs, perhaps they share a joke together. Cars pass nearby, their drivers oblivious to imminent danger. Someone might mention the weather. Then ... suddenly ... the unexpected happens: a machine explodes, the earth quakes, or a giant tsunami comes crashing down. Vancouverites fell back upon this type of narrative when they told the story of the Second Narrows Bridge collapse. A generic version of this story would begin like this:

The morning of 17 June 1958 dawned like any other day. The sun shone brightly over this young city on the Pacific. Above the waters of Burrard Inlet, on the Second Narrows Bridge, ironworkers sweated under the early summer heat. If this had been an ordinary day, the heat might have been something to complain about; but this was no ordinary day. At 3:40 in the afternoon, Vancouver's Second Narrows Bridge collapsed. The outermost span shook, tilted, and then plunged into the water below, taking with it another span and sixty startled men.

The *Vancouver Sun* and the *Vancouver Province* told the story in this way. So too have others since that time.[2]

In the immediate aftermath of the collapse, shock was the most common response. Witnesses responded with a mixture of incredulity and action. The surviving ironworkers and other workers on the site that day immediately began to help their fallen coworkers. Emergency crews and many Vancouverites nearby rushed to respond. In the political realm, the government called for a Royal Commission. Yet disbelief backed this action. The *Sun* remarked: "It couldn't happen. But it did." An immediate witness to the collapse, the operator of the older Second Narrows Bridge, which the new one was to replace, Alfred Engleman, later recalled, "Well, when I actually seen it coming down I couldn't believe what I was looking at, it was something that was – well, I never expected a thing like that to happen, I never realized what was happening." A boater who witnessed the collapse recalled, "It seemed to go down in slow motion. It was fantastic to watch it." In Victoria, Premier W.A.C. Bennett and Highways Minister Gaglardi responded in similar fashion. According to the *Sun*, Gaglardi guffawed in disbelief when a reporter first told him of the collapse. Bennett responded simply, "It was just one of those things. It seems impossible." This language of disbelief was both an effect of and a contribution to the era's high-modernist optimism.[3]

The collapse threatened the promoters' celebration of humanity's ability to control technology and the environment. Responses to the collapse were fraught with fearful references to the smallness of man next to the massive forces unleashed. The workers jumping off the bridge were "like flies." Contrasted with the usual expanding march of the bridge outward, the *Sun* noted that after the collapse, "All that stood against the sky ... was a huge steel W shape. A couple of giant waterchutes, their steel ends curling like gnarled roots with dead and dying men tangled among them, sloped down [into] the water instead of arching above it."[4] Initial reports repeatedly focused on the bodily pain and suffering, telling of cuts, bruises, and worse. The reports counterposed this horrifying reality to the utter inadequacy of safety equipment. For every brutalized body, a torn life jacket or safety rope lay to the side, seemingly useless.[5] In this language of a world turned upside down, the power of man to overcome – the essence of modernity's promise – had been thwarted. Could it be that, like the Sorcerer's Apprentice, Vancouverites had lost control of the forces that their modern engineering magic had unleashed?

This narrative style, with its emphasis on shock, is enticing: it has immediacy and impact; one minute all is calm and the next the world is in chaos. Yet we should attend as much to *how* this story is told as to its content. The accident-story genre tells us much by the meanings that it privileges and hides, by its silences as well as by its speech. This type of narrative assumes that the workplace is normally accident-free, that economic development is an inherently progressive activity that usually runs without violent incident. The shock comes from normality's interruption. Yet the narrative must *establish* the moment before the incident in this way. When such a narrative is not novelistic but social, existing in daily practice, then the support for this device may also be found in the social world.[6] The popularity and success of this narrative strategy in 1950s Vancouver depended upon a set of cultural beliefs and institutional practices with three intermingling features. First, infrastructure development occupied a special place in high-modernist ideology in the postwar years. This meant that when the bridge went down, its violence could be seen as having resulted from an already inherently progressive act and understood as an unfortunate side effect of progress. Second, the administrative system set up to deal with modernity's dangerous side effects, the Workmen's Compensation Board (WCB), turned workplace violence into a matter of discipline and management rather than politics. By regularizing workplace accidents, the WCB removed the issue from the political and public realm to such an extent that the bridge collapse could appear as an exception or aberration – not as one large incident among many, which it was. Finally, the ideology of manly modernism provided a further bond of social glue holding together this system of industrial modernity. All involved in the bridge collapse, from bridge workers and engineers to politicians and journalists, assumed that the risks involved in building the bridge were inherent features of masculinity. The aftermath to the bridge collapse, then, witnessed a public outpouring of these common assumptions about the benefits of modernity, its terrible risks, and men's prominent role in managing them.

The decision to build the Second Narrows Bridge was part of a larger process of turning Vancouver into a successful modern city. Bridges were essential features of transportation in a city like Vancouver.[7] Its downtown core is almost surrounded by water, and many other areas of the city are divided by various bodies of water, including the Fraser River to the south. As the city grew, so did the number and size of its bridges. Local governments had built the Burrard Street Bridge in 1932, and private interests with government aid had built the Lions Gate Bridge in 1938. Bridge building continued in the postwar years and included the Granville Street Bridge in 1954, the Oak Street Bridge in 1957, and the Second Narrows Bridge, the one that collapsed in 1958 and that was finally completed in 1960. Vancouver's rapid suburbanization depended upon the automobile, and the automobile required a whole infrastructure of roadways, including bridges. The Second Narrows Bridge that collapsed during construction in 1958 was meant to replace an earlier bridge that spanned the same part of Burrard Inlet, joining Vancouver and North Vancouver. The new bridge offered more lanes of traffic for commuters to and from the north shore. It also opened up the waters beyond the Second Narrows to larger ships. The earlier bridge had been built just above the water with a section that raised and lowered to allow ships to pass through, but it had proved unwieldy. A number of ships had crashed into it, knocking it out entirely between 1929 and 1934 and earning it the nickname the "Bridge of Sighs." When the Social Credit government announced plans to build a new bridge, it did so to help spur on these processes of suburbanization and industrialization and to provide Vancouver with a small share of the provincial public works largesse that the government felt was so important to the province's modernization.[8]

Even beyond the bridge's utility to the city, promoters of the Second Narrows Bridge emphasized the aesthetics of its modernizing potential. They gave it an aura of progress that seemed to be an end in itself. This is what the historian of technology David Nye has called the "technological sublime," indicating the sense in which major works of industrial modernity came to stand in for natural wonders that had previously created this sense of dangerous awe.[9] Promoters extolled the bridge as a symbol of the extent to which daily life in a modern British Columbia included daring feats of engineering and other technological advances as a matter of course. Newspapers spun stories of the bridge's technical gizmos and industrial inventions. From the size of massive girders to the movement of heavy cranes, few details escaped the notice of Vancouver bridge enthusiasts. The industrial and engineering press also boasted of "firsts": that the bridge was made of 16,600 tons of steel, that it was the largest structure in Canada to be erected by tension bolting, and that its centre span length of 1,100 feet was second in Canada only to that of the Quebec Bridge.[10] Perceiving an appetite for bridge details, these publications provided plenty of feed.

Building bridges could, however, cost lives. The Quebec Bridge that the Second Narrows Bridge was beating in the record books had collapsed twice during construction. Bridge building was no different than any other large-scale development project or industrial operation. It harmed as well as helped. In 1958, in British Columbia, 208 workers lost their lives on the job. And that was a good year. The 1959 total of workplace deaths was even higher: 262 people died on the job that year in British Columbia. The industrial development of British Columbia that fuelled the postwar boom and kept up hopes that the modernist project was on track in this particular corner of the Western world killed hundreds of workers every year. It was never clear who would be killed or when, but the fact that industrial development would take lives was a given. And the number of lives was not at all insignificant. The number of murders, for example, paled in comparison to the number of workplace deaths. The 208 workplace deaths in British Columbia in 1958 was greater than the total number of murders in all of Canada (198).[11] The persistence of a modernist appreciation for development – in both its utilitarian and aesthetic senses – demanded that this violence be neutralized. This is what the Workmen's Compensation Board provided. The era's high-modernist optimism depended on the fact that the WCB depoliticized and neutralized the potentially contentious issue of workplace danger.

The creation of the WCB is a subject that has yet to receive sufficient scholarly attention in Canada, so a brief account will be necessary here.[12] British Columbia established a Workmen's Compensation Board in 1917, after a series of earlier pieces of legislation beginning in the 1890s failed to provide a lasting solution to the problem of workplace safety in the province. The system itself – and the debate that led to its formation – resembled what had emerged elsewhere in North America and Britain in response to the violence caused by the Industrial Revolution and the inadequacy of existing laws to deal with its consequences. The legislation established the WCB as an independent body responsible for overseeing all matters related to workplace safety, including accident prevention and, most significantly, the compensation of workers for injuries incurred while on the job. Business agreed to finance the system in order to ensure stability in how awards were granted. While the older system generally favoured companies and accepted the notion of "implied consent," which stated that workers accepted risks when taking on a new job, the law worked erratically, providing some very large awards to the injured, with which businesses could find it difficult to deal. Even more important, the large number of injuries fuelled working-class radicalism. Both businesses and politicians appreciated how the WCB could dampen this potentially volatile aspect of class antagonism. For their part, unions agreed to the system because it provided regular financial compensation for workers. It also represented, as the American historians David Rosner and Gerald Markowitz argue, a recognition in principle (if not always in practice) "that workers have a right to a safe workplace, and it is the responsibility of society to guarantee that right."[13] The process of establishing a system of workmen's compensation did not go as smoothly as this summary suggests. The language of partnership and compromise masked significant differences over how the system should be run, how much it should provide workers, and which workers should be covered. But such disagreements lost their potency after 1917 because of the legalistic and bureaucratic context in which they were made.

While the WCB emerged from a heated context of class conflict in the early years of the twentieth century, once established, it worked to neutralize the political dimensions of workplace violence by making risk into a wholly managerial process. The WCB threw out questions of intent and blame. Instead, it focused on whether certain injuries and industries fitted into its administrative scheme and then determined, by referring to a series of tables and already agreed upon schedules, the level of compensation to be paid. The loss of a right arm was worth so much, the loss of a left arm so much, and the loss of both another amount again. The system closely resembled that used for disabled war veterans. Everything had its grid, its already agreed upon price. Politics was out, and bureaucracy was in.

This is, according to Karl Figlio, a particularly modern way to deal with calamity linked to the development of contract-based relations and capitalism. Whereas traditional societies place disasters within a providential scheme of reckoning in which everything has meaning, the modern way is to say that they are chance events that are best understood at the aggregate level. This is made possible by setting up a series of actions and events as natural and normal – in this case, the workings of industrial capitalism. "This field of natural expectation," Figlio argues, "is often invaded by (retrospectively) predictable but unforeseen events which can be treated routinely in the form of claims for compensation. No fault is assumed, in the sense of malice, yet one party is held accountable, *as if* he or she were responsible ... Motive is there, but in neutralized form; accountability without culpability."[14] In this rendition, the emphasis has switched from the individual incident to the broader system. Workplaces do not have dangers for which someone is blamed but risks that need to be managed. And this switch to focus on risk management involved an increased emphasis on the role of expertise and workplace discipline.

In practice, the WCB regulated industries by emphasizing self-discipline on the part of management and especially of workers. Although it was empowered to legally enforce sanctions against management, the board rarely used this option, preferring education over enforcement. Indeed, the WCB had little enforcement capability (for example, the ability to inspect work sites). Although the Act came into force in 1917, the board did not hire safety inspectors until the 1930s, and then only after numerous serious accidents in the logging industry forced their hand.[15] The chaotic years of the Second World War, with their increased industrial activity and many more accidents, demonstrated the need for safety inspection, and the board had hired twenty-one inspectors by the early 1950s. Yet, after substantial industrial growth in the 1950s and early 1960s, the number of inspectors had only risen to twenty-two by 1965, an increase of just one. With so few inspectors to cover so much industry, the board could only imprecisely ensure safe work practices. All involved – inspectors, businesses, and workers – knew that many work sites could not be visited regularly. According to long-time WCB inspector Jim Paton, successful inspection in these years depended more on "intuition" than on strict surveillance.[16]

Instead of enforcing regulations by legal action, the WCB tried to get workers to adopt a kind of rational self-discipline that matched the ideals of manly modernism. They called on workers to think ahead and to put "safety first." An image reprinted in *The Span,* the paper published by the bridge-building company Dominion Bridge, nicely captured the gendered implications of the safety message. It showed a broad-shouldered safety man giving a lesson in the proper way to hold a heavy object; in this case, the "object" is a female ballet student winking at the camera. The safety man would, the caption claims, "find no hardship in obeying this safety rule."[17]

Or would he? How did workers respond to the optimism of high modernism and the WCB's welfare capitalism? The particular way that the story of the Second Narrows Bridge collapse came to be told could have found its most serious critic in the workers themselves, in those who actually suffered from the violence of industrial modernity. Yet it did not. Workers remained relatively silent on the issue of workplace danger after the collapse and indeed for much of the 1950s.[18] In part, we have seen how the WCB system muted such criticism, turning it toward the amount of money to be paid in compensation rather than toward the extent of danger itself. Yet there was ultimately more involved in the workers' lack of safety politics than the WCB alone can explain. If we are to understand the response of Vancouverites, especially workers, to the collapse, we need to look at how gender figured into stories of the collapse.

Manhood, Sacrifice, and the Bridge Collapse

The Second Narrows Bridge collapse hit Vancouverites close to home. Seventeen men died in the collapse, and another died in the salvage operation. The sound of crashing steel could be heard in downtown Vancouver. The ground literally shook. If only briefly, the bridge collapse showed the advances of the modernist project to be ambiguous. Particularly striking about Vancouverites' responses to the collapse is how they used gender to make sense of the calamity. Despite its unexpectedness, the collapse fitted smoothly into an already existent way of representing modernity's dark potential, through the ideology of manly modernism. One man's letter to the *Province* nicely captured this link between masculinity and modernity: "I have felt a ... personal grief over the bridge itself, and all men who build bridges and the other vast edifices upon which so much of our modern life depends," he wrote. "They build bridges, and we commit our lives to those bridges every day, and we have utter faith in them, so much faith that we look upon the builders as mere ordinary men, forgetting that they work side by side with death."[19] The letter is telling for how it equates the everyday benefits of the modernist project with the sacrifices and risk taking of heroic masculinity. If these were not ordinary men, then they must have been extraordinary. And they earned this special status by the risks that they took on behalf of society at large. A number of postwar Vancouverites romanticized and valorized the risk-taking behaviour of the bridge workers and the kind of masculinity that it represented, the kinds of masculine traits that other critics feared were being lost in the postwar years. The bridge collapse, a moment of modernist crisis, served as a way to reassert this notion of rugged masculinity and the inherent masculinity of the modernist project.

Postwar manhood was defined, in part, as being able to manage and take risks. Reporters conveyed the magnitude of the disaster by showing how it inverted male stoicism, causing grown men to cry. The *Province* columnist Jean Howarth recounted how one survivor "laughed a silly little laugh and then passed his hand over his face, and when the hand came away he was crying." Another "big burly man," Howarth told readers, "kept digging tears out of his eyes with the heels of his hands." If men's tears unnerved reporters, so too did the bodies of the dead. While the workers may have been large and active in life, death emasculated their bodies. The bodies lay silent in lines on the rescue boats. Another, not yet recovered, hung "limp, suspended on a safety line on the collapsed span."[20] The power of such accounts depended on the notion that to be masculine was to be actively in control of one's emotions and of one's part in the modernist project.

This language of gendered crisis extended to men's position in the family as breadwinners. The American historian of fatherhood Robert Griswold argues that breadwinning has been the dominant masculine ideal throughout the twentieth century. "Supported by law, affirmed by history, sanctioned by every element in society," he notes, "male bread-winning has been synonymous with maturity, respectability, and masculinity."[21] This argument holds true for postwar Vancouver. In the wake of the collapse, Vancouverites saw the fallen workers as men and bread-winners interchangeably. The public directed the major thrust of its response toward ameliorating the economic plight of the widows. The *Province* and the Vancouver and District Labour Council established a charity called the Families Fund to raise money for the families of the fallen workers. Their appeals played upon an image of feminine dependency and masculine breadwinning. The *Province* deemed one widow, Mrs. Crusch, especially needy and included her story in many of their articles calling for donations.[22] With dependent children in need of medical treatment, poor health, and an elderly father under her care, Crusch fitted well into images of appropriate feminine need. The plight of Crusch and other widows spurred the protective breadwinning instincts of one young man to offer his breadwinning services to the Families Fund. "This may sound funny to you," he said, "but I think instead of making a donation to the fund, I ought to get the name of one of the families that's in the worst need and send them a cheque for $25 every month. You see, I'm not married, and I haven't any responsibilities, and it wouldn't hurt me to help a family like that."[23] In total, the Families Fund raised $50,000 for the families of the fallen bridge workers, demonstrating that Vancouverites supported the manly ideal of breadwinning with their pocketbooks as well as their hearts.

These fears of the threat posed by the bridge collapse, whether to men's emotional state or breadwinning capabilities, coexisted with assertions of some men's appropriately masculine response. The collapse challenged men to respond with vigour. When they did, the papers celebrated these valiant efforts and reasserted the link between masculinity and the control of modern risks. For example, when the bridge collapsed, twenty-two-year-old ironworker George Schmidt fell into the water amid the mangled steel. One of his legs had been sheared off just above the knee. According to the *Sun*, "He took off his belt and he made a tourniquet with it around his thigh. Then he lit a cigarette. He smoked it and waited and finally two men came along and lifted him out of the mangled steel into the rowboat. 'Thanks fellas,' is all he said."[24]

The workers' status as direct manly descendants of veterans emerged clearly in the public funeral held on their behalf. The funeral service had two parts, one of which took place in Empire Stadium and the other at the waters of Burrard Inlet in sight of the downed span. At the water's edge, Reverend George Turpin conducted a memorial service. Turpin also happened to be the reverend of Vancouver's veterans' hospital, the site of most of Walter Kirchner's cases. "Remember their courage," Turpin admonished. "It was the daily courage of men whose tasks take them to dangerous places. When the span is completed, it will be a giant memorial to loved ones who are gone."[25] As in war, men's sacrifices on behalf of the modernist project meant that they deserved respect and authority. Ultimately, it came back to doing a job, something men were supposed to do implicitly. "They died doing their job," one Vancouverite wrote to the *Province*. "Building a bridge so that we could cross from one side to another. They have died for us."[26]

This celebration in the public sphere and in the press of men's stoic risk taking mirrored the men's own sense of themselves as skilled craftsmen. Many workers presented safety regulations as a hindrance, as something that interfered with their own ability to manage the risks of the workplace. From this perspective, the regulations of the WCB amounted to workplace discipline. The class inequalities of the workplace belied the language of partnership in the company's and the WCB's appeal to industrious and safety-conscious manly behaviour. The ironic effect of these disciplinary strategies, however, was to make workers sometimes less, not more, keen on adhering to safety standards. At the Second Narrows Bridge worksite, safety became an area of contention between some workers and the employer, with the workers, not management, demanding fewer and less stringent safety rules. Workers presented safety regulations as an inconvenience and as a threat to their competence and skill. WCB safety inspectors encountered problems in enforcing rules that required workers to wear hard hats and life jackets. These two safety features directly related to two leading areas of injury and death in bridge building: being hit by falling objects and drowning.[27] In general, workers believed safety to be important, but their vision of themselves as exceptionally competent removed the need for such precautions in their own cases. When Dominion Bridge asked for its employees' opinions on the utility of educational games promoting workplace safety, the workers agreed that such policies were helpful. However, they distanced themselves from the need for education by saying that such measures would likely help younger workers and those who were less careful or skilled.[28] For workers, safety came through individual competence and skill, not just through following expert guidelines.

The conflict between, on the one side, the bureaucratic rationality of the WCB experts and company managers and, on the other, the workers reflected the broader tension between masculinity and modernity that was typical of the veterans' experience. It pitted regulations and rules against individual merit and character, working-class men against middle-class "experts." Yet, as with veterans, the situation is more complex than it might first appear. Workers and management may have disagreed over how safety could be achieved, but both supported the broader modernist project within which the danger was created. Workplace safety did not emerge as a major issue in labour politics in the 1950s. Just as the veterans embraced their role as risk takers, so too did the workers on the Second Narrows Bridge take up their own daring role. It is this final element, the shared belief in manly modernism, that allowed the story of the Second Narrows Bridge collapse to be told in the way that it was, as an aberration. Broad public support for the modernist project and the success of the WCB's welfare capitalism depended on the dominance of manly modernism as a gender ideal for working-class men.

Reasserting the Rational

In the aftermath of the collapse, Vancouverites searched for its meaning: they wanted to know *why* it had happened. They searched for answers from the engineering profession and its technical know-how. This quest for truth in technical knowledge and quantitative systems was distinctly modern. It treated accidents as preventable and subject to control. The basic questions became: Was it preventable? Who was to blame? What could be learned from this tragedy? These are the questions of risk management. In the high-modernist context of the 1950s, these kinds of questions dominated public debate over the collapse. What is striking is how postwar notions of masculinity interacted with this line of questioning. The workers' masculinity, with its connection to bodily risk taking, awkwardly fitted into the modernist emphasis on reason and objectivity. In their reticent and emotionless demeanour, the two joined at the point where stoicism and reason met. Yet working-class masculinity became attached to the modernist project only to be colonized, to be seen as other, as a fascinating difference from the middle-class norm. Just as moderns found the accoutrements of the exotic other to be fascinating and valuable (think here of the celebration of the noble savage), so too did postwar modernizers embrace working-class risk taking as a valuable but ultimately "othered" type of knowledge that had its own inferior place in the modern pantheon.[29]

Commentators rushed to prove that they exhibited the proper modern reasoned approach and that others showed too much emotion. According to the logic of manly modernism, such sacrifice demanded a restrained emotional response that was as stoic and rational as that given by those who had suffered. Reporting of the collapse mirrored an emotional style that the American historian Peter Stearns has called "American Cool." Stearns argues that the first half of the twentieth century saw a switch from an expressive emotional style to one that was restrained. Building on this work, Michael Barton has found that disaster reporting showed a similar transformation from one that focused on the intense emotional content of catastrophe to one that emphasized cool professionalism in its wake.[30] This hierarchy that located reason over emotion showed up repeatedly in political discussions of the collapse. Critics claimed that the government had strayed too far from a reasonable approach to infrastructure development. Robert Strachan, leader of the Cooperative Commonwealth Federation (CCF), called for the resignation of Highways Minister Phil Gaglardi. "It's now said his ideas are triumphs of imagination over engineering," Strachan said of the minister. "Is this collapse a result of his imagination?"[31] The *Sun* editorial page echoed Strachan's concerns: "there is an urgent demand that public uneasiness about the safety of major public works be allayed ... Too much talk has been attributed to the flamboyant highways minister about the 'triumph of imagination over the cold hard facts of engineering.' Too much has been heard about 'testing the curves' of new highways by ministerial car. In all the rush and bustle and the flying from place to place, some things may have been forgotten or gone astray."[32]

The government responded by appealing to the same cultural dichotomy. Bennett called Strachan's criticisms "wild" and "irresponsible" and alleged that the CCF leader was acting inappropriately in trying to make "political capital out of a tragedy." The *Province* labelled those who criticized the government as emotional. "The collapse at the Second Narrows ... was an appalling tragedy," the editors claimed. "But its causes will not be uncovered, and a repetition of it elsewhere perhaps thus averted, by emotionalism or political haymaking. It will be done only by a cold, dispassionate and microscopically thorough investigation by engineers." The defenders of Dominion Bridge, the company charged with the construction of the bridge, drew the same emotional boundaries. They emphasized the need to honour the workers and grieve over the loss of life, but they equally emphasized that emotion had no place in explaining the cause of the collapse. The *Province* praised ironworkers as a "tough and gallant lot" and argued that "the newly dead among them would spit with contempt if they could know that their deaths were being used in the meantime as the fuel for political emotionalism."[33] Both Dominion Bridge and the editors of the *Province* were likely concerned with very precise issues: defending profits, reputations, and political allegiances. However, it is significant that they chose to make these arguments by claiming that their own reason trumped their opponent's emotionalism. They invoked the workers' risk taking to silence critics. Then they turned to another type of masculinity and another type of knowledge: that of the reasoned, dispassionate engineer.

These different types of manly modernism showed up in the establishment of a Royal Commission. The government appointed Sherwood Lett, chief justice of the British Columbia Supreme Court, to head the enquiry. Lett then called upon John Farris Jr. (son of Senator J.W. de B. Farris, a prominent Liberal), to act as the commission's legal representative and upon J.B. Pratley as the commission's engineering consultant.[34] Later, after realizing that the companies involved in the disaster were taking on experts of their own, Lett also appointed two teams of engineers, one British (Ralph Freeman and J.R.H. Otter) and one American (F.M. Masters and J.R. Giese). The commission called on representatives from Dominion Bridge and from Swan, Wooster and Partners, the engineering firm that had drawn up the bridge plans. Where did the workers fit into this rendering?

Local unions had a different kind of commission in mind. They wanted a board of inquiry made up of three members, one of whom, they argued, needed to be a representative of labour. The three labour organizations directly involved in the collapse – Local 97 of the Ironworkers, Local 98 of the Painters, and the Vancouver–New Westminster Building Trades Council – argued that workers should be involved at the very top of the investigation into the bridge collapse.[35] They based this claim on two interrelated arguments. According to the Ironworkers' business agent Norm Eddison, workers spoke in a distinct language and had a special knowledge that was unlike that offered by engineers. The commission needed a union representative in order to translate this special knowledge into the technical jargon of engineering. Moreover, the ironworkers had earned their knowledge by their proximity to danger. Accidents and disasters like a bridge collapse were hard to predict. Often only a fine line distinguished an "engineering triumph" from tragedy. According to Eddison, ironworkers had a special voice because they were the men who walked this line between "triumph and life[,] and disaster and death." These men, Eddison argued, had "paid a price in death, injury and bereavement" for the privilege of representation.[36] Bennett saw things differently and refused to give in to labour's demands; the commission went ahead with Lett as the sole commissioner. Determined to have their say even without an official labour commissioner, the Ironworkers hired an engineering consultant, Harold Minshall, to act on their behalf.

The commission got underway in mid-July, a month after the collapse. From the beginning, it was clear that the different participants had contrasting notions of who could speak and about which issues. Lett divided the commission into two sessions. At the earliest session, he heard evidence from eyewitnesses. These included workers, company officials, and some local residents. The first meeting served as a fact-factory from which the engineers could draw information in order to make their judgments. Just as in the media response to the collapse, workers' role in the investigation was related to their stoic risk taking. Aside from their comments on the collapse itself, they were also asked about safety on the work site. And workers uniformly noted that the bridge had been safe. They had no problem with Dominion Bridge's adherence to Workmen's Compensation Board safety measures. Given that they linked their identity with the dangerous work that they did every day, the workers could not easily turn around and use the collapse as an opportunity to attack the company. Worker after worker came before the commission to agree with WCB officials, who reported that all the designated safety precautions had been followed. The company held weekly safety meetings. Safety inspectors did not find any problems at the site.[37]

The Royal Commission gave credence to workers' sacrifices but only in a limited way. The workers appeared mostly in the commission's first sitting as eyewitnesses. They were closest to the collapse. They saw it happen. They could speak about the facts. They could not, however, speak as experts. Sherwood Lett conferred this status only upon engineers, company executives, and Workmen's Compensation Board officials. One obvious way to see the distinction between workers and those whom the commission deemed to be experts came at the beginning of their respective testimonies, when Farris asked witnesses to state their backgrounds and reasons for appearing. For workers, the whole introduction lasted a few moments, taking up a couple of lines in the transcripts. When the engineers appeared before the commission, Farris questioned them much more extensively on their backgrounds, asking for an extended listing of previous experience that went on for quite some time and covered pages of the transcripts. Lett and his wife entertained the engineers when they arrived, some of whom brought wives and took the visit as an opportunity to combine vacation with work. The pleasantries and social mixing seemed to match the respect that Lett accorded their opinions and approach.[38]

While some ironworkers claimed expert knowledge, Lett (and commission counsel Farris) did not allow them to speak in this capacity.[39] Ironworker W.J. Stroud found the distinction confusing and pointed out the inadequacy of drawing such a clear boundary over what was a much more messy reality. When Farris asked Stroud the place of origin of a noise that immediately followed the collapse, the ironworker questioned whether his answer would be fact or opinion. Only experts could give opinions. Their conversation offers a telling pointer on the constructed legal basis of expertise:

> *Farris:* You are not here to give opinions, you know, you are here to give facts ...
> *Stroud:* It seemed like my whole testimony here would be based on my opinions, my knowledge.
> *Farris:* Certainly not.

To Stroud this seemed an odd distinction, given that many witnesses had given conflicting testimony. "Well, I can answer that if you will clarify one point for me," he said:

> *Stroud:* When I say the bridge went down five or six inches here, not far enough for me to grab hold of, is that a fact ... or is that an opinion?
> *Farris:* That is a fact. You say that as a matter of fact.
> *Stroud:* Somebody is wrong because we are all on oath here and some say four feet, some say six inches. Apparently we have established no facts here.[40]

Farris dismissed these reservations, seeing them as mere distractions. Yet Stroud had arrived at an important insight into the socially constructed nature of expertise in the commission. It is not clear whether Stroud would have offered a radically different interpretation of the collapse than that offered by the engineers, but it is clear that even if he had wanted to argue it, his opinion would not have been heard.

After hearing from the workers and other eyewitnesses, Lett recessed the commission to allow time for the engineers to conduct their inspections. They presented their reports when the commission reconvened in late September 1958. From this point onward, issues of engineering and corporate responsibility dominated the commission hearings. The two official teams of engineers, executives from Dominion Bridge and from Swan, Wooster and Partners, and two local engineering consultants all came up with the same essential explanation for the collapse. They blamed it on a fault in the design of False Bent N4, a temporary support structure that had been holding up the outermost bridge section as it moved outward and before it was supposed to be attached to the permanent pier. A mistake had been made in the design of the outermost support. This design fault caused the collapse.

Having decided the mathematical problem, the commission then moved on to the question of responsibility. The support had been designed by a junior worker at Dominion Bridge and then checked over by a more senior manager. Neither of these two engineers caught the fault. Both died in the collapse. The question of responsibility, however, did not die with them. What else could have been done? The consulting engineers claimed that a problem in the corporate structure of Dominion Bridge had also worsened the situation. The company had placed the building of the Second Narrows Bridge outside its normal corporate structure, a move that resulted in fewer engineers' having a chance to check designs such as those for False Bent N4. This organizational decision had terrible consequences. Moreover, the engineers believed that the consulting engineers, Swan, Wooster and Partners, should have checked over the design of temporary support structures. Although this check was not required by law, the commission's engineers noted that it was standard practice elsewhere and that, if it had been done in this instance, it might have prevented the collapse. So from discussions of worker sacrifice and stoicism, the commission moved on to issues of organization and technicality.[41]

The presentation of the Ironworkers union's engineering representative before the commission, Harold Minshall, demonstrated both the power and the limitations of working-class manly modernism. Minshall began by boasting of the particular character of the average ironworker, particularly in how he dealt with danger. These were special men, he argued, whose temperament prompted "them to follow this hazardous ... endeavour. The temperament ... of the structural man is that ... he finds a zip in life by building things and following that occupation, perhaps, where he could not work in a store or on a farm." Like the letter writer to the *Province*, Minshall wanted the commission to know that these were not ordinary men. They were committed by their very nature to the dangerous occupation of bridge building. When he dealt with the engineering details, Minshall did not substantially differ from the other engineers. He agreed that the collapse was caused by the improper design of False Bent N4. Yet he emphasized what he called the "human element" in the collapse. He noted that all scientific endeavours ultimately depend on human endeavour. Here, the physicality of the ironworkers mattered. No matter how complex or certain are the techniques, ultimately someone must put this into practice, and there is always a chance of disaster. This is the nature of "calculated risk." "It is in this bracket," Minshall argued, "that the competency of fellowman plays such an important role in our achievement." And this provided the crux of Minshall's and the Ironworkers' argument. They did not criticize the practice of bridge building or the danger inherent in their jobs. Instead, they claimed that they had done a better and different sort of job: they had proved themselves fit for the task; they were true manly moderns. "In the pursuit of surgery and aeronautics, as in engineering and many other scientific fields," he argued, "judgement, the antithesis of man's formal knowledge, prevails and proves the adage, 'The only world a man truly knows is the world created by his senses.' It is from this understanding that humility becomes of singular importance in life, ever remembering that it is by the Grace of God that we are saved from disaster and that disaster is never an Act of God." This is what Minshall meant by the "human element."[42] With the bridge destroyed and men dead, Minshall wanted everyone to know that the workers had done a good job.

When Sherwood Lett published his report in December 1958, six months after the collapse, his conclusions demonstrated how workers' risks could be subsumed within the larger narrative of postwar modernization. Lett agreed with the commission's engineers and found that the collapse had been caused by a design error in False Bent N4. He noted the problems in the organization of Dominion Bridge as well as the inadequate communication between the construction company and the consulting engineers. He recommended that, in future, all plans for temporary supports be reviewed by the consulting engineers. In his concluding remarks, Lett reiterated his epistemological basis, the need for rational investigation. "The precise cause of a tragedy of this nature must be determined," he argued, "not by conjecture or surmise, but by the accurate, scientific investigation of skilled and experienced experts."[43]

The engineering profession greeted Lett's report as a positive step in this education. They particularly appreciated his neutral, objective stance. A.H. Finlay of the University of British Columbia wrote to Lett, congratulating him on the report, noting that "the tone in which it is pitched lends a special dignity to the inescapable conclusions which you reached." Engineering publications and organizations produced articles on what exactly went wrong. The problem was a technical one. This mistake, if the case was studied appropriately, would not be made again. Progress would be made.[44]

Sherwood Lett later recounted how difficult it was for him to find fault with his friend, the consulting engineer Bill Swan, and with Dominion Bridge, his client for thirty years. No doubt, on a personal level, this was a difficult action for Lett to take. However, in a more general way, Lett did nothing to upset the boat. His report set the appropriate cool and rational tone. It also positioned workers in what was perceived to be their appropriate place. Lett wrote to the widows of the two dead engineers whose errors had been found to have been pivotal in causing the collapse. He reminded them of their husbands' bravery. "Those acquainted with bridge building and such projects, know that every engineer and steelworker on the job must take risks daily if the job is to be done," Lett told them. "I am sure it will always be a matter of pride for you to know that your husbands were the kind of men who asked no man to take risks which they were not prepared to accept themselves." This emotive private correspondence that praised stoic daring provided the perfect accompaniment to Lett's publicly legalistic report. In the postwar ideology of manly modernism, both stoicism and reason had their proper place.[45]

In the summer of 1959, one year after the collapse and with the bridge not yet completed, the Ironworkers union went on strike in British Columbia. While the strike involved many building sites across the province, that the Ironworkers had struck on the Second Narrows Bridge played a prominent role in the labour dispute. Dominion Bridge claimed that the bridge was in a dangerous state and that, if left for some time, the situation could be disastrous, perhaps even leading to another collapse. The company took the union to court and the court ordered them back to work on the bridge. The next day, however, workers did not show up. When the union ended up back in court, Justice Manson demanded to know why the leaders had defied his order. The union representatives replied that they had done no such thing. If individual workers decided on their own not to go to work because the site was unsafe, this was not the union's fault. How could the company and the courts force men to work on an unsafe site? If it was too unsafe to be left for the duration of the strike, then surely it was too unsafe for the ironworkers. Such arguments made good headlines, but Manson found little use in them. The judge found the union leaders to be in contempt of court, and the ironworkers returned to work on the Second Narrows Bridge.[46]

The debate over workplace safety fitted nicely into the union's strike strategy. The idea that working-class men took risks that others would not was a source of power, especially following so closely upon the collapse the year before. The union used the acceptance of danger as a negotiating tactic. A 1959 contract brief listed the types of dangerous practices that workers regularly accepted, including a lack of safety scaffolding, working under suspended loads, working at great heights without a platform, being exempt from many WCB safety regulations, and the constant danger of falling objects.[47] The Ironworkers union went so far as to note that fourteen of their workers had died at one worksite (the Second Narrows Bridge).[48] Then, instead of calling for better safety and less dangerous conditions, they demanded higher pay. In 1959, the tactic succeeded. When the companies and union finally settled, the workers received a much better deal. The same tactic showed up in a 1962 contract brief. The union argued that "No amount of wages can compensate a man for the loss of his life." But the brief continued, "it is obvious that the wage rate must reflect the fact that the members are constantly faced with risk of death. No other building trade, and few occupations in any industry face a comparable degree of risk. It is appropriate therefore, that ironworkers should be the highest paid of the skilled building trades."[49] Local 97 directly stated that there was no comparison between wages and life but then immediately went on to make such a comparison. The brief did not call for improvements in workplace safety.

The Second Narrows Bridge was finally completed in the summer of 1960, and the opening ceremonies displayed the same contradictory confluence of ideas about manly sacrifice and progress that had been a part of the entire response to the collapse. The ceremony was oddly discordant. With marching bands and the press in tow, Premier Bennett waxed optimistic. Linking the new bridge with the health of British Columbia generally, he boasted, "I have never seen our people so optimistic, so forward-looking." When a West Vancouver councillor asked for another bridge crossing between Vancouver and the north shore, Gaglardi replied, "When you need 'em, we'll build 'em." Gaglardi's reply revealed a matter-of-fact approach to progress even though his government never built a third crossing of the Inlet. With the bridge complete, anything seemed possible – or at least this was the impression that the government wanted to leave. Such optimism went together with a ceremony honouring those who suffered during the bridge's construction. Mrs. John Wright, widow of one of the fallen workers, unveiled a plaque in honour of the dead. One of the surviving ironworkers who had been injured, William Wright (no relation), cut the ribbon for the official opening. The *Sun* claimed that Wright did not quite fit into the festivi-· ties, noting how he "looked uncomfortable in his best brown suit, slightly crumpled and damp."[50] For once, the boosterish paper got it right: working-class sacrifice and high-modernist optimism did indeed make odd bedfellows.

The postwar economic boom granted mixed rewards. The Canadian economy experienced its single largest period of expansion between the end of the Second World War and the early 1970s. The real income of working-class Canadians, just like that of the ironworkers here, rose considerably. In British Columbia, this boom was in many ways associated with the kinds of infrastructure projects that the Second Narrows Bridge represented: government-led projects contracted out to private companies that were meant to foster capitalist growth. This grand vision did not, however, alter the basic inequalities of social life that had existed during depression and war. Despite the overall rise in Canadians' incomes, differences between income groups and classes remained constant. In 1951, the top fifth of Canadian families controlled approximately 40 percent of the national income, while the bottom fifth of families controlled only 6 percent. The same proportions held constant in 1971. As John Porter argued in *The Vertical Mosaic,* Canadian society was sharply divided along the lines of class and ethnicity, even if debates in the political sphere did not reflect these economic realities.[51]

Labour historians frequently refer to the postwar years as an era of Fordist compromise. After the heightened militancy of wartime, employers and governments provided a certain amount of union security in exchange for maintaining capitalist control over the workplace. Unions focused on wages and benefits, while corporations benefited from a more passive, bureaucratic, and legalistic unionism, constrained by continued employer resistance to reform and the unanticipated consequences of the new industrial-relations system.[52] The political timidity of the postwar consensus also had much to do with the Cold War political climate and the purging of Communists from most Canadian unions. By taking gender into account, however, we can add a new dynamic to this account of the postwar compromise.

The lack of a radical working-class response to the Second Narrows Bridge collapse (and to workplace danger in the postwar years more generally, we might hypothesize) came not just because of the structure of unionism, employer resistance, or the restrictive Cold War political climate, but also because workers and employers shared common cause in their support for the modernist project and the ideology of manly modernism. In the postwar years, the gendered threat to male authority came in the form of the memory of women's work during the war and in the rising percentage of women, especially married women, who were working outside the home. Male workers tried to stake out their own place as the responsible risk takers who facilitated economic development. They appealed to the same production-oriented mythology as did the newspapers, politicians, and employers but repositioned the actors so that working-class men came out as the heroes and experts. This tactic closely resembles what other historians have noted about how nineteenth- and early-twentieth-century unions appealed to male workers' role as breadwinners.[53] The dilemma of such a tactic is that it positioned workers alongside employers as breadwinners and as men, uniting employers and employees in their gendered identities. The same process occurred in the wake of the Second Narrows Bridge collapse, and it dampened the potential for a radical labour critique of workplace violence. The bridge workers' celebration of their role as manly modernizers meant that they shared in the broader ideology of the modernist project alongside their employers and middle-class politicians and engineers.

The risky endeavours of modern development served as sites for the construction not only of bridges and megaprojects, but also of class and masculinity. The contradictions of manly modernism in this context clearly worked along class lines, with the benefits of rational risk management being largely accorded to middle-class men, while working-class men suffered the indignities of regulation. Vancouverites' response to the collapse demonstrated that they associated working-class masculinity with fantasies of control and authority. Manly modernism defined as masculine the traits needed to control one's body and the environment in dangerous circumstances. It also defined as masculine the power and authority of the modernist project that such risks served. High atop the steel girders over Burrard Inlet, individual men performed acts that mattered. They put their own bodies on the line, taking risks that others feared to take. When the bridge collapsed, however, the hierarchies within this gendered discourse became apparent. Manly modernism had a role for the working-class ironworkers, but this role tended to be as romanticized risk takers. Modernist institutions like the WCB and the Royal Commission looked to engineers for the "real" truth of the collapse. And this truth centred not on risk taking but on rational knowledge, technical procedure, and the quest for the perfect system of risk management. .

If middle-class men benefited from their more easy association with manly modernism, this is not to say that the same kinds of contradictions did not affect them in different ways. Ironically, the very men who benefited from the risk-management ideals of manly modernism also wanted to be associated with the risk-taking traits of modernity's other masculinity. A number of middle-class men experienced similar kinds of alienation in the form of postwar suburban living and the forms of domestic and unadventurous masculinity with which it was associated. To deal with this alienation, some of these men turned to the mountains and to the sport of mountaineering, seeking in their leisure the kinds of risky behaviour that other men found on the job.

4
In the Mountains

Although he never mentioned it during the inquiry concerning the Second Narrows Bridge collapse, Harold Minshall had more in common with the ironworkers than a desire to give them a stronger and more legitimate public voice. In his professional capacity, Minshall represented the Ironworkers union at the inquiry into the Second Narrows Bridge collapse. He applauded the workers' skilled daring, backing up his praise with (and being allowed to speak because of) his engineering expertise. In his private life, however, Minshall was a member of the British Columbia Mountaineering Club (BCMC), a group of Vancouverites who regularly sought meaningful leisure on the peaks of nearby mountains. Minshall was both engineer and mountaineer, a man who praised the risk taking of ironworkers on the job even while he took risks of his own during his leisure time. Both risk manager and risk taker, someone who sought to both instil and escape the regulations of modern life, Minshall and others like him nicely encapsulate how manly modernism both reinforced and transcended class boundaries.

This chapter looks at the sport of mountaineering in postwar British Columbia and, in the process, shows how the mainly middle-class Vancouverites who took up this iconic modern sport dealt with some of the same types of conflicts that affected their working-class compatriots.[1] In a sense, we are moving from the risk takers to the risk managers, from the veterans and bridge workers to the engineers, experts, and bureaucrats. But we are not looking at these men while they are at work. Instead, we move with them to their weekends and holidays, to their leisure time, when they too sought risky endeavours as a means of defining their masculinity. Even those men who apparently benefited from their connection to the modernist project – the growing middle class of the postwar years – still found this experience to be as frustrating as it was promising. This is not to mistakenly equate the hardships of middle-class and working-class men or to confuse similarity with equality. But it does show that the tensions of manly modernism operated up and down the social scale.

Vancouver's mountaineers exemplified the contradictions of both modern life and manly modernism at mid-century. They sought to escape from, yet were inherently part of, a modernist ethos of risk management, rationality, and "newness." The BCMC represented mountaineering as an escape from what was becoming an increasingly suburban existence in British Columbia's Lower Mainland. As much as Canadians embraced suburban life as never before in these years, they did not do so without worrying about the consequences. Suburbs, critics warned, brought isolation, a loss of community, and an enervating existence in the in-between land that was neither city nor country.[2] They also threatened manhood. Magazines and books fretted over the henpecked man in these feminine spaces, with their lives dominated by concerns over children and neighbourliness.[3] These problems all seemed to find their solution in mountaineering: against the loss of community, men created a new community of mountaineers; instead of isolation, climbers found camaraderie and meaningful friendships; against the semi-naturalness of lawns and parks, mountaineers set the real rugged wilderness of mountains. The enervating nothingness of white-collar work paled in comparison with the life-and-death decisions climbers made on their way to the summit.

In rushing to escape some of modern life's problems, however, mountaineers did not really turn their backs on the ideal of the manly modern. BCMC members may have believed that wilderness leisure offered a more authentic experience, but they also insisted on modifying and controlling this experience in ways that showed they shared much in common with other exponents of postwar manly modernism. As much as they celebrated the wholeness of the wilderness experience, they also established a modern system of regulating nature, other mountaineers, and themselves. The BCMC set itself up as the arbiter of appropriate conduct in the bush, establishing rules of etiquette to better police the barrier between wilderness and civilization. In seeking an alternative to the artificiality that they saw in modern life, mountaineers were part of a process of modernization that brought the tension between authenticity and artifice with them into the mountains. The mountaineers' desire to set nature apart as something unique and unspoiled went hand-in-hand with their desire to then regulate and mediate the (socially constructed) authenticity of their environment.[4] As we shall see, they set up boundaries between wilderness and civilization, expertise and excitement, and other such categories only to take pleasure in their penetration.

Mountaineering in Postwar Vancouver

Wilderness has often been the preferred source of solace for those – from nineteenth-century doctors treating neurasthenia to the young Teddy Roosevelt – trying to maintain assumptions of a primal and powerful masculinity.[5] The initial popularity of mountaineering in Victorian England and Canada resulted from the notion that masculinity was threatened by modernity and needed to be retrieved in natural and imperial endeavours, preferably ones that fostered competitiveness.[6] In the 1950s and 1960s, the BCMC was less likely to link mountaineering with the notions of national, military, and racial greatness that had so marked earlier periods. Mountaineering continued, however, to offer middle-class men a version of masculinity that was connected with possibilities of control and power. On the peaks, mountaineers still maintained control, but this came through the regulation of one's body and environment. This was a manly modernism that offered a personalized power of discipline and desire tied to the creation of individual expertise.

The first Canadian mountaineering organizations were established in the early years of the twentieth century. They came fifty years after the so-called "Golden Age" of (English) mountaineering between 1854 and the disaster on the Matterhorn in 1865. And they came more than a decade after British and American climbers had, with the help of the Canadian Pacific Railway's Swiss guides, claimed a number of first ascents on Canadian mountains. In 1906, the Alpine Club of Canada (ACC) was formed by A.O. Wheeler (at the instigation of Elizabeth Parker) to ensure that Canadians could claim their fair share of first ascents on Canadian mountains. In the era of empire building, mountaineering served as one more way of expounding identity, conquering new territory, and as historian Peter Hansen argues, bolstering ideas of national and imperial masculinities.[7] It was in the context of these concerns over exploration and national "firsts" that the BCMC was established in 1907. Although it went by a provincial name, the BCMC was made up largely of Vancouver-area climbers.[8]

The early nationalism of climbing had faded by the post-Second World War era. While some still spoke of conquering mountains, especially when the BCMC organized a special expedition to mark British Columbia's centennial in 1958, postwar BCMC climbers only occasionally explained their actions in terms of national or civic pride. As we will see, however, mountaineers still connected their sport with masculinity, but this was a masculinity that sought escape in the experiential advantages of wilderness leisure. Along with other clubs, including the Vancouver section of the ACC, the Varsity Outdoor Club (based out of the University of British Columbia), the Vancouver Natural History Society, and (in the late 1960s) Simon Fraser University's Mountaineering Club, the BCMC promoted outdoor leisure as the perfect salve for the scars of modern life.

Clubs like the BCMC played an important role in shaping the experience of mountaineering. The BCMC brought people together to meet, socialize, and most important, climb mountains. Before the advent of guidebooks and a large system of marked trails, clubs provided prospective climbers with much needed information.[9] The club almost doubled in size in the postwar years, going from 150 members in 1945 to almost 300 in 1970. As well, the number of official club trips expanded each year between 1945 and 1970. In the 1940s, the club organized trips approximately every other weekend, although members often went on nonclub trips as well. By the late 1960s, the number of club trips had more than doubled, and a club member could attend one or more organized activities every weekend. Members visited a photo shop in downtown Vancouver that was owned by another BCMC climber and signed up for club trips on a register. While there, they could also sign up for regular training sessions in ice and rock climbing or for the annual summer camp. A monthly newsletter, *The BC Mountaineer,* brought everyone up to date with all the club's activities. It published lists of upcoming climbs and social events, reports of previous trips, club business, and miscellaneous articles and anecdotes. The newsletter also kept members up to date on who had married whom, a relatively common occurrence in the 1940s and 1950s especially. Overall, the BCMC represented a tightly knit community of climbers that grew considerably in these years.[10]

Part of the group's cohesiveness came from the relatively similar class positions of its members; the BCMC was a middle-class organization. While historians of British Columbia mountaineering and BCMC members themselves refer to the club as being more casual and open than the ACC, the difference was one of tone rather than kind.[11] Statistics on the class position of members from three different decades (1949, 1959, and 1969) show that a majority of members always belonged to the middle class. The BCMC was made up of professionals such as university professors, doctors, and engineers as well as small-business people and white- and blue-collar managers. Working-class members, who usually occupied skilled or semi-professional positions, included lithographers, technicians, and teachers. Certainly, the club was not exclusive. A few members had unskilled jobs, working as labourers or drivers. But these climbers always made up only a small minority of the overall number of climbers. Perhaps most telling is who was absent from the club. Very few climbers worked in forestry or on the waterfront, two of Vancouver's major industries. And those who did work in such industries tended to do so in skilled or management positions.[12]

The location of climbers' homes followed the trends of Vancouver's middle class. Those members who did live within the city of Vancouver disproportionately lived on the affluent west side. Increasingly in the 1950s and 1960s, BCMC members moved away from the city altogether and into the suburbs. In 1949, fewer than 1 in 6 BCMC members lived in the suburbs compared to 1 in 2 or 3 in 1969. Adding to this general trend of suburbanization was the large number of climbers who lived in areas of Vancouver that, although inside the city limits, nonetheless closely resembled suburban communities.[13] With their majority middle-class membership and their increasingly suburban lifestyles, BCMC members were those in the postwar years most able to benefit from postwar affluence. They were also, as we shall see, those most keen to escape its environmental and gendered ambiguities.

Civilization and Wilderness

The natural environment sought by Vancouver mountaineers underwent dramatic changes in the postwar years. In 1945, British Columbia was still a collection of regions mostly isolated from each other by geographical barriers, united in name only. While transportation links such as railways, ferries, and roads had been breaking down these provincial barriers for quite some time, the process was slow. "For many British Columbians of mid century," notes historian Jean Barman, "the province as a geographic entity simply did not exist."[14] Yet this isolation quickly came under attack in the 1950s and 1960s, especially with the election of the Social Credit Party under W.A.C. Bennett. Seeing as his mandate the economic development of the province, particularly of its interior regions, Bennett promoted infrastructure as the main tool of development. Picking up from where earlier governments had left off, Social Credit embarked on a massive program of infrastructure development that included highway expansion, the extension of the provincial railway (the Pacific Great Eastern), and bridge building. The government emphasized breaking down barriers between the economically underprivileged regions of the interior and the better-off areas of Vancouver and southern Vancouver Island.[15] All these developments tended to diminish the barrier between civilization and wilderness and to reduce the distance between mountains and streets.

This infrastructure development not only led to industrial growth, but also facilitated an expansion in the numbers of tourists visiting the province's wilderness areas for recreation. The postwar "good life," so popular with Bennett and many British Columbians, included more leisure time spent in the wild. The era saw the emergence of the forty-hour work week as the standard in many industries. This meant that more workers had more time in which to pursue their leisure out of doors.[16] Increased ability fitted in nicely with increased desire. A range of family experts, both academic and popular, encouraged postwar families to spend more time together on "fun" outings. In the era of "togetherness," fathers were expected to spend more time with their families. They were not, however, to break down expectations of gender difference between men and women. Veronica Strong-Boag has shown how suburbanization in these years was an inherently gendered process. It separated men's and women's places, putting women in suburban homes, often without access to a car and far away from families and friends. Yet even as it had these effects on women, contemporaries also worried about the effects that suburbia had on men. Spending time outdoors, whether camping, fishing, picnicking, or even in the backyard having a barbecue, became an acceptable way for men to spend more time with their families while still asserting that, because such activities occurred out of doors in the "wilderness," they were acceptably masculine.[17]

Throughout the postwar years, the BCMC expressed contradictory views on the shifting relation between city and mountain life that was accelerated by these changes. Should they welcome the new highway up to Mount Seymour, or should they see it as something that would destroy their privacy? Would it open up the hills to new mountaineers and to a more respectful attitude toward the wild or would it bring in the wrong kind of nature lovers, those whose only use for trees was as scenery to be viewed from the car window? On the one hand, the club wanted to control this crossing. Trips needed rational planning and care. From this perspective, building roads and expanding facilities made sense; it made getting to the mountain easier and encouraged more wildlife recreation. On the other hand, mountaineers wanted to cross over into wilderness to get away from civilization. To truly experience the climb meant going beyond the certainty of regulations and roads. It meant completely losing oneself in nature's difference. The club was pulled from both sides. They wanted to explore, to achieve, to go further. Opening up the mountains meant that they could go further more easily. Yet they also wanted isolation. They wanted to maintain the exclusivity of the peaks, where being alone in nature provided the meaning that seemed to be missing from life in the city. Mountaineers wanted both to erect and to penetrate the barrier between civilization and wilderness. Perhaps not surprisingly, they invested great importance in this boundary, regarding its transgression as the essence of mountaineering and (we should add) of modernity.[18]

In 1973, the BCMC helped to publish a pamphlet called *Get Back Alive! Safety in the BC Coast Mountains*. The pamphlet was indicative of much of the club's postwar thinking about the wildness of the mountains. *Get Back Alive!* told local hikers that the mountains were not just an extension of the city or a play-field of steep hills. On the way up a mountain near Vancouver, civilization seemed so close. It was almost there – around a bend in the road, hiding behind that big patch of cedars. Yet the boundaries between city and mountain life could not be measured by the nearness of road or city. A few thousand feet (a few hundred feet) could transform a rocky outcrop from a scenic view into a place to die. After leaving the highway or getting off the ski lift, the mountaineers warned, it is only a short distance before "you cross, probably without noticing the change, the line between civilization and wilderness. Easy access breeds a false sense of security and, for the unwary, the crossing of this invisible line often means going from safety into danger." The differences between home and away needed to be acknowledged and respected: "Mountains are rough and violent places, where humans are mere specks of potential fertilizer on their flanks."

A good mountaineer was humble before this great divide between the routines of human comfort and the whims of unpredictable nature. "Humans are soft and vulnerable animals," they warned. "A falling pebble or a slight stumble can kill the strongest man." And those who needed warning were often not the strongest men. Postwar life, with its family cars and roadside picnics, had opened up the forests and hills to many people who did not recognize their own softness. The north shore mountains, the peaks overlooking Vancouver and lying within just a short drive of downtown, killed more than a few who trundled up their slopes, especially in the fall and spring, when sunny days turned into cold, rainy nights. It was so easy to get lost, to go down the wrong path, to slip on a rock and slide down to a part of the mountain that you did not know and from which you could not escape. Not that you would think this when you headed out. It would be only a short jaunt – a little healthy exercise in the city's steep backyard. So many others managed to climb and hike without incident. More and more trails traversed the mountain sides. The highway up to Seymour had just been paved. The local ski slopes were installing lifts. The mountains were so accessible, so civilized, so safe.[19]

Some in the BCMC fretted over the consequences of opening up the wild areas too much – and to the wrong sorts of people. Long-time BCMC member R.A.M. Pilkington lamented the extension of the highway to Seymour in 1951. "I cannot help feeling that in giving the mountain to the public the government is taking it away from the mountaineers," he wrote in the *BC Mountaineer*. "Part of the joy of mountain climbing is to be in the unspoiled high places away from ... the presence of people. That is why it is worth while to struggle up a mountain instead of strolling in Stanley Park ... Let no one think for a moment that I am opposed to progress. The general public has as much right to be dirty in the mountains as upon the beaches ... But to some of us who knew the mountain twenty years ago it seems rather a pity."[20]

As more and more Vancouverites came to the north shore mountains in the postwar years, the club's mountaineers increasingly sought their leisure elsewhere. The BCMC may have been among those pushing for greater local wilderness protection and promotion, but when the newcomers arrived, the BCMC left.[21] The club owned two cabins on the north shore mountains directly by Vancouver, one on Grouse and the other on Seymour. Many social activities, including the annual turkey dinner, took place at the cabins, which served as gathering places and starting points for local climbs. As road access to the mountains improved, allowing club members to go up for a day and return the same night, and as more locals came to the mountains, increasing the number of break-ins and hiking and skiing traffic, the cabins declined in importance. Members stayed there less, and the club decided to sell the Seymour cabin in 1962 and the Grouse cabin in 1965. Contemporaneous with this abandonment, the club began to build new smaller huts in more remote locations. Instead of being social gathering points, these new huts served as bases from which to launch further exploratory trips. And they were, at least initially, much more isolated.[22]

BCMC climbers thirsted for isolation and novelty. They fetishized "firsts" – the first ascent of a peak, the first trip up a new route. In their desire for virgin climbs, postwar mountaineers blended older imperial ambitions of conquest and exploration with modernist desires for ongoing advancement and progress. British Columbia was one of the few places that still offered many new climbs. Most peaks in other parts of the climbing world, especially Europe, had already been climbed. The opportunity to be the first (or even the second) to the top was lost. In their later lives, BCMC climbers recalled this as one of the best aspects of local climbing – the ability to be the first person to ascend a peak. The mountains were not always high or very difficult, but they had not yet been climbed. And a first ascent also meant the opportunity to name a peak. Names had to be cleared through the government, but the possibility of naming provided a thrill. Ralph Hutchinson's recollections serve as appropriate for most serious BCMC climbers: "I could see all these mountains, you know, stretching all the way down Pitt Lake, and I was asking the knowledgeable ones, 'What's that one called?' and they said, 'It's not got a name.' 'Has it been climbed?' 'Probably not.' And so ... the major interest from then on, was on the unclimbed peaks."[23] The possibility that such mountains had already been named by British Columbia's First Nations did not seem to occur to Hutchinson. This was a colonialism of silence, not so much devaluing First Nations' peoples outright as simply not considering their presence at all.

Some mountaineers from other places looked down on what they believed to be the amateurism of British Columbia alpinists. Postwar climbing in the United States had turned to the open face of the mountain, seeking more and more difficult routes to the top, as climbers were no longer satisfied with the easiest or most direct. The same process is central to mountaineering writ large; with fewer unclimbed peaks, mountaineers turned to improved technique and new routes to satisfy their need for firsts.[24] In this context, the British Columbia climbers appeared to be out of date. Yet really they were just climbing to the local context, taking their firsts as others had done before. The desire for novelty was the same in both places. By the later 1950s and early 1960s, BCMC climbers also sought the more difficult ascents. They spoke derisively about "tourist routes," frowning upon the less challenging approaches, referring to them as mere "slogs."[25]

By desiring the isolated mountain and valorizing what had not yet been tried, however, mountaineers created a dilemma for themselves. They sought the isolated place only to end its isolation. Their desire to get to new places gave them a sometimes ambivalent attitude toward the mechanisms – roads, planes, industry – that eventually ended this cherished newness. Pilkington may have lamented construction of the highway to Seymour, but others in the club had lobbied hard for it. They wanted the easier access to the cabin that a good road provided. Without the modern encroachment on wild areas, through aerial-survey maps and photographs as well as logging and mining roads, many BCMC trips would not have been possible. The *Climber's Guide to the Coastal Ranges of British Columbia* (for which BCMC members had given much material) provided information on the reliability of government maps and the usefulness of logging roads.[26] The technology of transportation significantly helped mountaineering exploration in British Columbia. One BCMC climber saw the coming of the bush plane after the Second World War as a major impetus for the sport.[27] At the club's 1970 turkey dinner, members watched a film on the provision of a drill site in the Yukon. The *BC Mountaineer* ignored the impact that such a development would have on the natural environment and instead noted that the film gave members some good ideas about potential snow-climbing trips.[28] Of course, the club did not always ignore the potential environmental consequences of industrial development. They lobbied for wilderness protection and against the logging of many wilderness areas. Their desire to access the bush, to always go where no one had gone before, however, created potential tensions. The best a mountaineer could hope for was to always be at the front of the exploration machine, enjoying the fresh unspoiled view before giving it up to the reaping mechanism that came behind.

The BCMC presented itself as an ideal organization to assist with policing human incursions into the mountains. This desire to regulate and to impose systems of order marked the modernity of mountaineering, the point where the desire to get away showed itself also to be a civilizing mission. When the climbers went to the hills, the modernist project went with them. After setting up wilderness as something distinct from humanity, they went about protecting and reinforcing this distinction. Dangers came in a variety of forms, including the possibility of stranded and injured hikers and of despoiled, litter-ridden mountain sides. To combat this problem, the BCMC worked to create a system of trails that would mediate the spaces where humans and wilderness met. A lack of public trails, they argued, caused many of the hiking accidents that Vancouverites read about in their papers each year. The growing popularity of hiking, and the Lower Mainland's growing population, meant that more inexperienced climbers were heading to the hills, and some were ending up in well-publicized mishaps. And BCMC members became directly involved in such accidents in their work with the Mountain Rescue Group, a volunteer organization of local climbers meant to help the police and military with accidents in the mountains.

The new hikers did not always treat the wilderness in the way that the BCMC might have preferred. They left garbage, destroyed sensitive vegetation, and presented a danger to others. After a death on Seymour in 1970, BCMC executive member Dr. Joyce Davies wrote to British

Columbia's minister for recreation and conservation to impugn his government for its lack of funding for trail construction: "Similar tragedies have occurred in the past and most certainly will occur in the future unless action is taken to remedy the deplorable conditions which prevail."[29] The club did not wait for provincial-government funding. By the time of Davies' letter, the BCMC had already been seriously building trails for more than a decade. They hosted trail-building weekends where members volunteered their time to clear and mark trails. In 1963, the BCMC and other local outdoor groups came together to form an organization that became the Mountain Access Committee. Many of the trails in British Columbia, and especially the Lower Mainland, owe their existence to the work of this committee. The club also helped to create a guidebook on mountaineering in the coastal ranges of British Columbia and a guidebook on local trails. Both books served, and continue to serve, as important tools for local amateur hikers.[30] While most mountaineers wanted to escape the regularity of trails, they also believed that trail construction would ensure that the wild areas would remain relatively unspoiled.

The existence of an extensive system of mountaineering etiquette demonstrated that the policing concerns of the BCMC also extended to the community of climbers. The BCMC, older members especially, often emphasized the importance of mountaineering etiquette. They published lists of rules and commandments, some of which were humorous but all of which demonstrated a belief in a set of regulations for the bush. One of the worst, and most common, infractions involved climbers who dislodged rocks and debris onto others below them. A club trip to Mount Shuksan in 1956 was cut short by another group of climbers who "seemed not to be hindered by any considerations for the ones who were there already." The *BC Mountaineer* reported how the disrespectful climbers overtook the BCMC group, whose members were soon "busy dodging rocks of all sizes which were coming down in increasing numbers. Helga got hit and let go one of those blood curdling screams which knocked the leader almost off his feet and which would have put to shame any Hollywood stuntman. Fred and Arnold had barricaded themselves behind an enormous wall of ice and refused to leave their fortress, so after a hurried long-distance (3 ropes) consultation with the leader they decided to turn back to camp from that point. They had of course to wait another 2 hours before the air was clear."[31] This may have been a remote location, but the danger came from its occupation, not from its isolation.

Leadership provided one of the main ways to foster appropriate mountaineering behaviour, at least among one's own group if not among others. When the BCMC went on climbing trips, the leader always went first, and the endman, the second in command, came last. The leader was in charge. He – almost invariably a he – decided the route, the timing, and when the club would turn back. In practice, this was not a rigid hierarchy. Poking fun at the leader's troubles was one of the enjoyable things to do on a trip and especially when writing the report of the trip later. When Jim Addie followed his lecture on snowcraft techniques at the Grouse Mountain cabin with some practical demonstration, the *BC Mountaineer* felt duty-bound to report that "the leader's insistence that his followers follow in his exact footsteps in true mountaineering style seemed a little unreasonable when some of his footsteps took him up to his neck into rotten snow."[32] Another report sarcastically suggested ways to endear yourself to the leader: "Every few minutes ask the leader if he knows where he is going. Try to elbow past him and reach the peak first. When he has the rope wrapped around twice and tied in four knots about the stoutest tree on the mountainside, be sure to ask him if it is safe."[33] The joking put a human face on the hierarchy – mountaineering was, after all, supposed to be fun. Behind the joking, however, lay a belief that a mountaineer's experience of the wilderness should be mediated by clear organization and lines of authority.[34]

The BCMC often turned back to people and civilization at the very moment when something went wrong in the wilderness. This is a key theme in modern acts and stories of exploration – whether mountaineering tales or episodes of *Star Trek*. They are as much about what is left behind as what is sought. And the BCMC's discussion of mountaineering risk was no different. Mountaineers endeavoured to go to places where others had not gone and to get there by routes that others had not taken. Yet the risks that they faced – and the reasons that they were willing to face them – tended to diminish the distance between themselves and others. They wanted to escape the petty restrictions of everyday life, yet if trouble came, they suggested rules, organization, and more knowledge (less mystery) as the solution. Despite, or more accurately because of, the uncertainty of the distinction between wilderness and civilization, the club emphasized it all the more.

Expertise and Excitement

This process of turning away from civilization and then, almost surreptitiously, turning back toward it again matched postwar ideas about the state of modern manhood. Men were presented as occupying both a threatened and a powerful position. In one sense, postwar affluence allowed middle-class men to feel more secure in their role as family breadwinner. Yet security had its drawbacks: suburban domesticity and white-collar work were not the stuff of rugged, active men. Even though sociologist William Whyte's criticisms of the "Organization Man" were addressed to Americans (especially the concerns about competitiveness and the frontier), he could still find a receptive audience among Canadians, who were also concerned that suburban life robbed men of their natural vigour. Sociologist Michael Kimmel argues that postwar men were caught in what he calls the "Goldilocks dilemma." They could not be too conformist, nor could they be too rebellious or wild. Caught in the middle, they increasingly sought "fantasy thrills" through leisure and entertainment. "The more boring and dull the routine of men's work became," Kimmel claims, "the more exciting and glamorous were their fantasies of escape."[35]

BCMC discussions of their sport – especially of its risky nature – mirrored these doubled-edged concerns over manhood. Mountaineers constructed the nature of their sport in a quite similar way to that presented in Kimmel's "Goldilocks dilemma." Mountaineers had to achieve a balance between reason, control, and safety, on the one hand, and emotion, experience, and risk taking, on the other. The BCMC's discussion of their sport vacillated between these paired concerns: the thrill of pushing forward versus the recklessness of pushing too far, the responsibility of knowing one's limits versus the boredom of knowing them too well. The difference here lay in the fact that mountaineers did not just watch movies about this kind of masculinity, but also enacted it upon themselves. In mountaineering, as in bridge building, men could make consequential decisions that mattered. Masculinity could continue, in a very potent if fabricated way, to be connected with the power to control bodies – in this case, the mountaineer's own. The possibility of manly and mountaineering control lay in finding the right balance between expertise and excitement.

Although the club was open to both men and women (there were no formal barriers restricting activities of either sex), mountaineering was definitely a gendered sport. Men dominated the club by numbers alone. They always made up the majority of climbers. More significantly, a climber's sex could often be an indicator of skill and experience. Women were much more likely to be "graduating" members, those who had not yet completed the required number of specified club trips in order to qualify for full membership. In 1949, 1 in 3 female climbers was a graduating member, compared to only 1 in 7 male climbers. Although the relative number of female full members increased over the 1950s and 1960s, the same process occurred with the men as well.[36] Such differences in membership details had practical consequences for climbing trips. On a number of club trips, the group divided upon reaching the approach to the summit, with one party taking the most difficult route to the top, while another stayed behind or tried an easier ascent. Often, the groups divided by sex, with most women staying behind. The same gendering worked in the planning of longer, more ambitious trips. A small group of advanced male climbers tended to dominate these exploratory trips. In this way, the division in the club between climbers and hikers, seemingly one based on skill and willingness to embark upon difficult climbs, also became gendered.[37]

The same process influenced the operation of the club's executive. Women were much more likely than men to organize the club's social activities, while men planned the climbing activities. The club's Climbing and Ski Committee, responsible for determining when and where the BCMC would climb, did not have a female member until 1967. And it was not until 1971 that a woman, Esther Kafer, became the committee's chair. Kafer's case is illustrative, for it shows that even when female climbers were very advanced, the gendering of skill continued. She later recounted how club members referred to her by the diminutive tag of "girl." When she went along on difficult trips, she was often the only woman. This gendered division between the serious and the casual was not completely rigid, nor did it divide only on the basis of sex. Some women like Kafer went on the ambitious trips, earning a special reputation; some men did not engage in serious climbing, or not to the same extent as the most prolific climbers. But this did not stop the gendering of mountaineering expertise. Exceptions proved the rule.[38]

Beyond numbers, the very notion of skill was constructed in a way that matched contemporary ideas of what it meant to be masculine. Cool rationality infused the BCMC's idea of mountaineering expertise. Nothing was more important in a crisis than unemotional and unfettered assessment. Eric Brooks told new climbers that good mountaineering required the proper mindset as much as technique. The "true mountaineer" needed refined judgment and experience. In dangerous situations, he "become[s] cooler and more full of resource when bad weather sets in." He is able to "estimate bearing power of snow with a single thrust of the axe."[39] To such a man, "panic is the enemy."[40] Ian Kay argued that mountaineering was similar to that other risky modern activity, driving an automobile. In other contexts, the BCMC might have eschewed comparisons to such an urban pursuit, but Kay saw through to their mutual demand for rules-based self-discipline. "To drive a car safely we must know the rules of the road, so it is with climbing, we must know the rules of the mountain. A driver that can anticipate conditions is a safer driver than one with a quick reaction, this fact also applies to mountaineering."[41] This appeal to responsibility and preparedness fit nicely with many elements in the postwar era's political culture, from ideas of containment in the Cold War to the breadwinning duties of fathers. Men, the family experts (and, in this case, the mountaineering experts) claimed, needed to be responsible. The language of disciplined mountaineering matched the language of disciplined masculine citizenship.[42]

Discipline called for planning and preparation. Accidents happened when you failed to prepare. In 1958, when the BCMC joined with the Vancouver Section of the Alpine Club of Canada to climb Mount Fairweather to mark the British Columbia centennial, they employed the language of national and martial masculinity. Paddy Sherman, one of the organizers (and later editor of the *Vancouver Province* and biographer of W.A.C. Bennett), compared mountaineering preparation to that of a military undertaking. The expedition members, he noted, had devised their "plans of attack" and had held a "council of war."[43] More often in the postwar years, however, preparation was more about individual expertise, competence, and responsibility. The *BC Mountaineer* hearkened to this point in the aftermath of a hiking death on the north shore mountains in 1956. "Rather than acquire knowledge the hard way," it argued, "it is as effective to listen to others and prepare and act accordingly ... Simple uncomplicated preparations that everybody knows about, but so few act upon."[44] This same outlook inspired the club's involvement in the Mountain Rescue Group. This was a volunteer organization set up by local climbers to assist the police and military in saving stranded climbers. Preparedness was the Mountain Rescue Group's mantra. They extolled its virtues for the amateur climbers whom the group often had to save. They also believed in its usefulness for themselves; the group's organizers continually tried to maintain an up-to-date list of all those available for rescue operations, emphasizing the need to be prepared.

The BCMC often criticized recklessness. When they spoke to young climbers or the public, they advocated safe and responsible climbing. "The idea," according to the *BC Mountaineer*, "is not so much to get to the top, as to get back."[45] Mountaineering was an exercise in rational risk management. "To every climber comes the moment when he must decide, is this mountain, today, worth my life? If your answer is NO, we will ... be full of respect for the immense powers of destruction attending our every step. If your answer is YES, stop a bit and think of the rescue party that must come if you are injured, spending their time, money and equipment, taking risks for your benefit they would not take for their own pleasure. If your answer is yes, think further: are you worth the lives, time and strength of your friends, your rescuers?"[46] Here is the reasoned, cautious approach to risk: evaluating options and choosing carefully. In the postwar years, when a range of public figures, from psychologists to politicians, advocated responsibility as the hallmark of manhood, this aspect of the club's approach to risk would likely have found fertile ground. While club members rarely publicly challenged other experienced climbers' decisions, if they did, they did so on these grounds. When a 1960 ascent of Mount McKinley ended in tragedy, Paul Binkert claimed that the "accident serves as another reminder to climb always with a feeling of responsibility." He quoted a line from a *Life* magazine article on the incident: "They suffered the penalties which the mountain inflicts on the weak or the rash."[47] The climbers certainly were not weak, so that left rash.

Mountaineers knew of what they spoke; no doubt these attributes did lead to greater safety. The very instrumentality of the attributes and the context in which they were championed nonetheless reinforced connections between masculinity and expertise. Calls for an unemotional and unornamented approach to risk carried gendered implications. Many scholars have noted how the language of modernity has been gendered. Masculinity has, for much of the modern period, been connected with reason and essence, while femininity has been connected with emotion and ornament. To focus on anything but the instrumentality of a situation has often meant to lose sight of its essence, to give in not only to danger but also to emasculation and femininity. The BCMC's description of mountaineering danger picked up on this longer history and, in emphasizing the divisions between recklessness and responsibility, gave it meanings particular to their sport in the postwar years.[48]

Club members and the press both used and reinforced these notions of masculine expertise when they evaluated the cause of accidents. In late June 1952, the twenty-nine-year-old BCMC climber Vera Taylor suffered a near disastrous fall on a club trip to Holy Cross Mountain. According to the *BC Mountaineer,* Taylor and some other "girls" were being shepherded down the mountain on a rope between "experienced climbers." "Part way down, Vera Taylor, apparently growing tired of this slow method of progress, left the rope and attempted to glissade," a technique whereby a climber slides on her bottom to cover long distances at greater speeds, using her ice axe as both a brake and a steering mechanism. Taylor lost her axe and lost control, bowling over someone else who tried to break her fall, before finally coming to a rather violent stop against an outcrop of boulders. She was still unconscious when the report was being written twelve days after the incident. Like many who suffered serious injury, Taylor later returned to climbing. In the interim, the club and the press referred to her youth and femininity in explaining the incident. At the next BCMC executive meeting, the club claimed that the Taylor accident should serve as a warning for young and old alike. The young needed to respect and obey trip leaders, and the older, experienced climbers needed to take the mantle of leadership seriously. The local papers contrasted Taylor's femininity (articles in both the *Vancouver Sun* and the *Province* began with almost identical sentences, reporting that she was young and attractive) with the skill and experience of the male rescue workers who brought her out of the bush. Taylor was not alone in being unfavourably compared to the male rescue workers. Many of the young men who found themselves stranded on local mountains each year suffered the same fate. The papers emphasized the Mountain Rescue Group climbers' experience, skill, and determination at the same time as they told of how the climber in trouble had failed to take the necessary precautions. The expert mountaineer served as an ideal against which those involved in accidents could be compared.[49]

In practice, however, whether on a weekend club trip up the Lions or on an expeditionary venture into the far reaches of the province, BCMC climbers often treated danger a little more lightheartedly than they suggested when talking to the press or giving instruction to young climbers. So long as everything turned out all right in the end, so long as no one ended up in hospital, they laughed at rocks falling from above or at a slip on the cliff face. Enduring these tribulations made mountaineers special. R.A.M. Pilkington's short mountaineering poems provide a typical flavour:

A boulder bounding off an alp
Landed on poor Willie's scalp
Rotten luck! But anyhow
Willie is broad-minded now

or:

> George fell down a deep crevasse
> He's in cold storage now, alas
> His mother's ailing, sad to tell
> But George is keeping rather well.[50]

A little fall was good ammunition for campfire jokes or reports to the bulletin. Jim Teevan's friends seemed to enjoy ribbing him after an eventful trip up the Tomyhoi in 1948. "It will be a trip that one of our party will long remember," they reported to the *BC Mountaineer*. "Someone knocked loose a rock from above a small bluff. The rock hit Jim Teevan on the side of the face and he received a cut which required four stitches from the First Aid man. Five minutes later Jim started to sit down on a ledge and his feet went out from under him. A slide over rock and snow for about fifty feet resulted and back we went to the First Aid man to have Jim's scraped arm bandaged. If he intends to use up our First Aid Kit this fast we shall have to charge him double rates."[51] Mountaineers often faced minor incidents like the ones faced by Teevan. They dealt with the recurrences by poking fun at them, minimizing their significance.

Club members did not want to be injured, but they wanted to climb and knew that climbing involved danger. They went ahead with it anyway. They took risks. By 1961, a Canadian team had yet to climb Mount McKinley, North America's highest peak. A British Columbia team, including climbers from the BCMC, decided to make an attempt. The 1961 expedition to Mount McKinley had all the elements of a classic mountaineering story: a remote mountain, an attempt to achieve the first Canadian ascent, risks taken, hardships endured, and in the end, success. To achieve this success, the climbers suffered severe hardships. Two climbers lost a number of toes to frostbite. They had to be emergency airlifted off the mountain. Serious hospital treatment and physical therapy followed. The press wanted to know whether they would climb again, to which BCMC member Jim Woodfield replied: "Climb again? I jolly well hope to." And he did. So did Ralph Hutchinson, another BCMC climber who lost toes on the McKinley expedition. With a new, adjusted boot, he was back climbing the next year.[52]

The BCMC's ambivalence toward danger – cautious one moment, carefree the next – came from how it sought to play with the contradictions of risk and modernity. Experience of risk is risk's ultimate arbiter. One can judge the risk taker only by engaging in risk oneself. In its emphasis on doing and experiencing, mountaineering bridged the divide between the 1950s fears of excessive rationality and bureaucracy, on the one hand, and the more radical 1960s critics of the dehumanizing effects of the "system," on the other. Mountaineers were not necessarily radicals, but especially for men, their interest in climbing came, in part, from how it spoke to these concerns. It offered a powerful and meaningful (if artificially constructed) life-and-death experience that postwar critics claimed was absent from most middle-class men's lives.[53] In an article entitled "So you climb, do you?" Jim Woodfield tried to answer the question of why a mountaineer climbs. It is a question that climbers often faced and by which they claimed to be frustrated. To ask why one would climb implied that you could not possibly understand.[54] Woodfield went through – and rejected – several stock responses: "Because I enjoy it – open to question: because it is good for me – priggish: because I want to – avoids the question: because of the pride in achievement – sounds a bit pompous: because struggle is good for man – sounds Marxist." External concerns did not define the mountaineer. Rather, the true importance of mountaineering lay beyond ego and risk, in the realm of meaning. Woodfield offered an existential answer to why he climbed. In a modern world so fast-paced and open to change, mountaineers found meaning in the simplicity of mountaineering. Climbing offered a primal experience. It freed "the fettered soul of civilized man so that he can rejoice in the primeval silence of a great forest, and hear the joyful lullaby of a spilling stream, or know tranquillity atop a mountain as he absorbs the breadth of valley, ridge and peak unfolding in disappearing array to the mysterious horizon." Woodfield pitied those who had never climbed and who therefore had never known "the deeper satisfaction which so outweighs the strain of a pack-in, that reduces all rigours of element or nature to insignificance, that teaches a person to value the permanent truths of life."[55]

This embrace of primary experience, and the stoicism that it engendered, originated not only in mountaineering experience, but also in postwar gender relations. In the context of contemporary fears about the emasculating effects of urban and suburban life on contemporary manhood, mountaineering provided a meaningful salve to notions of modern manhood. Mountaineers endured danger, they left the city, they went out into the wilds just as many in the postwar period believed that men had always done. Norman McKenzie, president of the University of British Columbia and member of the Massey Commission, highlighted the sport's enriching potential in modern life, arguing that mountaineering "gave its followers a chance to get away from the undesirable influences of city life."[56] The club itself offered the same arguments, suggesting that climbing, like hunting and fishing, offered a healthy outlet for youthful energy and thus acted as a deterrent to juvenile delinquency.[57] BCMC members often jokingly questioned why they kept up with climbing. Early mornings and rainy days seemed to inspire such doubts. "On being roused from the down warmth of his sleeping bag at 1:30 a.m. and sent forth into the darkness with a half-cooked and hastily eaten breakfast lying soggily on his stomach," one climber reported to the *BC Mountaineer*, "the most ardent mountaineer may perhaps be excused for wondering if he shouldn't take up golf."[58] Yet it was just this version of manhood, the golf-playing, suburban father, against which mountaineers defined themselves. Paul Binkert used the stereotype of suburban man to jokingly chastise those who did not climb. In a mock biblical/prophetic tone, he wrote of those who made excuses not to go climbing, "to cut their lawn, to paint their houses, to wash their windows." Such people should repent, Binkert wrote: "Ye are no longer worthy to call yourselves mountaineers for whilst you are squatting here, gaining weight and losing agility the mountains are still out there waiting in their eternal beauty for the worthy ones."[59] By accepting the risks of their sport, by venturing out of the city, mountaineers adopted an alternate version of masculinity to the "Organization Man," that stereotype of postwar manhood that so many pilloried.

British Columbia mountaineering changed in the late 1960s and 1970s. In 1967, the BCMC began to grade the difficulty of club trips, using a system of numbers and letters. The system first assessed the strenuousness of the climb from A to C and then combined this with an assessment of the grade's steepness and difficulty from 1 to 4.[60] This marked a greater interaction between local climbers and the systems of organization and classification more widely used in the North American and European mountaineering world. It represented a movement away from making first ascents of unclimbed peaks and toward calculating more difficult treks up those mountains that had already been climbed. It increasingly called on climbers to head to the open face of the rock itself. When commenting on the changes in mountaineering, BCMC members later spoke of specialization and the decline of the wilderness mountaineer. According to the individual mountaineer, such a process could be seen either as an important step in the professionalization of their sport or as a slip-up that led to the loss of some intangible wholeness.[61]

Although BCMC members understood these changes within their local context, such a transformation is endemic to mountaineering's history. From the sport's earliest origins, we can trace a change from wilderness mountaineering, in which half the battle is simply in getting to the base of the mountain, to more specialized mountaineering, better serviced by transportation routes and technology and with a focus on specific aspects, such as rock or ice climbing. In her introduction to accounts of early British Columbia mountaineering expeditions, Susan Leslie's perspective is typical of that of many postwar mountaineers. She celebrates the progress made in the past, the many first ascents. At the same time, she also mourns the loss of novelty and the environmental costs of growing human leisure in the wild. This contradictory celebration and mourning of progress is not tied to any one historical period. Already in the late nineteenth century, a group of German climbers called for a more pure mountaineering separate from the large military-like expeditions so popular among the English.[62] The conflict between authenticity and artifice, between purity and corruption, has been endemic to mountaineering. Whether we are discussing postwar British Columbia, Victorian England, or the late-twentieth-century Everest expeditions, mountaineering, like the larger process of modernity of which it is a part, pushes forward while both destroying and mourning what it leaves behind.

In the reflections, conduct, and regulations of Vancouver's postwar mountaineers, we can see some fairly clear links with what others saw as both the possibilities for and the dilemmas of modern manhood. In mountaineering, men encountered the long-term historical dilemma (mentioned earlier) that the sociologist of masculinity Michael Kimmel humorously called the "Goldilocks dilemma."[63] Men were called upon to be daring risk takers, to engage in a dangerous activity where their decisions mattered. At the same time, they were also expected to be responsible risk managers, carefully planning and preparing for every eventuality, developing a sophisticated expertise about how to survive in the mountain wilderness. The BCMC defined manhood and the ideal mountaineer in a doubled way: as that which was at the heart of rational, rules-based modernity (i.e., the engineers, scientists, and in this case, expert mountaineers) and as that which served as modernity's opposite (i.e., the primal and experiential traditional man).

These contradictions were inextricably linked to the mythology of progress that reigned supreme in the postwar years. Gendered notions of manly risk taking and risk management emerged in tandem with widespread support for the modernist project. Many in the BCMC wanted to protect wildlife and the natural environment; they wanted to conserve wilderness. They also, however, shared a gendered belief that put manhood at the centre of modernity, both in the need to escape its hollowness and in the ability to control its risks. In their understanding of risk, mountaineers showed themselves to be true modernists. They offered the creation of expertise as the solution to the danger that they faced. Like those of other modernists, from nuclear scientists to car safety experts, theirs was a limited form of expertise that never questioned the belief in progress or in achieving more "firsts." Refinement, a better tuning of the machine, was all that was needed. The risks that mountaineers faced on the rocks may have seemed at some remove from industrial modernization, but the shared language of modern manliness demonstrated that the mountaineers had much more in common with the boosters of the province's postwar modernization than they might have cared to admit.

The doubled nature of mountaineering's modernity and of postwar ideas of masculinity is nicely symbolized in one man: Fred Lasserre. As the first director of the University of British Columbia's School of Architecture, Lasserre was a key figure in promoting architectural Modernism in the province. This architectural style emphasized visual aesthetics and the bird's-eye view over practical usefulness; it sought a clear separation in physical space between buildings meant for living, working, and learning. With the almost authoritarian role that it gave to the architect's original vision and its dogmatic insistence on the perfectibility of this vision, Modernist architecture later became subject to the same kinds of criticisms that were levelled at the modernist project more generally. While at work, Lasserre was one of the modernizers. Aside from this architecture, Lasserre also enjoyed mountaineering. He, too, took up a sport as a form of solace, as a way to "get away to the mountains to free himself from the over-bearing details of administrative work." In his leisure, he took up the sport that promised an escape from the negative aspects of modern life and a different kind of masculine identity. Lasserre died on a climbing expedition while he was in England in 1961 to research public-housing architecture.[64] Lasserre was not alone in incorporating this ironic connection between the risk taking of mountaineering and the management ethos of high modernism into his own life. This irony infused the project of mountaineers in the postwar years, just as it represented one of the key tensions of modern manhood.

These tensions did not, however, always work themselves out in situations where the risks taken and the men involved were socially valued. Another key risk management project that accelerated in the postwar years was the effort to medically and psychologically determine what to do with criminals. When twenty-four Vancouver men committed capital murder in the postwar years, a number of experts stepped up to help interpret their actions and their masculinity, demonstrating that the creation of a thoroughly modern masculinity (mediated by middle-class experts) also extended to definitions of men's deviance.

5
Before the Courts and on the Couch

There is a moment in Robertson Davies' 1954 novel *Leaven of Malice* that amply conveys the mixture of skepticism and confusion with which some Canadians treated psychological knowledge in the postwar years. Norm Yarrow, a psychologist on the student-guidance staff at the local university approaches Professor Vambrace of the Department of Classics with the aim of giving him some parenting advice. Conversation begins with that most popular of psychological issues in the postwar years, the Oedipus Complex:

> "I take it that you've heard of the Oedipus Complex?"
> "I am familiar with all forms of the Oedipus legend."
> "Yes, but have you understood it? I mean, as we moderns understand it? Have you got the psychological slant on it?"
> "Mr. Yarrow, I should hardly be head of the Department of Classics at this University if I were not thoroughly acquainted with all that concerns Oedipus."
> "But the Complex? You know the Complex?"
> "What Complex are you talking about? All art is complex."[1]

Robertson Davies is having fun here. He is satirizing both the professor and the psychologist, playing up the crotchety snobbishness of the old-guard professor even as he mocks the naive eagerness of the psychologist. This disjointed conversation, however, is more than just one funny section from the early career of a Can Lit star; it also speaks to the growing power of psychology and psychiatry in postwar Canada and to the sometimes ambivalent responses that this expertise elicited. It is noteworthy that the psychologist in *Leaven of Malice* seeks to interfere with paternal authority, that he tries to give Professor Vambrace some advice on how to be a better father. In these years, a growing number of psychiatrists and psychologists played increasingly prominent roles in discussions about what it meant to be manly. They repackaged the meanings of masculinity, medicalizing its language and positioning themselves as the ones best able to explain anything from fatherhood to a Greek myth.

Capital-murder cases provided one of the most significant and effective venues in which these experts would position themselves as those who could speak about masculinity in a scientific fashion. Between 1945 and the late 1960s, Vancouver courts sentenced twenty-four men to hang for murder. Capital cases dealt with the most serious form of crime, calling forth the harshest penalty from the criminal justice system. The horrific nature of these killings stretched the credulity of many contemporaries, making them wonder how one could commit such violence. They sought explanations and solutions, and increasingly in the postwar years, psychiatrists and psychologists provided the kinds of answers that many involved in such cases, from judges and lawyers to relatives of the killers and the general public alike, adopted as official explanations. The fictional Professor Vambrace may have been skeptical about the young psychologist, but when it came to dealing with murder, many postwar Canadians turned to just such experts to make sense of the murderers in their midst.[2]

In this chapter, we move from the celebrated cases of men's violence and risk taking (during war, on the job, at leisure) to one extremely important situation where Vancouverites turned toward a variety of experts to manage the risks posed by men's violence. The continuity lies in the emphasis on the need to control and manage risk and in the ambivalent relation of masculinity to this process. In the earlier chapters, a masculinity rooted in notions of bodily competence and daring came up against, and only imperfectly blended with, the ideas and practices of manly modernism that valorized reason, objectivity, and abstract knowledge. In this chapter, a similar process is at work. All of those convicted of capital murder in postwar Vancouver were men. Much of the discussion in capital cases, especially about commutation, centred on the murderer's manhood, on whether he had been or could become a good man.[3] Vancouverites considered some types of men's violence to be, if not acceptable, then certainly understandable. Discussions about which murderers should have their death penalties commuted to life imprisonment hinged on gendered beliefs that certain kinds of men, under the right (or wrong) conditions, could quite naturally (and more reasonably) be violent.[4] Just as with veterans and ironworkers, however, a number of experts entered into the decision over when this was the case. Psychiatrists and psychologists came to define much of the language through which Vancouverites discussed the norms of, and the deviations from, manhood.

To speak of the medicalization of masculinity may at first seem odd. Beginning in the late nineteenth and moving into the twentieth century, a growing number of doctors and other health professionals engaged in a process of medicalizing womanhood. This process included early public health campaigns around maternal and infant mortality, efforts to improve the health of women workers in industry, and the growth of a network of professional advice givers on the best methods of motherhood. With success in many public health measures in the early twentieth century, doctors, psychologists, and social workers increasingly came to focus on the emotional and psychological aspects of mothering at mid-century. While many of these campaigns were led by those who sought to improve women's lives and health, they also had the effect of setting up a new kind of expertise (often dominated by men) about how to best fulfill and define a woman's duty.[5] This chapter suggests that it might be useful to think about whether (and to what effect) a similar process of medicalization of manhood occurred.[6] Throughout the twentieth century, a number of professions, from medicine and social work to psychiatry and psychology, came to define how to best be masculine. And while most of these professions were dominated by men, they often did not share the same notions and practices of masculinity as did those whom they treated. The professional development of some men often went hand-in-hand with the disciplining of others.[7]

Crime and Mental Health in the Postwar Years
In the postwar years, the criminal justice system as a whole moved slowly but steadily toward a greater emphasis on the rehabilitation and "correction" of offenders. This was based on a sense of optimism that criminals, especially the very young, could be remade into good citizens. While such beliefs had always made up one part of the criminal justice system in Canada, they were increasingly backed up by actual resources in these years. The federal government's 1938 Royal Commission on the Penal System of Canada marked a point of transition from which, after the interlude of war, governments at all levels took their direction. Governments constructed new prisons of varying security levels, developed rehabilitative programs, established more lenient parole schemes,

and began to provide better resources for prisoners, including libraries and sporting and leisure facilities.[8] One of the most noteworthy features of these initiatives is the extent to which they empowered a new group of experts to take on the task of correction.

In the postwar years, the criminal justice system increasingly relied on experts in the fields of psychiatry, psychology, and other related professions such as social work. In 1950, the British Columbia Gaol Commission called for a number of rehabilitation measures, including expanding parole and probation, establishing training programs for all inmates, and, significant for our purposes here, hiring a full-time physician and psychiatrist. In the early 1950s, the province's main penitentiary, Oakalla Prison Farm (where all those convicted of capital murder in Vancouver stayed until their sentences were either carried out or commuted) took on Dr. Ernest Campbell as a consulting psychiatrist. Moreover, the gaol's physician, Dr. R.G.E. Richmond, was also a psychiatrist and regularly gave reports on the psychological state of convicted killers. That 1,248 psychological tests were administered on Oakalla inmates in one year, between the beginning of April 1958 and the end of March 1959, gives some evidence of the extent of psychological and psychiatric influence.[9]

The trend toward rehabilitation within the criminal justice system matched similar trends within the mental health professions, emphasizing the possibility of improvement and reflecting the desire of mental health professionals to take active roles in shaping public policy. Postwar psychology, as Mona Gleason has shown, increasingly turned toward behavioural explanations of mental illness, emphasizing the events within individual life cycles that caused mental problems and that could, at least theoretically, be treated. Since the late 1930s, the umbrella organization of many of these professions, the Canadian National Committee on Mental Hygiene, had been moving slowly but steadily away from its earlier emphasis on eugenics. After the war, with the public revulsion at the "discovery" of the Holocaust, the impetus away from such genetic explanations became all the more pronounced. Psychologists' involvement in the war effort, providing and administering psychological tests to volunteers and recruits, boosted the status of their profession and fostered its growth. In 1939, Canadian psychologists separated from their American counterparts and formed the Canadian Psychological Association. Interwar efforts to work through schools and to establish child-guidance clinics continued and expanded in the postwar years. Indeed, a number of those convicted of capital murder in these years were already known to officials not only through their previous criminal records, but also through the Vancouver Child Guidance Clinic.[10]

Psychiatrists had different but equally compelling reasons to pair up with the rehabilitation efforts of the criminal justice system. Eager to present themselves as professionals with scientific credibility, psychiatrists in late-nineteenth- and early-twentieth-century Canada focused their efforts on classifying the mentally ill. They saw a rigorous system of classification, in which individuals were matched and labelled according to symptoms, as the key to professional credibility. Beyond this ability to classify, however, early-twentieth-century psychiatrists struggled to prove that they could actually do something to improve mental illness, that it could be cured. Beginning in the 1920s and 1930s, psychiatrists increasingly turned to interventionist somatic treatments, including insulin-shock therapy, artificial-fever therapy, and lobotomies. The psychiatrist at British Columbia's Oakalla Prison Farm, Dr. Campbell, began performing electric-shock therapy on inmates in the 1950s. The emergence of neuroleptic drugs in the mid-1950s expanded the trend in physical therapies in a whole new direction. More broadly, the psychiatric profession increasingly moved to a more community-oriented model of medicine in the postwar years. Although the transition was never wholly complete or without contrary arguments from some psychiatrists, the trend nevertheless moved away from the asylum and toward strategies that prevented and treated mental illness within the community. Throughout this period, in other words, psychiatrists sought ways in which to show that their profession could do more than simply keep the mentally ill locked up in asylums. Involvement in the criminal justice system provided them with just such an opportunity.[11]

When Vancouver murderers were arrested for their crimes, then, they came into contact with a system that sought to find out a great deal about the kind of people they were. This concern with the individual was strengthened even more by the seriousness of the sentence imposed in cases of capital murder. The rehabilitation decision found its most profound crisis in the case of capital murderers: either commute the sentence and hope that the prisoner could be made into a successful citizen or allow the law to take its course, which meant revoking for all time the possibility of correction. Before deciding to go ahead with a death sentence, officials in Ottawa collected information on the offender and presented it to Cabinet for a final decision on whether or not to commute. This information included transcripts of the court proceedings, a letter from the presiding judge, and documentation from various agencies, including the police and anyone else who would have relevant knowledge of the offender's background. Anyone could write to the government, and this information was collected to be used in the final decision. This often included letters from friends, neighbours, and relatives calling for commutation. It also increasingly included information from experts such as psychiatrists, psychologists, and social workers.[12]

Medicalizing Manhood

Mental health professionals entered into capital cases in a variety of ways. The most direct intervention came when they appeared as witnesses in murder trials. One or more psychiatrists appeared in seven of the twenty-four cases. This typically happened when the defence put forward a case of insanity, provocation, or lack of intent due to intoxication (usually mixed with the fact that alcohol exacerbated the accused man's mental illness). The Crown then often responded by calling psychiatrists of its own. Even in other cases, psychiatrists entered the fray before the trial by determining whether the accused was fit to stand trial. In several cases, letters from these doctors made their way into the capital-case file. The government also frequently had psychiatrists see those who were sentenced to death if there was any suggestion of mental instability, and their letters, too, made it into the case files. Making the final commutation decision also involved gathering as much information as possible about the personal history of the convicted man. The Remissions Office in Ottawa often retrieved this information from social workers and psychologists who had worked with the men in various institutions, including child-guidance clinics and mental hospitals, or from organizations such as the Catholic Children's Aid Society and the Provincial Probation Branch. At many stages throughout the capital case, in other words, various experts were called upon to give their assessments and knowledge of the convicted man.[13]

Some sense of the respect granted mental health professionals in capital cases comes from how other officials picked up their language. In providing their histories of the convicted men, Remissions Office officials invoked the language of psychological testing, especially intelligence tests. One man was noted to be "in the average age group, in general intelligence," while another was of "better than average intelligence and has no record of any previous mental illness."[14] In a 1945 case, the remissions officer quoted the jail surgeon to note that the prisoner's "mentality is normal, if not good."[15] In 1953, Justice A.M. Manson took it upon himself to instruct the jury on the defence of insanity even though the defence lawyer had never mentioned such a possibility during the trial. Manson decided to do this after reading a letter that had been found on the accused when he was arrested. "It [was] a strange letter," Manson noted, "indicating from beginning to end that the man was labouring under a persecutory complex." The judge had suggested that the defence seek out "one of the leading psychiatrists in our City," and although he thought that this had been done and even though the defence lawyer still did not make the case for insanity in trial, the judge instructed the jury on this defence nonetheless, "out of an abundance of caution."[16] And while one psychiatrist earned Manson's opprobrium, for the most part Manson and other judges treated psychiatrists and their knowledge with a good deal of respect. In his regular letter to Ottawa after a 1958 case, Manson reported about a psychiatrist who appeared in the trial: "One of the medical witnesses, Dr. Tyhurst, was, if I may say so, an outstanding witness."[17]

Manson and others found mental health professionals to be "outstanding" or just plain useful partly because such experts helped to explain the causes of illegal killing. The American historian Karen Halttunen notes that when modern explanations of murder – those emphasizing secular concerns such as an individual's poor upbringing or the neglect of self-government due to an excess of passion – emerged in the late eighteenth and early nineteenth centuries, they frequently failed to offer satisfaction. "Again and again," she argues, "such liberal explanations of the crime failed: some men and women murdered despite their good religious and moral upbringings; some murdered without any discernible motive; and some killed coolly and dispassionately." While Halttunen is concerned with how this failure led to the rise of other ways to talk about murder, those focusing on horror and mystery, this same failure also helps to explain the increasing turn to science and psychological explanations. Some may have despaired of rationally explaining murder, but others turned to more credentialed sources. Contemporaries looked for explanations that would help to explain how someone could kill, and in the postwar years, they increasingly turned to medical explanations.[18]

The best proof of some kind of medical explanation was an actual physical problem. A number of cases included debates over whether the killer had a somatic problem, some physical malady that was traceable and measurable, that explained his actions. The defence obviously had much to gain from such a finding, so they frequently brought in experts to suggest as much. The most common suggestion was some form of bump on the head. When Joseph McKenna stood accused of shooting another man with almost no provocation at the Mayling Supper Club in 1957, the defence called his mother and other family friends to help explain his history of strange and erratic behaviour. They claimed that it began after he was knocked down by a car when he was a small boy. From then on, he had "difficulty sleeping and was a very unsettled boy."[19] Another mother used the same tactic but claimed that the "bump" had been delivered by the police when they arrested her son for drinking on a fire escape with a girl. "When I saw him at the jail the next day he was swollen up like a football. An esray [sic] was taken at the General Hospital, no bones were broken but Bob suffered a nervous trouble ever since."[20] While most of these men were unable to use such somatic defences effectively (i.e., they were still found guilty), one Italian man, Gino Casagrande, used his own "brain damage" to successfully argue for more lenient treatment. If Casagrande was to be believed, he had had some very tough luck. When he was young, his brother hit him on the head with a rock, knocking him unconscious for two hours. When he was fifteen, he fell while ski jumping, breaking his back and remaining unconscious for some time again. To top it off, he fell fifty feet while serving in the Italian army, was knocked unconscious for thirteen hours, and spent four months in hospital during 1950 and 1951.[21] The psychiatrist, Dr. Tyhurst, ordered a number of tests, including neurological exams and psychological testing, and reported to the court that Casagrande had suffered "brain trauma" and "post-traumatic constitution." Tyhurst claimed that such an individual had "a predisposition to react explosively to situations, characterized by a very great irritability after alcohol sometimes leading to acts of violence."[22] The judge later recommended commuting Casagrande's sentence, citing a number of reasons, including the history of brain damage.[23]

More commonly, psychiatrists turned to behavioural explanations for a murderer's action. These experts sought to explain why murderers had failed to meet the ideal of the disciplined modern man who kept his cool, reigned in his passions, and acted responsibly. We have seen how this ideal of the rational, stoic, and competent man pervaded many aspects of postwar culture including claims of veterans, postwar reconstruction efforts, and notions of the kind of men responsible for postwar economic development. This ideal entered into capital cases as a question mark, as a presumed norm whose absence needed explanation. Experts, lay witnesses, and court officials medicalized this ideal in a variety of ways, one of which was through the language of maturity. This approach suggested that there was a step-by-step way to adulthood with a variety of different levels and stages at which individuals could go astray. Officials could explain, or at least label, a murderer's actions by categorizing him as "immature." The most common diagnosis of the out-of-balance male character was the psychopathic personality. Many of the men sentenced to death in the postwar years were said to be "aggressive psychopaths." Dr. Richmond, the surgeon at Oakalla Prison Farm, described an aggressive psychopath as "one who is aggressive, impulsive, requires immediate gratification of his whims; he is unable to form lasting relationships; he is anti-social, not deterred by punishment and not profiting by experience; they are inclined to be grossly egocentric, that is, self-centred; emotionally they are immature, undependable, with impaired sensibility to the feelings of other people, and subject to alcohol or drugs."[24] Such a figure contrasted with almost all the postwar ideals of middle-class masculinity. While men could be impulsive and aggressive, middle-class manhood was defined at this time by one's ability to restrain such primal attributes. Manhood was achieved by passing through the steps to maturity. While, in this sense, all men had the potential to become psychopaths in that much of this definition was consistent with the dark possibilities that were said to lie within men, they actually became modern men by disciplining these alternate life paths. In the capital cases, psychiatrists stepped into the limelight to explain and diagnose this manly failure in the language of science. Notably, experts maintained that psychopaths were not mentally ill (they did not suffer from a disease); rather, their problems were behavioural.

The turn to environmental explanations for murder marked the real coming together of the legal system and mental health expertise. Almost all those involved in murder cases, with the exception of the police, who were more prone to focus on plain wrongdoing, drew upon environmental explanations for murder. They borrowed the language of mental health expertise to try to make sense of murder. In the postwar years, psychologists and psychiatrists identified the spectre lurking in the background of abnormal personalities as an unhealthy family. In theory, psychiatrists focused on the pathological and deviant characters who came from such families, while psychologists focused on creating "normal" families. In these cases, however, such disciplinary boundaries blurred, as all experts invoked the same notions of healthy and unhealthy family life.[25] Justice Coady's comments about a young man convicted of murder in 1952 were typical: "The accused is a young man and while his past record extending over a period of some years is not good, there may however be something in the background – a lack of family training and such like, which would explain to some extent at least his past criminal record."[26] In another case, Coady noted: "It does not appear that this boy had any of the advantages of a proper bringing up."[27] Justice Manson projected similar sentiments about a murder in 1947. According to Manson, the young man was "just one of those unfortunate products of a society which does not care for its youth as it ought to."[28]

The figure of the bad mother loomed large in references to unhealthy family backgrounds both in trials and in psychological discourse. Philip Wylie's *Generation of Vipers* (1942) popularized a form of mother-bashing that many other family experts took up in the postwar years. Wylie and others suggested that great dangers stemmed from the possibility of overmothering, from women's too strong attachment to their children, and especially from young boys' inability to form proper masculine attachments in such situations.[29] These experts presented the mother as the most important figure in a child's development; if she did not fulfill her duties (following the guidelines of psychological expertise), terrible consequences could result. Not surprisingly, many looked to the role of mothers in setting the unfortunate paths that their sons followed, which took them to that most terrible of delinquencies: murder. In 1945, one killer's brother-in-law drew attention to the man's overmothering after his father died at the age of seven. "Brought up by his mother, he was the apple of her eye, too much so," he claimed. "I am afraid Bill was showered with too much attention and so grew up without the responsibility a young man should have."[30] In 1947, the barrister for a convicted bank robber and murderer wrote to Ottawa to let officials know of his client's family background. The mother had "been an inmate of Essondale Mental Hospital for over six years," and given this fact, he recommended that his client "be examined immediately by a psychiatrist."[31] When Roger Graham's defence lawyer informed officials of his client's "sordid" background, which included a homosexual father who had also prostituted out his mother to friends while their children sometimes watched, the lawyer noted that the mother was obviously "inferior in intelligence or in morals" for not restraining these practices or herself.[32]

. Fathers did not escape unscathed in this search for scapegoats. In the postwar years, psychologists argued that fathers played important roles in shaping the mental and emotional development of children. While a father was not to take on the role of primary caregiver, he was expected to set an example as disciplinarian, wise advice giver, and masculine role model. Officials pointedly noted that the fathers of many of the men convicted of murder had not been present during their sons' youths because of either death or family breakdown. Roger Graham's father came in for as much blame as his mother. His lawyer reported that the father was a "complete homosexual" and a "complete sadist." Graham claimed that "his father at all times displayed towards him complete animosity and subjected him to such tortures as holding his head under water to see what length of time would elapse before he might drown." After his son was arrested for murder, Graham's sister reported that the father said, "I hope they hang the 'S-OF-A-B.'"[33] This background was enough to explain Graham's behaviour to the Oakalla psychiatrist, Dr. Richmond. After receiving the information about Graham's family background, he explicitly linked the problems of the father and mother with psychological issues and murder. "I note from your enclosures the bestial background of the home," he wrote. "I think your suggestion of psychopathic tendencies is apt – Graham must have an immense amount of hostility towards his father, and no doubt this is released in many explosive incidents, culminating in murder ... He appears to be a case of violent hatred engendered from an early age, so understandable in the light of the psychopathic father and inadequate mother."[34] When men like Graham failed to act in a self-disciplined fashion, Richmond and other mental health experts had explanations ready to hand, upon which many drew. Bad families made for murderers.

Although family problems were the primary explanation that mental health officials gave for a murderer's wrong turn, they also emphasized the importance of other institutions and organizations of character formation. The late nineteenth and twentieth centuries saw the origins of a number of organizations meant to strengthen the character of young boys, to make sure that they could be built into strong men in a modernizing context that was seen to be threatening to traditional virtues of self-discipline, hardiness, and resourcefulness. Reformers responded to what they saw as a threat to gender by creating such organizations as the Boy Scouts, Fresh Air camps, and organized sporting leagues.[35] Contemporaries often looked to a murderer's background to see whether he had participated in such activities. A probation officer reported on Harry Medos' lacklustre involvement in the Kivan Boys Club in 1941. The officer claimed that "Medos used to lean against the walls watching activities, but rarely participating. The subject was persuaded to take lessons in the art of self-defence – but he quit after being struck once." Such actions showed a lack of willingness to engage in the strong character-building activities of mid-century masculinity. After noting a number of other problems, the officer suggested that Medos might have "psychopathic traits."[36] The stepmother of another murderer explained his childhood problems in part by noting that he "did not attend Scout or church activities."[37]

In other cases, the previous involvement of a convicted man in these kinds of activities served as an indicator of his good background and potential for correction. When twenty-year-old William Gash killed a man on the Langara Golf Course, a number of officials spoke up about his strong character. Gash had been volunteering as a boxing instructor at the Sunset Memorial Centre. The director and assistant director of the centre wrote letters on his behalf and noted his good character. The director claimed that problems in Gash's family background, "the lack of his parents' understanding of his life," helped to explain his actions and that "he was partly insane when he took the action he did."[38] Other letter writers on Gash's behalf mentioned his community involvement as an example of his potential for rehabilitation.[39] In 1957, Calvin Klingbell's hockey coach from his home town of Kelowna wrote in to speak for his good character. The coach claimed that Klingbell had always shown respect in his appearance, equipment, and treatment of other players. And "while he no doubt received minor penalties," the coach concluded, "nothing comes to mind where he showed that he could be difficult."[40] Another letter writer claimed that "he isn't a criminal of nature; [he] must of [sic] lost his mind."[41]

This interplay between the norms of manliness and mental illness spread throughout the trials. Quite often, the kind of man that a murderer could claim to be – or could be presented as being – mattered a great deal in decisions over guilt and commutation. A murderer's breadwinning capabilities and work ethic provided the most common test of manhood. Being a man meant being a good worker.[42] Perhaps the most commonplace form of this assumption came in the insistence of newspapers to refer to murderers by occupation. Most of the men convicted of capital murder had very spotty work records, holding few jobs for any length of time. In 1962, the *Vancouver Sun* insisted on calling Eric Lifton "a former cook"[43] even though Lifton came to be in trouble in Vancouver after stealing another man's credit card and travelling to various locations in Europe and North America, not working at all. He had also been an intermittent university student in the United States and had served a brief stint in the US army. To say that Lifton was a cook was to say very little, yet local papers insisted on the convention in this and all cases. Stating a man's job mattered.

Some prosecutors emphasized a man's spotty work record as a way of making the murderer look bad during the trial, linking his manly failure to illegal and horrific violence. This worked especially well in murders that resulted from robberies, where the Crown could make a direct connection with the unwillingness to work and the decision to kill. In a 1947 case involving two bank robbers/murderers, the prosecutor cross-examined the common-law wife of one of the accused (itself a contentious issue in this period) lingering over the men's unwillingness to work. He asked the woman, M. Peterson, in what context the plans for the robbery had been discussed and then played dumb to get her to elaborate her position:

> *Peterson:* Well, I think the whole thing led up the fact that Douglas Carter was working nights and I guess he didn't fancy the idea and they were talking about holding up a bank, that's all.
> *Prosecutor:* What connection would that have with Carter working at night? I didn't follow what you mean. What is the connection between Carter working at night and holding up a bank?
> *Peterson:* I guess possibly he thought that wasn't a very nice position to have, or something like that; working nights didn't appeal to him.
> *Prosecutor:* What did you mean – the bank would be held up at night?
> *Peterson:* No.
> *Prosecutor:* I must say I don't follow you. If you will explain what you mean by that?
> *Peterson:* I gathered they meant it would be an easier living than working.[44]

The prosecutor had not just stumbled upon this tactic. Two men were accused of the murder, and the prosecutor asked the same questions in both trials.[45] In both of these cases, officials explained this failure to achieve the breadwinner norm within the parameters of postwar psychological discourse that emphasized environmental and behavioural problems. Medos, it should be remembered, had a mother who had been in a mental hospital, and his lawyer and the judge brought up this issue to officials in Ottawa. A large campaign to save the life of the other convicted man, Bill Henderson, who was only seventeen, centred not just on his age but also on his poor family background. Many organizations and individual Vancouverites wrote in to call for commutation, including the United Church Women's Social Service Council, the painter Lawren Harris, former provincial leader of the Coopérative Commonwealth Federation E.E. Winch, and the local Council of Women.[46] They drew upon the behavioural explanations of mental health expertise to explain Henderson's violence and to save his life. In the end, Cabinet called for a new trial for Henderson and for the law to take its course with Medos.

Contemporaries presented balance and discipline as well as bread-winning as main features of masculinity and, in doing so, mirrored the psychological discourse of the day, which emphasized the many ways that one could go astray on the path to maturity. The notion of the "teenager" first appeared in the postwar years, partly as a result of social changes, including changes in the education and work patterns of youth, and also as a result of the work of mental health professionals who argued that adolescence was a distinct and troublesome biological pe-riod in one's life. These experts, and the society at large, projected their gendered fears of the future onto discussions of adolescent develop-ment. They saw the potential downfall for girls in issues of sexual im-propriety, while for boys they feared the improper taming of aggression. The path to proper manhood meant steering clear of being either too feminine or too masculine.[47]

Discussion of murderers frequently invoked these ideas about manli-ness. Manliness needed to be tamed and controlled. Murderers who con-veyed the least amount of threatening masculine aggressiveness generated sympathy. Often this was the case with young murderers. In 1954, Mr. S. Jenkins, pastor of the Pender Christian Mission, wrote to the minister of justice on behalf of one young man: "He never had an easy road in life as he was slight and almost feminine looking in appearance, with the mind of a boy and the responsibility of a man."[48] In the case of the nineteen-year-old Henderson, a judge used similar logic: "It is impossi-ble to understand why [Henderson] got mixed up in an attempt to rob a bank with arms. The boy does not look like a killer and he doesn't even look like a boy of courage. If anything, he has rather a weak face."[49] When another man killed a bank manager, his defence counsel empha-sized his status as a "weakling" in an attempt to explain away his re-sponsibility for violence.[50] These kinds of statements made a direct link between masculinity and violence that the authors considered threaten-ing and then distanced the particular murderer from this type of mascu-linity. In doing so, they represented a backhanded compliment, absolving inherent evil in the enactment of violence while taking away the mur-derer's manhood. The other side was also problematic. Being too manly was just as bad as being unmanly. When James Carey and Joseph Gordon faced murder charges for the death of a Vancouver police constable, the two men's relative strength of character played a role in how the judge interpreted the murder they had committed. Justice Manson claimed, "Gordon is rather proud of his criminal record, seemingly. He is a strong character. Carey, on the other hand, I would regard as a somewhat weak character, a follower rather than a leader."[51] A local woman wrote to Carey's lawyer to offer assistance in fighting for commutation. "James Carey has a decent face," she wrote, "a good face and one can judge a great deal by a man's face. Joe Gordon, in my humble opinion, judging as justly as I can, is another kind of man altogether than Carey. He has always been a bad one. He will always BE a bad one."[52]

Other commentators found more sympathy for aggressive male youths. They accepted a basic notion that men were naturally aggressive and in certain circumstances would lash out in violence. Written pleas to spare the lives of young murderers appealed to the government's understanding of "the natural animal spirits of young boys"[53] and spoke of the "thousands of fine hardworking men in Canada ... who look back on the days of their wild oats with a smile."[54] Defence counsels often appealed to assumptions of a natural and allegedly harmless masculine aggressiveness. In 1955, when death resulted from a fight between two young men amid a gathering of Vancouver youth, the defence lawyer argued for the normalcy of this behaviour. "Thousands of incidents of this kind probably occur every night throughout Canada," he argued, "but this one ended in a fatality."[55]

These kinds of arguments assumed that men were prone to violence and that this merely needed to be appropriately directed. A woman calling herself "Another Grandma" suggested work and the military as possible outlets. She wrote to the minister of justice to ask that he spare one young murderer. He "could work and learn the Golden Rule and become a good man," she suggested, "maybe with the next war he would be useful."[56] Another plea for the same young man's life noted the link between the army and the need to tame youthful masculine aggression: "I can see my brother at seventeen just before I left England wanting to be called into the Army," wrote Doris Boynes. "All I can hear him saying is, 'Wait until I get into the Army I'll show you how to kill em!' You and I know what killing means but to the minds at that age it's all adventure."[57] In these cases, age served as a defence. The convicted boys and men had not yet learned to discipline themselves, to redirect their impulses toward socially useful ends.

The distinction between disciplined and unruly violence pervaded newspaper coverage of murder trials. In the wake of a violent 1947 bank robbery, newspapers printed alarmist stories about young men and guns. "Raiders, even the youngest of them, handle guns with complete confidence and familiarity," the *Vancouver Daily Province* told its readers. It warned that a criminal leader – akin to the character Fagin in Dickens'

Oliver Twist – was training impressionable Vancouver youngsters. The problem was not violence with guns in general. The paper celebrated one of the police officers in the same case. It recounted how, in the gunfight with the three robbers, Detective Hoare had used his wrong hand to "kill one of the trio and to wound another at a distance of 100 yards." In a parallel to its fearful stories about trained criminals, the paper claimed that "Detective Hoare's excellent marksmanship, right hand shots even though left handed, were definitely not just lucky breaks. The officer is one of a small group of police who started the Vancouver Police Shooters Club ... and Detective Hoare is one of the most enthusiastic members ... If it had not been for Detective Hoare's constant practice, there might have well been three dead officers and three escaped suspects."[58] A picture accompanying the story showed Hoare pointing his gun directly at the camera.[59] The postwar ideal of manhood lay in finding the middle route between the weakling and the brute.

The sexuality of a murderer also mattered a great deal to Vancouverites, and here, too, psychiatrists played a major role in setting the language of public discourse. In 1948, the federal government added a special amendment to the Criminal Code regarding "criminal sexual psychopaths." A few years later, in 1954, the Royal Commission on the Law Relating to Criminal Sexual Psychopaths took up the same controversial subject yet again. It does not appear as though there was an actual increase in this type of crime. Rather, as Estelle Freedman has argued, North Americans' concern over sexual psychopaths at mid-century was part of an attempt to define proper heterosexual relations by casting out people and actions deemed abhorrent and, in the process, by normalizing those actions not deemed so. The castigation of sexual psychopaths played a role in establishing the norms of masculinity as heterosexual within certain prescribed limits. It was also, as Elise Chenier has argued about the Canadian experience, a successful effort on the part of psychiatrists to medicalize the language of sexuality and to promote their role as its monitors.[60]

This was especially evident in possibly the most sensational murder trial of postwar Vancouver, the killing of Ferne Blanche Fisher by Frederick Roger Ducharme, a tragedy that the coroner and police quickly identified as the work of a "sex maniac."[61] In early November 1949, workers found Fisher's body on the shores of False Creek. As in most cases involving a female victim, questions immediately went to her own sexuality, but friends and relatives described the forty-five-year-old spinster as a religious, happy, good worker who had regular habits and was not suicidal.[62] The evidence of sexual assault and the fact that part of her body hair had been shaven off drew speculation, and the press made comparisons to a similar case in which another woman's "nude and hairless body [had washed] up on the rocks of a lonely beach at West Vancouver."[63] Police Chief Walter Mulligan warned of a possible sex maniac loose in Vancouver.

Even before he became a suspect, concerns over Ducharme's sexuality played a significant role in how police treated him. In early December, almost a month after the as yet unsolved murder, two police officers patrolling an area not far from the waterfront spotted what they later referred to as "a person ahead of them who at the moment may have been male or female." The police report described the capture:

> The object [Ducharme] dashed across the street behind the Coca Cola plant followed closely by the officers who were firing revolver shots to stop it. Two employees of the plant who saw the fleeing object, jumped it when the police shouted to them to do so. It was then found that [the] accused was wearing only short underware [*sic*], a shirt, long rain coat, a pair of rubber boots and a silk scarf draped over his head like a girl ... they found [the] accused had a shoe lace wrapped round his penis which he told them he had to wear to keep his penis down as he got delirious when it got up.[64]

Police initially had no evidence linking Ducharme with the Fisher murder but kept him in custody for mental examination. In a subsequent search of his home, they found key physical evidence linking Ducharme to Fisher and only then charged him with the murder.

All involved in the trial, including Ducharme himself, invoked the language of mental illness to explain his odd sexual behaviour. Dr. J.P.S. Cathcart, the chief neuropsychiatrist with the Department of Veterans' Affairs (and the doctor repeatedly called upon to perform psychiatric examinations of all convicted capital murderers for the Remissions Office), visited Ducharme in his Oakalla cell in June 1951. Cathcart noted a number of features about Ducharme that he thought could indicate a certain kind of unmanly personality. Cathcart wrote, "I noticed that his finger nails were rather long, particularly the thumb nails ... I have an idea that the nail picture fits in with a lot of other things about this man, including the significant female trophies that were found in his float house."[65] In an earlier letter, Cathcart took up this same theme after reading one of Ducharme's diaries. He wrote to Ottawa claiming

"Ducharme reveals an unusual interest in some intimate female details which, while it doesn't prove anything in connection with this particular crime, nevertheless it does suggest that he fits into a group or type that would be perversely interested in that direction."[66] Justice Manson picked up the language of the psychiatrists who frequently appeared in his court when he claimed, "My own view is that this man is definitely a psychopath of some description, with an inclination to sexual misbehaviour."[67] Ducharme himself attempted to play up his troubles to earn sympathy and respite from conviction and later execution. In diaries and letters later released to the press and the courts, Ducharme took up popularly known themes of medical deviance, describing himself as a man "very much alone in [his] own world" and a "lone wolf" (perhaps a reference to Freud's "wolf man" case study).[68] His defence attorney made a similar plea in his closing address to the jury, admitting to the jury that Ducharme and his friends were "a group of exhibitionists, who live in floathouses and to whom I will refer as a nest of perverts." But he went on to argue, "Even if you believe Ducharme did this murder knowingly, he is a type of man whose background and personality is timidity, a fool who hasn't got the courage to go around asking for what he wants. Psychiatrists tell us he should not be in an insane asylum. Do you think he is mentally right? Is he normal?"[69] The correct answer here was that he was not. The jury disagreed with this reasoning, finding Ducharme guilty of murder, but the references to medicalized sexual oddity no doubt lingered.

Vancouverites could (and did) racialize these notions of appropriate manly conduct, seeing some races as more or less likely to fall astray in different directions. When a black man killed one woman and mutilated another with a hammer in 1953, his race served to explain the violence and to mark him as unmanly. Charles Matthews, an African American boxer who had been living in Vancouver, had fallen in love with Peggy Bowen, a young woman from Vancouver's African Canadian community. Some members of the community disapproved of Matthews, and Bowen called off their relationship. Matthews blamed the break-up on Los Angeles Smith, the sister of his boxing trainer and the woman in whose home he had boarded. Early on a weekday morning in March 1953, he went to her home. He first went to an upstairs apartment where Jocelyn Wallberg lived with her husband. Wallberg was preparing to leave for work, but she recognized Matthews from his time at the Smith home and let him in to borrow a pen. Matthews beat this woman with his fists and a hammer and left her for dead. He searched for a trap door that he believed led into the Smith home below. Not finding it, he eventually entered the downstairs home from the front door. Once inside, he also beat and killed Smith with a hammer. The woman in the upstairs apartment, Wallberg, survived and acted as the star witness at Matthews' trial.[70]

The sheer brutality of the murder as well as the issues of home invasion and a love affair would have been sufficient to make this a sensational case. But the element of race trumped the others. Commentators on the case picked up on the trope of the too manly black male that pervaded North American culture in the early years of the twentieth century.[71] This was the idea that black men were overly sexualized and masculine because of their allegedly primitive state. While such race-based claims were becoming less popular in the postwar years, they nevertheless dominated public and institutional discussions of this case. Newspapers wrote of the love affair between this "Negro" and his "Negress."[72] Justice J.V. Clyne neatly summarized the general racialized language of black primitivism in his comments on Matthews' general character. "He is obviously an emotional, undisciplined youth of twenty years of age," Clyne wrote, "and in my opinion is not very far removed from the jungle ... I think that he is a primitive who became so furious by being deprived of what he wanted that he committed a very brutal murder and was careless of consequences."[73] These sentiments reflected not only one judge's candour, but also the general tone of expert opinion. The psychiatrist sent to examine Matthews, J.P.S. Cathcart, quoted Clyne's comments on Matthews' "primitivism" in his report to the Remissions Office. He noted that "His Lordship has supplied the simplest and most accurate summary of the case" and then went on to quote Clyne's characterization of Matthews as primitive.[74] In no other cases did judges or psychiatrists refer to a murderer as "primitive"; they instead opted for the language of immaturity. Medicalization seems to have offered a way for older ideas about racialized manhood to continue by giving them a scientific shine appropriate to the postwar years.

Matthews' response to his medical explainers is worth dwelling on for what it suggests about the power relation between psychiatrists and the convicted and the effect of medicalization on notions of masculinity. Most of the men convicted of capital murder turned to psychiatrists and other professionals for assistance, either directly pleading insanity or indirectly doing so by invoking medicalized language and expertise to earn commutation of their death sentences. They, or others on their behalf, sought the language of mental health expertise. Unable to make the case on their own, they gave themselves up to the power of a growing expert class that promised to make the case on their behalf. Matthews did not go along on this ride willingly. During the trial itself, he shouted at one of the psychiatrists, E.A. Campbell, who appeared as a witness. After the trial, the government sent Campbell to inspect Matthews before the commutation decision, but the prisoner refused to see him, claiming that he did not want to see any more doctors. In reports on Matthews' behaviour in jail, Oakalla medical officer R.G.E. Richmond described watching Matthews as he would watch a wild animal in a cage. "Tonight," Richmond wrote to one of Matthews' psychiatrists, "I was able to observe an attack by him on a guard who had found him in a corner of his cell, hidden from adequate watch. He felt provoked at being disturbed and in a rage reacted violently ... He resents constant vigilance."[75] We get this report in the language of the watchers, those looking in. Yet we can also get hints of the perspective of the one who was watched – striking back, resenting the psychological gaze that so neatly labelled him throughout his trial and afterward. As Matthews' response to his doctors suggests, some men found the medicalization of masculinity to be uncomfortable.

The context in which Matthews and others were punished changed over the postwar years. Beginning in the 1940s and 1950s, a small but significant minority of Canadians – religious leaders, intellectuals, and humanitarians – called for the abolition of the death penalty. In Vancouver, prominent citizens, such as the writer Eric Nicol and even the warden of Oakalla Prison Farm, Hugh Christie, advocated an end to the noose. This movement gained force in the late 1950s under Conservative prime minister John Diefenbaker's government; the former defence lawyer commuted the sentences of fifty-two of the sixty-six cases that came before Cabinet. Lester Pearson's Liberal government continued with a similar policy until 1967, when it legislated a five-year trial abolition of the death penalty for all cases except those involving the murder of law enforcement officers. Despite rising murder rates and a majority of the population who still favoured hanging, Trudeau's government extended the ban in 1973 and finally abolished the category altogether in 1976. The last executions in Vancouver took place in Oakalla Prison Farm in 1958, and the final Canadian hangings took place in Toronto's Don Gaol in 1962.[76]

From capital-case files, it is difficult to know why the remissions officer in Ottawa recommended that one man should be hanged and another spared. This became impossible after 1957, when all Vancouverites convicted of capital murder had their sentences commuted. What is clear is that the files themselves (the evidence used to make these decisions) contain a number of assumptions rooted in historically particular ways of thinking about what it meant to be both masculine and violent. More often than not, those who died before 1957 were those who least matched contemporary standards of appropriate manly behaviour. After 1957, officials made the same kinds of judgments but to different effect. The postwar movement to abolish the death penalty criticized this type of "discretionary justice." While politicians and the courts emphasized the rationality and even-handedness of capital punishment in line with a long history of the rationalization of punishment, the all too human prejudices that actually affected who the state executed provided plenty of targets for criticism.[77] Ultimately, the state was found lacking in the aspect of modernity that it found so important in the men it judged: unbiased reason.

Psychiatrists, psychologists, social workers, and other mental health experts entered into this debate as those who could ostensibly speak in a rational and objective fashion. Both supporters and critics of capital punishment drew on the language of psychology and psychiatry to give their claims scientific legitimacy. In doing so, these experts became key spokespersons on the men with whom they dealt and on masculinity and manly deviance more generally. The main features of postwar psychological discourse, the emphasis on behavioural, environmental, and family problems, infiltrated all aspects of capital-murder cases. As with veterans and ironworkers, murderers found that their manhood was being defined by a group of experts.

The image of the good man that comes out of these cases shows strong continuities with what came before and after. Murderers could be construed as masculine to the extent to which they presented themselves as good breadwinners, heterosexual, white, responsible, and civilized. All of these men had great difficulty making this case. Many were long-time criminals who had rarely kept regular work; a large number were recent immigrants or of an ethnic lineage (African American, Chinese, eastern or southern European) that made them suspect to the narrowly defined white majority; and others had "mixed" sexual pasts in which they had engaged in such things as homosexual acts or adulterous liaisons. And of course, as killers, they began the race to respectability a good deal behind the starting line. Nonetheless, their defence lawyers, relatives, and the murderers themselves tried to show that they had acted in manly ways. The extent to which postwar killers successfully presented themselves within the normative bounds of postwar manhood mattered a great deal in the outcomes of their trials and in Cabinet's commutation decisions.[78]

What is striking here is the extent to which postwar psychiatrists and psychologists inserted themselves between the men and the decision makers, redescribing the norms of manliness in the language of mental science. Capital-murder cases served as sites of professionalization, as venues through which these experts spread their authority. And this professionalization was quite successful. Those seeking to explain a murderer's actions – including judges, lawyers, newspapers, and many members of the public – frequently invoked the language of psychiatry and psychology. This meant that, in practice, a group of experts with their abstract language became significant mediators of manliness in capital-murder cases. Thus, while in earlier periods a man's failure to live up to his breadwinning obligations might have been seen as a social, economic, or moral problem, the turn to psychiatric knowledge in capital-murder cases also made this a *psychological* failure, perhaps even evidence of an individual's pathology. The decision over where the boundary lay between reasonable violence (that which was understandable if unwanted) and outright deviance came to be made through the language and with the involvement of psychiatric and psychological experts.

Many of the men convicted of murder embraced these experts and their diagnoses. Giving themselves up to scientific explanations of deviance offered them the chance to escape the noose. But as with the other postwar men who found their masculinity caught up with the decisions of experts – whether bureaucrats with the Department of Veterans' Affairs (DVA) or safety officials with the Workmen's Compensation Board – capital murderers sometimes found the blend of the manly and the modern to be a mixed blessing. Their similarities with these other postwar men were not just thematic; at least in the case of one man, the personalities also overlapped. Working for the federal government's Remissions Office, the psychiatrist Dr. J.P.S. Cathcart interviewed a number of the convicted men to determine their mental states before Cabinet made its commutation decisions. It was Cathcart who wrote of Charles Matthews' primitivism and who diagnosed the sexually odd features of Frederick Ducharme's personality. Cathcart also happened to be chief psychiatrist first for the federal Department of Pensions and National Health in the 1930s and 1940s and then for the new Department of Veterans' Affairs in the late 1940s and early 1950s. In this capacity, Cathcart helped to set DVA and Canadian Pension Commission policy toward psychiatric casualties of war. He argued that the main cause of mental illness in war was not the actual battle experience but the background characteristics of individual soldiers. He used the same kind of environmentalist explanations that dominated psychiatric evaluation of capital murders to make sense of mental illness in soldiers and to minimize the entitlements of veterans to state aid.[79] He represented just the kind of interfering expertise that Kirchner and other veterans criticized in their 1947-48 Royal Commission. Cathcart's work in both instances represented a growing tendency for the norms of masculinity – whether in its celebrated or castigated forms – to be mediated through the language of expertise.

6
On the Road

At their 1960 annual meeting, members of the Vancouver Traffic and Safety Council listened to an impassioned keynote speech by W.A. Bryce, executive director of the Canadian Highway Safety Council. Bryce told the audience of local business leaders, labour organizers, school board notables, and civic officials something they often told themselves: that the world was a dangerous place and that the danger they faced was new. "Life in the world today is not the casual easygoing existence that our grandfathers knew one hundred years ago or even fifty years ago," he claimed. "Yes, life today – on the streets or in the skies – does not guarantee that we shall all die in our beds." Although Bryce spoke primarily of those who died on the streets in car accidents, he also put the problem into a larger context, comparing it to the risks of the nuclear age. The modern age gave birth to the threat of the traffic crash and the nuclear war; such dangers were the progeny of modern technological life. In both cases, he warned, one could easily become "baffled and frustrated" by the apparent dearth of solutions. Yet Bryce decried such fatalism. Although modern technologies created many problems, they also offered solutions. He admitted to having no immediate solution to the atomic threat but claimed that "highway accidents ... are a different matter. They are within our experience – we do know their cause and we can provide their cure."[1]

What was Bryce's cure? How did he hope to eradicate the harm caused by the automobile age? If attendees at the annual meeting wanted a novel approach, they were surely disappointed, for Bryce's solutions mirrored what local traffic-safety advocates had been arguing since the early years of the automobile. He called for a smattering of different programs, from more education to better enforcement, all of which fitted neatly into the range of accepted traffic-safety discourse. Safety experts,

Bryce included, held that individual drivers caused accidents and that
the best way to stop accidents was to find better ways to encourage self-
discipline. This approach reflected a technologically deterministic view
of modern life, a view based on the assumption that humans, not technology, needed to change.[2]

What made Bryce's speech memorable (and the reason we are dwelling on it here) was the way that he grasped for the profound in his final
words. Wrapping up his speech, he quoted (selectively) from Rudyard
Kipling's poem of paternal advice "If":

If you can keep your head when all about you
Are losing theirs and blaming it on you
If you can wait and not be tired by waiting
If you can fill the unforgiving minute
with sixty seconds' worth of run
Yours is the Earth and everything that's in it
And what is more, you'll be a man, my son.

At the end of the poem, Bryce added a line of his own, rewording the
message of manhood achieved so that it matched the requirements of
the automobile age. "And what is more," he claimed, "you'll be a good
driver, a good insurance risk, with a low insurance premium and a long
life expectation."[3] Overlooking the line's merit as poetry, Bryce's addition is a telling pronouncement on the connections between traffic accidents, risk, and masculinity in the postwar years. Bryce called on traffic
experts to create safe drivers as the best way to eliminate traffic accidents. And how did one make good drivers? The answer was simple:
you turned them into good men.

Although we frequently connect men and driving with such dangerous activities as motor racing or drag racing, one of the more compelling, if counterintuitive, connections that postwar Vancouverites made
was between men and safety. In these years, ideals of the good driver
and the good man – ostensibly separate categories – shared many characteristics. Their point of convergence was in their shared support for a
disciplined character, one that stressed diligent awareness and foresight
as the epitome of responsible behaviour. This ideal of the reasonable
and responsible man is longstanding, and one of the ways that it has
continued to exert such force is by being continually rewritten into new
codes of behaviour. Earlier in the century, it was more likely to be ut-
tered along with moralistic calls for good character and self-restraint,[4]

but in the postwar years it fitted itself into the language of technocratic risk management. In these years, a group of experts assumed that the traits of the ideal middle-class male were also the traits of the ideal driver, and they mapped one set of characteristics onto the other. In this way, a set of instructions that allegedly applied to both sexes equally in actual fact became imbued with a gender ideology that saw good driving as a kind of masculine achievement. The safety experts updated the ideal of the reasonable man. As we have seen, the secular version of masculine restraint was not endorsed without some ambivalence, but endorsed it was. And the connections between the ideal of the manly modern and the ideal of the safe driver are striking. To the extent that knowing how to handle a car was an important and privileged type of knowledge (which it was), the ideal of the reasonable man became important and privileged, too.

As the 1950s turned into the 1960s, however, a number of critics began chipping away at the automobile's pedestal. On the international stage, Ralph Nader criticized the traffic-safety approach, which blamed drivers for accidents, suggesting instead that the technology itself caused many accidents. In a similar way, Jane Jacobs became the spokesperson for a large movement against automobile-centred urban planning in the United States and Canada, a movement that, in its emphasis on the local, directly challenged the basic principles of high modernism that had dominated urban planning for most of the postwar years and earlier. Vancouverites took up the ideas of both Nader and Jacobs in order to challenge the place of the automobile in their own community. They did so most prominently in the late 1960s, when a diverse group of citizens defeated plans to build a freeway through the city's Chinatown. This type of mid- to late-1960s criticism represented a significant challenge to (although certainly not a total rejection of) the ideological dominance of automobile-centred high modernism, as well as to the experts who told people how to deal with its negative side effects, such as traffic accidents.[5]

What, then, happened to the ideal of the reasonable man? We have already seen the kinds of tensions that resulted from manly modernism's contradictions, the reaction of some men against its disciplinary tendencies. As we will see in this chapter, when automobile-centred high modernism came under attack, the ideals of masculinity with which it was bound up also came under attack. The 1960s criticism of automobile-centred modernity was not just about cars, but also about the kind of man who sat behind the wheel.

Automophilia

Safety experts could not have chosen a more important symbol of post-war modernity with which to associate idealized masculinity. The car symbolized the central features of postwar modernity: suburbanization, consumption, nuclear family "togetherness," and most important, technological progress. Almost as a whole, postwar society embraced a technologically deterministic set of values that historian Pam Roper has called *laissez-innover*. Postwar Canadians' reactions to technological controversies such as the unemployment caused by automation, she argues, "were guided by their beliefs in the widely held precept that societies could not, and indeed should not attempt to control the pace of technological change as it might impede progress."[6] In this era, mechanization and technology went hand in hand with what was modern and therefore good. This even extended into the realm of culinary arts, where "processed" became synonymous with good taste. (This was, after all, the era when jellied salads could be considered fine food!)[7] Although some critics of technical society existed, their criticisms largely called for better machines, for a tune-up (but certainly not an overhaul) of the modernist project itself. Perhaps no other object better symbolized the technological optimism of the postwar years than did the automobile.

It is hard to exaggerate the extent to which North Americans and Vancouverites embraced the automobile in the postwar years. Although the automobile was invented in the previous century and mass ownership developed after the Great War, widespread car ownership truly took off after the Second World War.[8] The number of car registrations increased dramatically immediately following the war and continued to increase throughout the postwar years. This increase resulted, in part, from the city's growing population as more and more migrants (especially from the Prairie provinces) came to British Columbia. It also resulted from the increased ability of Vancouverites to buy vehicles as wartime plants converted back to civilian production. Joy Parr's cautious note about Canadians' more hesitant entrance into postwar consumer culture of domestic goods did not seem to hold true for the car. With the removal of wartime restrictions on production and consumption, Vancouverites seemed eager to take to the roads in their cars. In 1946, General Motors placed advertisements in the *Vancouver Sun* apologizing to customers for the slow delivery of ordered vehicles. Claiming that the conversion of plants was still slowing up production, they promised their customers that the company would soon be able to match the high demand.[9]

Beyond just the rise in the number of cars (which was significant), other developments suggest a social transformation. Organizations and institutions that focused on the automobile grew in importance in the postwar years. Provincially, the Social Credit government of W.A.C. Bennett considered highways to be such a priority that it split that section off from Public Works to create the first Ministry of Highways in 1955. The organization that represented British Columbia drivers, the British Columbia Automobile Association (BCAA), achieved full independence in 1952, splitting off from its sister tourist organization. A spokesperson for the BCAA explained the move by arguing that "motoring has long been a necessity for thousands, not a luxury ... When roads and automobiles become so vital for such a large proportion of the population it is important that there be an organization big enough and strong enough to protect the interests of those who operate motor cars."[10] Drivers were prepared to flex their muscles.

Automobiles changed the very basis of Vancouver's urban life. Many of these changes had been well under way before the war, but the period's widespread adoption of the automobile meant that the changes became fully realized in the postwar years. The car fed the process of suburbanization that was so characteristic of the era. Earlier Vancouver suburbs had depended on the streetcar; not so the postwar suburbs. Along with new developments in housing construction and home financing, the car was an essential catalyst to the development of a number of suburban areas, including Burnaby, Coquitlam, Richmond, and the north shore. Transportation to and from these communities was by car. Within the city itself, suburban-type communities expanded, filling in the sparsely populated urban hinterlands. The car, in other words, led to the filling-in and expanding-out of Vancouver. The city adopted the car so wholeheartedly that it decided to get rid of its earlier system of streetcars. A whole grid of street car lines once joined different Vancouver neighbourhoods, but the city ripped these up between the late 1940s and early 1950s, replacing them with a trolley-bus service. In taking on this kind of auto-centred growth, Vancouver was much like other large Canadian cities. It largely avoided the American problem of inner-city slums caused by white middle-class flight to the suburbs, even while the area's population shifted to represent the relative growth of the suburban areas over that of the centre.[11]

The automobile played a large role in the era's orientation toward family life and leisure. These were the baby boom years, when the sheer growth in numbers of new couples and young children meant that family life took on a renewed importance. Family experts extolled the virtues of "togetherness." All of these new families, the experts encouraged, should spend time together in enjoyable activities. This could include backyard barbecues and new hobbies. It could also include outings in the family car. Car companies advertised the size and roominess of their vehicles to assure families that there was plenty of space. The Standard Motor Company of Canada was typical when it told potential buyers in capital letters that its 1950 Vanguard was "NOT TOO SMALL." Small cars were the exception. In the family-focused postwar years, size mattered, especially in seating area.[12]

Aside from its usefulness to the family, the car also symbolized the democratization of the promises of power and progress inherent to the modernist project. Advertisers tried to sell cars by appealing to their status as modern consumer products that provided prestige. Partly, this came by emphasizing the elegance, beauty, and styling of a car. Companies brought out new models every year, encouraging purchases by emphasizing newness, even when not much had changed. A car's power was also important. Postwar cars came with large engines: V8 and V6 were standard. Companies made sure to tell prospective buyers just how much horsepower their engine could produce. In 1952, Oldsmobile celebrated its "Rocket" engine. Coining phrases with which only a dedicated car enthusiast would have been familiar, the company told readers that "The 'drive' is Oldsmobile's Hydra-Matic Super Drive, with the new 'Super' Range to bring out the 'Rocket's' surging power!" Yet, despite all this power, the driver would be able to have "effortless command of the car." Advertisers played up the idea that driving was an empowering activity. It was both incredibly powerful and easy to do. The Monarch, for example, had an easy task of getting this across because of its name; the company claimed that the car was "every inch a king" and that it allowed drivers to "ride like a king." The Monarch was not alone in emphasizing the great freedom and power of the automobile. Partly, this was just hyperbole, but it also reflected deeply held cultural values. The car produced an incredible amount of power at the flex of a toe. It was, as the German critic Wolfgang Sachs has argued, "a material reproduction of a culture" that set up the individual as sovereign and presented other social ties as subordinate.[13]

The individual behind the wheel of a car, however, was largely understood to be a man. As Virginia Schaff has argued about an earlier period, the automobile's promises of power and speed were gendered masculine. Women entered car advertisements largely as objects or symbols of

style and elegance. Although families may have used the cars on outings and although women may have driven cars, advertisers clearly
imagined the typical buyer as male. Pictures of cars in the advertisements usually showed men driving the vehicle. When women were pic-
tured behind the wheel, the vehicle was less likely to be in an action or
movement-like pose. The woman, like the car, was the object to be
viewed. Some advertisements emphasized recognizably masculine
themes, including a western cowboy theme for the Ford Falcon in 1960
and a shooting range theme for the Mercury Comet in 1962. Advertisements frequently described the car's features in a masculine language
laden with technical jargon that was meant to convey the automobile's
modernity.[14]

Clay McShane argues that the car served as a kind of masculine geta-
way from the troubles of the modern world. It offered opportunities for
action, adventure, and escape from a bureaucratic and industrialized
world.[15] What McShane has picked up on is the connection between
the automobile and the thesis of threatened manhood. We have seen
this before in the way that masculinity has been said to be harmed by
modernity just at the moment when it is also being connected to it.
While it is true that cars could be seen as a form of manly escape from
modern hassles, McShane is only half right in seeing it as an escape
mechanism. Those who gendered the automobile as masculine in the
postwar years were also connecting masculinity with the modernist
project, creating a cultural bond between technological mastery, progress,
and masculinity. To the extent that men became acted upon by modernist expertise and organizers, they no doubt would have wanted to
escape in their cars. But as we shall see below, many in the postwar
years defined the rational risk-management expertise of automotive technology as in alignment with the ideals of manly modernism.

Managing Modern Risk
The shiny golden age of the automobile had a rusty underside. The
number of car accidents in Vancouver doubled between 1945 and 1950,
rising from 3,500 to just over 7,000. Although these numbers levelled
off over the following years, they still tended to rise, reaching a high of
more than 17,000 in 1968. The number of vehicles involved in accidents showed an even greater increase, going from 6,020 in 1945 to
15,007 in 1949. Many more Vancouverites crashed their cars with each
passing year. While many of these were minor incidents, some were
fatal. The number of traffic deaths varied from year to year, ranging

from a low of twenty-six in 1955 to a high of fifty-one in 1966. Cars may have allowed for the "good life," but they also ended life. Such incidents generated a great deal of attention. Local papers regularly followed the ups and downs of traffic-accident and injury numbers, linking small increases and decreases to the success or failure of traffic-safety initiatives. On at least one day each week, Vancouverites could pick up their morning papers and see stories on the front page that detailed the car culture's travesties in their own community.[16]

How did Vancouverites respond to automobile accidents? Perhaps not surprisingly, Vancouverites, like other North Americans, treated car accidents in a very modern way. Safety experts emerged along with the automobile to help explain and deal with its dangers, and they treated car accidents as events that needed to be managed. Just as the automobile itself was a great example of modern control over the environment, its downside seemingly called for an equally modern system of control. Almost uniformly, mid-century safety experts did not aim to control the technological environment. Instead, they called for a greater system of personal control and called on Canadians to adopt a whole new modernist mindset based on risk-management principles. Safety experts considered it their job to overcome a lack of knowledge about the causes of accidents so that they could be thoroughly known, studied, and ultimately controlled. In this reckoning, car accidents were not dangers to be faced but risks to be managed. Given the car's status as a symbol of the modern in this technologically determinist age, the danger that cars posed was interpreted not as a sign that the technology itself was problematic but that drivers had not yet learned to become thoroughly modern themselves.

The acceptance of automobile accidents as an unfortunate by-product of an otherwise useful technology has a long history. The automobile took its first victim in New York in 1899. In its early years, critics attacked the car for the danger it brought to the roads; they argued that it was too fast, too unreliable, and altogether too dangerous. Criticism subsided, however, with the growth in car ownership, especially by the upper middle class, and with its transformation from an object of opulence into one of affluence. A rising group of traffic-safety experts arose to claim that the solution to the accident problem lay in the application of scientific rules and research. While the reasons for the decline in outright criticism are hard to pin down precisely, it was clearly the result of contingent historical circumstance, not just the inevitable effect of new technology. The British historian Sean O'Connell claims that the risk-management approach to car safety overtook more radical criticism because of the broad social usefulness of the automobile. "With motoring offering new freedoms to many in the middle classes, large numbers of jobs for working people and increasing financial revenue for the government," he points out, "it became convenient for all concerned to place their hope in the claims being made by the emerging 'science' of road safety. So, a belief that education and propaganda, better roads and safer technology were better alternatives than legislation made mass car ownership a palatable option, salving anxieties about the deaths and injuries that continued unabated on the roads." From its earliest days, the economics of the car industry created strong incentives to dampen criticism.[17]

Safety expertise in postwar Vancouver inherited this economically related risk-management legacy. It is not that there was no criticism of car accidents. Quite the opposite; many people felt that car accidents were a grave problem. A slew of local safety advocates suggested all kinds of ways to prevent accidents. But the kinds of people who became interested in the problem and how they spoke about it meant that they tended to blame individuals rather than technology. No one seriously suggested reducing the number of cars as a way of reducing the number of accidents. Safety work was always about making the car more palatable, about easing its place into everyday life. Safety advocates were car advocates.[18]

Industries and individuals with a vested interest in boosting the car's public image dominated the main local safety organization, the Vancouver Traffic and Safety Council (VTSC). Although it later included domestic safety under its mandate, the VTSC largely concerned itself with the problem of traffic accidents. Its directors and members included representatives from such organizations as BC Motor Transportation Ltd., the BC Motor Dealers Association, BC Electric, the Vancouver Board of Trade, the Downtown Business Association, the BCAA, the Taxicab Owners' Association, and McKinley's Driving School. In this way, the VTSC was similar to the national safety organization, the Canadian Highway Safety Conference (CHSC), founded in 1954 and also controlled by automobile-related business interests. In Vancouver, a VTSC representative sat on the city's Official Traffic Commission (OTC), a municipal board set up to deal with all local traffic issues. Other safety officials who sat on this board included the city engineer, chief constable, city solicitor, aldermen, and representatives from the BCAA and the Downtown Business Association. The organizations that typically appeared before the OTC to speak on traffic matters included the Board of Trade, the Junior Board of Trade, the local Council of Women, and parent-teacher organizations. More broadly, the British Columbia Medical Association (BCMA), political parties, and the federal and provincial governments all, in greater and lesser capacities, spoke on the place of car accidents in Vancouver.

What is striking is not only that corporations and government boosters dominated car-safety expertise, a subject already neatly outlined by Ralph Nader, but also *how* they did so, claiming that the solution lay in the achievement of a new kind of human mastery over technology. The safety experts turned to the individual, demanding a disciplined, modern technological expertise. Experts used a variety of devices to make this point, hoping to convince drivers to take control of the automobile. One of the more popular tactics was to compare the automobile to a wild animal that needed taming. "A lion in the streets knows nothing of the rules of civilized behaviour," claimed Ethel McClellen. "But when a human being takes his place behind the wheel it becomes the most dangerous killer at large in our modern world." Mixing his metaphors, J.C. Furnas made the same point in his much cited *Readers' Digest* article: "The automobile is treacherous, just as a cat is. It is tragically difficult to realize that it can become the deadliest missile. As enthusiasts tell you, it makes 65 feel like nothing at all. But 65 an hour is 100 feet a second, a speed which puts a viciously unjustified responsibility on brakes and human reflexes, and can instantly turn this docile luxury into a mad bull elephant." Here, Furnas presented the car as a cat, a missile, and an elephant. All these threats, he claimed, needed to be tamed, to be put to good use by the car experts' vision of the ideal modern citizen cum circus ringmaster.[19]

Although they may have used animal metaphors, safety advocates went to great lengths to convince drivers that the problem they faced was modern. They worried that modernity created a sense of ease that minimized vigilance. The *Canadian Motorist* warned that this "push-button attitude" could make drivers "act like a machine – unthinkingly."[20] British Columbia's Superintendent of Motor Vehicles, George Hood, blamed the rise in car accidents after the Second World War not on the increased number of cars on the road but on the problems of individual drivers. "Until such time as every motor-vehicle driver and pedestrian accepts his personal responsibility to obey the rules and regulations made for the purpose of protecting life and property," he argued, "we shall continue to have this wanton loss." Almost twenty years later, Sam Kershaw, executive director of the BC Safety Council, expressed the same sentiments. "The problem," he argued, "is man's behaviour in the mechanical age ... The realization that an automobile even at its best is a fast, powerful, inanimate machine, guided only by the judgment and control of the man behind the wheel, is proof enough that traffic accidents are thus as preventable as the individual driver wants or knows how to make them."[21]

The problem called for a particularly modern subjectivity that closely followed the ideology of manly modernism. Drivers needed to be excessively rational and aware to keep their attention tuned to all the latest gadgets and instruments. The automobile was a delicate instrument that called for a delicate touch. "In this very delicacy of touch," one safety advocate warned, "lies the danger of wavering of attention. We have definitely arrived at the era of finger-tip control in cars, but a keener mentality is required if safety is [to be] the end product." As a solution, he argued that drivers needed to become thoroughly engaged with their car. They needed to blend the technological and the psychological, the car and the mind. Safe driving meant monitoring the many gauges and buttons so that you not only drove safely, but also could enjoy what he called the "thrill of performance."[22]

This blend of modernist subjectivity and technological performance came across clearly in the key mantra of traffic-safety experts, the "Three Es." Safety experts argued that if enough steps were taken on each of these Es – engineering, education, and enforcement – traffic accidents could be eliminated. Although ostensibly about three different methods of achieving the same goal, the three Es shared a common ideology that blamed accidents on the individual (on what they called the "human factor") and that attempted to inculcate the proper modernist subjectivity to overcome these human faults.

Writing on the first of the three Es – engineering – demonstrated the broad faith in automotive technology in the postwar years. In the "Three Es" approach, engineering safety meant attending to how the design of cities and cars contributed to either creating or preventing accidents, including such things as the role of street signs, parking metres, one-way streets, and steering systems. Engineering car safety was largely the realm of engineers and the technically minded, especially Kenneth Vaughan-Birch, Vancouver's city engineer. He advised Vancouver's Official Traffic Commission on a steady course of incremental changes, including the provision of parking metres in 1946, the development of more one-way streets, and a slow increase in the number of traffic lights, stop signs, and pedestrian crosswalks. Like other municipal engineers, Vaughan-Birch tried to balance the desire for free-flowing and speedy movement against safety concerns and local interests. The OTC managed the car accident problem at the microlevel: parents complained of unsafe intersections for their children; businesses wanted special parking measures that would interrupt traffic flow; residents near dangerous intersections wanted traffic lights. Against these calls for more regulation, the OTC sought to achieve its main goal of maximum traffic flow.[23]

When Vancouver officials looked at the car itself, they tended to do so only as another way to get at drivers. Before cars could be licensed in Vancouver, they needed to pass a safety inspection. Vancouver's safety officials prided themselves on the city's inspection station, a rare institution in these years and one that became province-wide in 1964. Such an emphasis on the role of the vehicle itself in the accident problem was uncommon in Canada and seemed to be a significant innovation. Yet the station was not as radical as some claimed. It tested only upkeep of the individual car, not the safety of the technology itself. It assumed that cars were safe when they came out of the factory. Whenever safety officials debated the cause of car accidents, they could – and did – argue that cars themselves did not cause accidents in Vancouver. After all, they claimed, the cars had passed inspection.[24]

Engineering features that made cars safer – such as seat belts or collapsible steering columns – were the realm of science fiction and idealistic futurism, a hoped-for possibility that might sometime make life better but could not be expected right away. Seat belts for cars were almost unheard of until well into the 1950s, and companies did not begin to put them regularly in cars until the early 1960s. A 1952 *Maclean's* article quotes an executive of the Automobile Dealer Association of Canada on the idea of putting safety belts in all cars: "Never heard of such an idea. People would get the idea that automobiles are as dangerous as planes. They'd be afraid to buy cars."[25] And they did not need to be afraid because cars were safe. In 1957, an official with the Canadian Highway Safety Council claimed that "today's motor car is about as safe as it can be made."[26] Even those who hoped that engineering could reduce the number or severity of car accidents still believed that individuals ultimately caused accidents. Articles on possible new safety features inevitably ended by claiming that they would be for naught unless individual drivers changed their attitudes. Companies were benevolent overseers who wanted to make cars safer but who were constrained by costs, technology, and the ever important consumer, who simply did not want the new features, which looked funny, made for awkward driving, or were simply too expensive. Even worse were car owners who failed to take care of their cars properly, creating the very kinds of design and

engineering problems that would never arise under the care of a responsible driver.[27] A 1959 *Maclean's* article on eight ways to reduce traffic
accidents did not mention engineering at all.[28] So little criticism was
directed at the car that in 1964, one year before Ralph Nader showed
the dangers of the Chevrolet Corvair, *Canadian Motorist* gave the Corvair
a glowing review, mentioning safety not at all. The Corvair was, according to the magazine's reviewer, "a car to delight the hearts of those
motorists (bless them) who still believe that motoring can be fun."[29]

The other two Es, education and enforcement, picked up where engineering left off, moving right to the individual and trying to inculcate
the proper modernist approach to technological risk. Education was the
number-one weapon in the battle against car accidents. The fronts included exhibits by the VTSC at annual events like the Pacific International Motor Show and the Pacific National Exhibition, traffic-safety
drives sponsored by the police and advertised in local newspapers, safe-
driver pledges, and leaflets handed out by the Junior Board of Trade.
The BCAA, VTSC, and the provincial Department of Motor Vehicles
showed safety films and gave talks to schools and community groups.
Many officials wrote articles in local papers and national magazines
explaining that the "human factor" caused almost all accidents. Children came in for special attention with school safety-patrol programs
and traffic education for tykes held in local parks on miniature streets.
Local groups called for the retesting of all drivers and for pedestrian
education, especially for the very old and young. But it was high school
driver education, the one program that never came into being, that
safety advocates truly wanted. Whenever the accident toll took a turn
for the worse, this was the default solution. Private companies, including the local McKinley Driving School, long-time supporters of the VTSC,
offered courses to all Vancouverites. This was not sufficient. If only there
were universal driver-education courses in the schools, they believed,
accident numbers would really drop.[30]

Educational boosters saw their work as a kind of civilizing process. In
his speech to the 1956 VTSC annual meeting, Vancouver alderman H.D.
Wilson asked: "What happens to us when we get into our cars and take
over the job of driving? It would appear that many of us lose our powers
of reasoning completely. How many of us become ill-mannered, boor-
ish, impatient, irritable – almost all of those characteristics which we
dislike in others and, under ordinary circumstances, control within ourselves? Why can't we be drivers and normal people at one and the same
time?"[31] The VTSC used education as a way to teach self-control and
responsibility. And while both men and women could be responsible,

the concept held special importance for postwar men. Psychologists linked the achievement of responsibility with the achievement of manhood. According to such advice givers, men were to accept the responsibilities of breadwinning, give up the wayward days of bachelorhood and youth, and become a man in the process.[32]

This emphasis on responsibility translated well into public policy over car accidents. Throughout the 1940s and 1950s the government sought ways to ensure that drivers were financially responsible, that they had either insurance or sufficient money to pay for any damages caused by their accidents. This goal spurred on the British Columbia Department of Motor Vehicles to establish its first Drivers' Education Division in 1953.[33] This was not driver education as it might be conceived conventionally; it was more retributive then preventive. It targeted "habitual offenders" and "accident prone" drivers. The department formally reviewed these drivers' records and either sent warning letters or suspended licences altogether. By instituting this system of targeted driver education, provincial authorities wanted to reduce the number of accidents either by re-educating problem drivers or by removing them from the road altogether. They put administrative force and a regulatory apparatus behind the need to be responsible.

The last of the "Three Es," enforcement, picked up on this retributive element. Law enforcement was the partner of education in the postwar safety debate; it worked with the same goal in mind but through different means. Legal measures were, as one VTSC member called them, "education by enforcement."[34] Pamphlets and newspaper campaigns were the carrot, and tickets and criminal sanctions the stick, of accident prevention. Of course, other motives guided some enforcement enthusiasts. It is hard not to see the institutional will of the police (a desire for more resources and more power) behind the almost continual call for more traffic officers. Police forces used the automobile to get resources, and they were, in turn, transformed by the need to police the automobile.[35] Yet these bureaucratic desires coexisted with a belief in the individualistic nature of the problem and with the desire to regulate behaviour to fit with the demands of modern technology. Those who advocated enforcement believed that if only the bad drivers could be stopped, if only the bad human spark plugs could be replaced, the engine of progress would run smoothly.

The main villain in the safety debate was the drunk driver. The postwar years saw a consistent campaign on the part of many safety advocates to smear drunk drivers, those considered to play the largest role in creating accidents. Safety advocates had a tough job. Drinking and driving, at least in moderation, was not seen as a significant problem. Even early attempts to stop drinking and driving still allowed for consumption, the amount depending on the type of alcohol. The law also made distinctions based on the amount consumed. There were two offences, one for driving while intoxicated, the most serious offence, and another for driving while impaired. Lawmakers debated the need for two offences but maintained the distinction throughout this period because they believed that juries would let too many drunk drivers free if a guilty verdict meant jail time. Then there was the question of how to measure drunkenness. In the early postwar years, the law relied upon the judgment of police and other witnesses. Did they believe the driver was drunk? If so, how seriously? Because of this method's unreliability, there were very few convictions for either category of drunk driving, especially when compared to how much of a role safety advocates believed that it played. Contemporary estimates linked alcohol to anywhere from 30 to 90 percent of all accidents. Something had to be done. The police wanted to use scientific tests, machines that could measure drunkenness at the site of an accident. Vancouver police began using a tool called the drunkometer in 1953, and the breathalyzer was first introduced into Canada in 1956. But the law treated this evidence skeptically. Courts did not accept test results as definite proof; they could only corroborate other evidence. Even still, drivers could refuse to take the tests.[36]

Drinking and driving became such a problem because of the extent to which drinking made rational, risk-management behaviour harder to achieve. Since at least the mid-nineteenth century, drink had been a significant symbol in discussions of civilized behaviour, especially modern manly behaviour. Being able to handle one's liquor appropriately was linked to the achievement of manhood. Earlier, temperance and women's activists had based their appeals on the fact that many men could not meet these ideals and that women suffered as a result. The discourse on drunk drivers served as a modern way to continue these discussions. Advocates did not call for outright abstinence, but they did demand personal control and fretted over the consequences of its absence. Drinking's effect on one's ability to be modern was significant here. The British Columbia Medical Association warned that alcohol made a particularly bad mix with driving because drinking robbed people of their most civilized skills. The BCMA claimed that there was a drinking cycle in which social skills were lost one by one, with those learned most recently (such as driving) going first. "In this progression of events," the group argued, "the functions concerned with safe driving, such as co-ordination, judgement, self discipline, and control," would be taken away by only a few drinks.[37] Drinking could steal a driver's modernity.

What is striking is how the drunk driver and other "problem drivers" matched the usual bogeymen in the closet of postwar manhood. Although they frequently claimed that anyone could be in an accident, safety experts nonetheless tarred bad drivers with characteristics considered to be unmanly. Most significant, safety advocates claimed that bad drivers failed to be responsible. The "Hit and Run Driver" was a good case in point. In 1962, Hal Tennant warned Canadians about the dangers of identifying too closely with this figure in thinking that anyone could be in the situation of needing or wanting to escape from the scene of an accident. He seemed to think that philandering was the common excuse and expected that his readers would sympathize with the driver who rushed off for fear of being caught at infidelity. But he said that this kind of thinking could not be sustained. In the "automobile age," Tennant warned, "Nice Guys never run away."[38] The *Vancouver Province* agreed with Tennant's assessment. It reported 1,508 accidents in 1959 and claimed that the most common reasons for leaving included impairment, driving without a licence or insurance, having someone else's wife in the car, or driving a stolen vehicle. The paper also noted that it could be just plain panic, a sure sign that one had not maintained self-control.[39]

This controlled and disciplined citizenship could not just be assumed; it had to be achieved. In the 1940s and 1950s, the figure of the juvenile delinquent served as a lightning rod for Canadians' fears that this discipline was endangered. While the female delinquent garnered concern for her sexual behaviour, the male came under scrutiny for his inability to contain his aggression and be responsible.[40] This made the male juvenile delinquent a central figure in concerns over traffic safety. D.G. Dainton blamed accidents on poor young drivers who drove recklessly and did not care whether they got into an accident because they had a cheap car. This kind of driver, Dainton argued, "has no position of responsibility, either in a job or in the community ... He drives recklessly, devil-may-care, flouting the highway code, and expecting everyone, motorists and pedestrians, to give him right of way at all times. Everything he does when driving leads to accidents."[41] Dainton directly connected social responsibility with driving responsibility, the process of becoming a man with the task of good driving.

The gendered nature of traffic-safety discourse becomes clear when we compare it to postwar ideas of masculinity and femininity. In giving his account of the differences between the sexes, Benjamin Spock, the most popular childrearing expert of the postwar years, described young boys in a way that matched the ideals of the safety experts. He claimed that boys instinctively expressed a "love of machines and gadgets for their own sake" and that, robbed of the ability to have children, they expressed creativity in such things as building model planes and scooters and "designing futuristic automobiles and planes." The "urge to play at being fierce and intrusive comes more naturally to most boys" because they are more aggressive. He then linked these traits to risk taking: "Most men and boys seem to be courting danger a lot of the time ... It's boys who go out too far on thin ice and climb cliffs and it's men who take risks in boats and cars ... For a man a car is a symbol of his ambition to be a powerful person: in reaching his goals, in competing with other men, in impressing women."[42] Another Canadian psychologist suggested that it was fathers who taught "rational judgment" and "logical thinking."[43] Spock and other experts claimed that, when properly controlled, their natural proclivity for rational action, for creative engineering, and for taking risks helped boys to become men. This same development, this achievement of balance between risk taking and risk management, also just happened to be what the safety experts held to be the solution to the traffic-safety problem.

Ralph Nader, Radicalism, and the Critique of Manly Modernism

The VTSC, *Canadian Motorist,* and others presented technological problems such as car accidents as a failure to be fully modern. From this perspective, the rise in the number of car crashes represented not a problem with the technology but a sign that drivers had not yet fully adopted a sufficiently modernist mindset. So their work in the 1940s and 1950s consisted of creating this type of driver through programs of engineering, educating and enforcement. Even during the 1950s, however, alternative currents of thought suggested different ways to understand traffic accidents, technology, and the modernist project more generally.

Although postwar Canadians remained optimistic about technologies such as the automobile (and the modernist project generally) throughout the 1950s, it is also possible to read some signs of anxiety that foretold future troubles. This uncertainty galvanized itself most forcefully around the issue of the atomic bomb. With the explosion of the two atomic bombs over Japan in 1945 and the subsequent importance of that technology in the Cold War, nuclear power became a great, if troubled, symbol of North American modernity, of humanity's power to radically control the environment as never before. The historian Margot Henrickson argues that nuclear anxiety overflowed in the era's popular-culture products, including teenage science fiction films, pulp fiction, and rock'n'roll.[44] Canadians imbibed significant levels of American popular culture during this era, and there is also some sense that anxiety, both about the nuclear threat in particular and about technology more generally, was also prominent in 1950s Canada. The popular British Columbia nature writer Roderick Haig-Brown raised his voice against the untrammelled industrialization of the province's wildlife. European immigrants in these years created the beginnings of a health food movement that would later take off in the counterculture of the 1960s. And other critics fretted over the fluoridation of the water supply in many municipalities, including Vancouver.[45]

Similar anxieties surrounded the hyper-rational manly figure that was to guide this technological modernity. Such unease expressed itself most clearly in several aspects of the era's (male-centred) youth culture. The popularity of hot-rod culture, for example, showed how youths took up the concerns of their parents (the celebration of the automobile) and then twisted the ideals around until they became a form of rebellion. With their emphasis on showmanship and aggression, hot rodders represented the antithesis of the responsible man. In the representations of this mode of popular culture, hot rodders came across as those who celebrated not safety and certainty but danger and risk taking. Most Vancouverites would have known about this culture only through films and books, but its popularity nevertheless suggests a reluctance among the youth culture to embrace the gender ideals of their parents. This reluctance further showed up in popular coming-of-age books of the period, from J.D. Salinger's *Catcher in the Rye* (1951) to Mordecai Richler's *The Apprenticeship of Duddy Kravitz* (1959). Such works criticized the hypocrisy of adults and made heroes of anti-responsible male youths.[46] Like the critique of technology in the 1950s, this gendered dissent rarely expressed itself outright in politics. Yet it nevertheless revealed a shared sense that not all was well with the modernist project and its gendered ideals.

Although differently expressed, this culture of anxiety matched up with the worries about manly modernism that we saw in earlier chapters. The rebellious sentiments of youth culture mirrored mountaineers' desire to escape suburban certainties, bridge workers' distrust of safety regulations, and veterans' animosity toward bureaucracy and psychiatric expertise. They all suggested that the modernist project could hurt as well as help and that the ideal of the manly modern was as much trouble as it was good. In the mid-1960s, a number of critics of car culture took up these anxieties about modernity and turned them into a much more radical and systematic critique than had previously been offered. Whereas earlier critics still accepted the basic premise of the modernist project (and the overall benefit of expertise, technology, and its gendered links), a growing number of radicals in the 1960s came to criticize the modernist project writ large. They noted the negative attributes of modern expertise – its often one-sided inability to see the fullness of life, its disciplinary chafing – and denounced its negative effects on communities and individuals. In essence, the 1960s critics of modernization picked up on the concerns of earlier manly moderns that the system was out of whack and, in response, sought to shift the balance, opting for less certainty and reason, more risk taking, and less risk management.

The publication of *Unsafe at Any Speed* in November 1965 cracked open the fissures in the debate over car accidents. It is often unwise to accord any one person or event too much significance, yet Nader seems to deserve it. After 1965, you could hardly talk about car safety or car accidents without discussing – or at least refusing to discuss – Ralph Nader.[47] In *Unsafe at Any Speed* Nader reversed the logic of what he called the "safety establishment," the claim that drivers caused most accidents. Automobile makers wanted the public to blame drivers for accidents when, in fact, Nader argued, the car was really to blame. Cars were designed to be dangerous. At the very least, they were not designed to be safe. Nader began his journalistic indictment with the story of a woman who lost her arm when her Chevrolet Corvair flipped over after its rear tire popped off while the car was going around a bend – a quirky, dangerous trick that Corvair tires were prone to performing under the most ordinary conditions. In a suit brought against General Motors, the company settled out of court when a mechanic testified against the Corvair, arguing that the car, not the woman, was to blame. Yet, in a number of cases in the following years, the company continued to argue that similar accidents were caused by driver fault rather than by improper design. The company sold optional kits to fix the problems with the car's rear suspension but did not warn potential buyers of the car's danger and, most important, did not permanently fix the flaw until 1965, six years after the accident.[48]

According to Nader, the Corvair was not an exception. In *Unsafe at Any Speed,* he showed repeated examples of automobile makers' covering up mistakes that risked drivers' lives. Moreover, he argued that the companies dominated the safety establishment, turning its critique away from car design, that the companies also dominated the engineering and standard-setting professions, that very little science on the safety of cars was done, and that, when it was done, stylistic details overrode concerns about safety. In essence, Nader claimed that the automobile makers managed a cover-up of phenomenal proportions, one that turned the public's eye away from the real cause of traffic injuries: car design.

Nader not only criticized what he called the "safety establishment," but also found fault with the kind of men who promoted the driver-focused safety consensus. He criticized the safety advocates' technologically focused, bureaucratic form of modern manliness. He populated *Unsafe at Any Speed* with men who failed to act because they had subsumed their knowledge of what was right within their company's interests. Their loyalty to company and a superficial modern life that emphasized style over substance meant that they refused to acknowledge the dangers of the automobile that Nader exposed. He also ridiculed the safety focus of the automobile companies, which refused to improve safety features and instead called on everyone, including children, to be constantly aware of danger. Responding to a letter suggesting safety improvements in cars to prevent children from getting hurt in accidents, one General Motors engineer suggested: "I make it a practice to train them [his sons] so that at the command 'Hands!' they would immediately place their hands on the instrument panel if standing in the front compartment." The engineer went on to say, "Even now when one of them is in the front seat, at the command of 'Hands!' they brace themselves. I frequently give these commands even when there is no occasion to do so, just so we all keep in practice."[49] Here was the continual refrain of those in what Nader called the safety establishment about the need for constant vigilance. Clearly, Nader suggested, this hyper-rationality and caution were inadequate and were rooted in a perspective that was itself partly to blame. This kind of argument picked up directly from the 1950s fears over the "Organization Man" and the consequences of bureaucratic suburban life for modern manhood. If one was going to criticize the main symbol of postwar modernity, Nader's tactics showed that it was necessary to criticize the ideal of masculinity with which it was associated: modern manliness.

Nader's critique of automotive technology and its makers spread to Canada and Vancouver. The British Columbia Medical Association drew directly from Nader to express their own frustration with automobile companies. "One has only to read the recent book 'Unsafe at Any Speed' by Ralph Nader," the committee reported in 1966, "to realize the 'designed-in-dangers' of the North American car. One simply cannot buy a relatively safe car made in North America ... The car manufacturers seem only to be interested in sales and in designing eye catching ornamental, super speed missiles."[50] The BCMA's Traffic and Safety Committee had initially been created to determine guidelines for medically unfit drivers, a task that had them focusing exclusively on the individual's role in car accidents. Yet the committee had gradually expanded its focus throughout the late 1950s and early 1960s to the point where they advocated the mandatory introduction of seat belts, child restraints, and the use of helmets for motorcyclists.[51] Canadian politicians had occasionally taken up the case of car accidents as a cause in the House of Commons before this time (most notably T.L. Church in the 1930s and 1940s), but they did so with greater aplomb after 1965. In 1966, the member of Parliament for Brome-Missisquoi called on the federal government to create a national research centre to investigate automobile safety and to create a prototype safety car (both solutions offered by Nader and already underway in New York State). The minister of transport, Paul Hellyer, announced a Highway Safety Program in 1967. Over the next few years, the details of this program came to include a Motor Vehicle Traffic Safety Office, which established standards for automobiles, and a Motor Vehicle Safety Act, which put these standards into force.

Those who still held to the older safety consensus now presented themselves as embattled by the forces of unreason. If others attacked the benevolence of modern technology, these experts found shelter behind one ideal of manly modernism: reasoned objectivity. In 1965, *Canadian Motorist* complained that a great deal of "criticism, some of it unmercifully vitriolic, is being hurled at the automobile manufacturers these days." They particularly disliked the tone of the criticism and called for "a reasoned approach to the problem, no brickbats of blame, no self-conscious sloganeering."[52] This was the modernist return to rationality against the emotionalism of its critics. Phil Gaglardi, British Columbia's minister of highways, was characteristically even more direct. "When Nader tries to tell the United States of America that automobiles are more unsafe than anything else," he told a meeting of police chiefs, "I say he's a nut." Returning to the individualistic theme that so dominated postwar safety expertise, Gaglardi claimed, "it takes 10,000 nuts to hold an automobile together but just one behind the wheel to disintegrate it."[53] Here, Gaglardi brought it back to sanity and reason. To criticize the car, so this line of thinking went, was itself a crazy act.

Yet it was an increasingly popular form of madness. While Nader and others questioned the car, a number of Vancouverites went further and began to challenge automobile-centred and expert-led urban planning. In the postwar years, the growth of many cities in North America had been shaped by modernist urban planning that called for the removal of urban "blight," for redeveloping such areas with the extension of large-scale social housing, and for building freeways to facilitate increased traffic flow into and out of the city due to expanding suburban areas. The United States led the way in this type of development, but similar schemes had garnered the support of officials in Vancouver by the late 1950s. In many respects, Vancouver was a logical match for these urban planners. In the 1930s, centrist and right-wing political forces had come together at the municipal level to prevent the left from taking control of City Council. The resulting party, the Non-Partisan Association (NPA), governed the city for the next thirty years. The NPA established a bureaucratic form of expert government that gave free reign to administrators and their plans. Kim Livingston notes that City Council was "dominated by members of the development, business and planning communities" and that "its essence was technocratic, corporate and paternalistic, where decisions were made by 'experts' in an undemocratic but 'objective' manner."[54] Two different schemes of these planners came together in the 1960s to force a re-evaluation of this kind of modernist planning. The first was an urban renewal scheme that sought to remove urban blight from the area just to the east of the downtown core, an area that included Chinatown. The second was a plan to build a freeway through the centre of the city and directly through Chinatown. Both plans would have dislocated thousands of residents, many of them Chinese, and led to the destruction of a huge section of one of Vancouver's oldest areas. While two phases of the urban-renewal scheme had gone ahead in the early 1960s, a collection of Vancouverites banded together in 1967 to defeat the freeway plan.

The antiurban renewal movement of the 1960s represented a significant challenge to modernist planning and to the notion that development worked best when led by experts alone. How activists voiced their discontent was significant. They drew upon the anti-organization-man rhetoric of those men who had been frustrated by their experiences with the modernist project in the 1950s. The antifreeway activists included in their critical repertoire an attack on the kind of men who were behind urban planning in Vancouver. They especially disliked the "bureaucrats" and "authoritarians" at City Hall and in the city engineering department. One of the prominent activists, Setty Pendakur, used the term "bureaucrat" as an epithet for his opponents in his chronicle of Vancouver's freeway debates, *Cities, Citizens, and Freeways*. Pendakur and other activists urged a more participatory, democratic decision-making process in urban planning. They presented the agents of manly

modernism – bureaucrats, engineers, and planners – as the villains thwart-
ing their quest for a more involved democracy. The manly modern ideals of the automobile planners worked well so long as the modernist
project and the automobile remained the main determinant of urban
planning. Freeways allowed for maximum penetration of the city by the
car and for the free-flowing movement of traffic, unimpeded by other
social and physical obstacles. However, when other social determinants
came into focus, as the Vancouver activists insisted they must, then the
pure simplicity of freeway design became an authoritarian imposition
of 1960s high modernism.[55] And the manly modern, the expert who
put forward these plans, became not the hero but the enemy.

Vancouverites and other North Americans who fought similar urban-
redevelopment schemes could look to Jane Jacobs, whose *The Death and
Life of Great American Cities* (1961) offered an alternative vision of urban
planning. Jacobs eloquently outlined the inadequacies of modernist
design that sought to impose automobile-inspired order. She argued that
cities were being made unliveable by an expertise that privileged visual
and aesthetic order over the actual messy orderliness of real life. She
also challenged the idea that cities and citizens should continuously
make way for more roads and cars, arguing that building more roads
would lead only to their being filled by more cars. Commentators have
noted the gendered nature of Jacobs' ideas. James Scott argues that the
bird's-eye-view style of planning came mostly from male planners without roots in the actual communities nor contact with those who lived
there. But as a woman, Jacobs spent more time at home, watching the
neighbourhood. She could see its development first-hand, learn its rules
and practices, and then base her critique on this lived experience. While
it may be true that a man could have (and others did) come up with a
similar type of critique, her analysis was certainly gendered. Given the
strong link between modernist planning, automobiles, and masculinity
in the postwar years, her challenge had gendered repercussions; like
Nader and the Vancouver antifreeway activists, Jacobs' work challenged
the commonsense status of modernist knowledge and the gendered hierarchies that went along with it.[56]

In 1943, Leonard Marsh released his famous *Report on Social Security,* which
has been heralded as the cornerstone of the postwar Canadian welfare
state. Although most of its suggestions did not immediately come out
in government policy, the report nevertheless captured public attention
as the Canadian version of the Beveridge Report, the British plan for postwar reconstruction. Marsh offered a gendered vision of reconstruction

aimed at getting men back into their place as breadwinners and ensuring a successful economic transition in which the wartime hopes and demands for greater social justice received just reward in government policy. He also represented a vision of expert-led governance in which a number of social planners in Ottawa and other centres would guide social policy and bureaucratic practice. Less well known, but equally important for Vancouverites, is another report that Marsh published six years later. Having moved to the University of British Columbia, Marsh conducted a study of urban blight in Vancouver. In 1949, he published his study, *Rebuilding a Neighbourhood,* in which he called for an urban renewal scheme for the city that focused especially on the eastern side of the downtown core, the area including Chinatown. Marsh's plans did not see immediate action, but they were taken up in 1957 in the city's plans for urban renewal. In that year, the planning department for the city's Housing Research Committee published its *Vancouver Redevelopment Study.* The committee called for a wide-scale urban-renewal scheme, the same scheme against which many Vancouverites would organize, and whose final stages they would defeat, in the late 1960s.

The different fates accorded the two Marsh reports nicely capture the changes in attitudes toward automobile-centred modernity and ideas of masculinity that occurred from the 1950s to the 1960s. The first represents the origins of postwar planning and optimistic expert-led development. It looked forward to a postwar period in which a social-security system, organized by rational planners, supported a nation of breadwinners. Although many aspects of the report were not implemented (at least not right away), its ideals of masculinity were carried forward in the postwar celebration of responsible breadwinning as the hallmark of manhood. When Marsh's second report finally began to be implemented in the 1960s, however, something had begun to change. A new range of critics had emerged who were more eager to challenge modernist planning and the style of manhood that it celebrated. A variety of individuals and groups from the famous (Ralph Nader and Jane Jacobs) to the local (Setty Pendakur and the Chinese Benevolent Association) argued that the experts did not actually have the best interests of all in mind. Couching their arguments in a language of participatory democracy and anti-authoritarianism, the car critics and antifreeway activists challenged the notion that these experts were working for the universal good. Was the problem not, they asked, the masculinity of the experts themselves – too obsessed with control and rational manipulation and less caring about human interaction and community participation? Perhaps the Organization Man was not to be pitied but to be feared.

This transition from 1950s unease to 1960s anger, from the reception of the first Marsh report to that of the second, represented not so much a break with the past as the logical progression of an idea already present in the first period. Safety advocates presented the automobile as a safe technology and blamed its dangers on the failure of Vancouverites to adopt the proper modernist mindset. Yet this ideal of the hyper-rational individual, disciplined by expert systems (in this case, the technological apparatus of the car), created problems even as it offered solutions. A range of men of the postwar years fretted over the consequences of modernist discipline, over the downside of being a modern man. As the logic of this modernist discipline spread itself throughout postwar society, others began to fret about the same kinds of dilemmas. They, too, questioned the value both of modernist expertise and of the kinds of men who offered it. Using the same kinds of arguments as did the men whom we read about earlier, they suggested that there was something wrong with a universalized notion of the reasonable man. The similarity in the argument – indeed, the progression from one to the next – is striking. In challenging the logic of the modernist project and manly modernism, these 1960s activists drew upon and radicalized a critique first expressed by the men in the 1940s and 1950s who had benefited from the unchallenged normality of being called a modern man.

When historians discuss the revolutionary changes in gender relations of the 1960s, they usually dwell on such topics as the sexual revolution, the increase in married women workers, rising divorce rates, and the generational conflicts of the baby boomers.[57] However, the changes to ideas about what makes a good man also had their origins in other, less overtly gendered transformations. In the postwar years, the very language of masculinity had been embedded in the practices of modern life. That being a good man and a good driver were quite similar achievements seemed not worth mentioning; it could simply be assumed. However, when critics attacked the benefits of this modern technology and its experts in the 1960s, their attack also affected the ideals of masculinity bound up with this modernist vision. The change is perhaps clarified if we return to W.A. Bryce's speech with which we began. In 1960, Bryce could pass off a mangled version of Rudyard Kipling as the answer to traffic safety; by the end of the decade, there were plenty of critics around to tell him that it was nothing but bad poetry.

7
Conclusion: Manly Modernism in Hindsight

There is a voice from the postwar years that is instantly recognizable. It is a man's voice, and it is perfectly calm. This is the voice of early television and radio, the voiceover that tells us where we are at the beginnings of movies, the talking head that explains matters of science and truth, the speaker who tells us that, while all seems well in this country, town, or city, there is in fact something more sinister at work, which could be anything from mental illness to communism. We might identify the voice with a person. For many Canadians in the 1940s, Lorne Green, "The Voice of Canada" during the Second World War, took on this role. But regardless of the actual person behind the voice, its character remained the same: steady, calm, authoritative, and male.

I first became aware of the voice as something worth thinking about in and of itself while listening to parenting-instruction programs at the National Archives in Ottawa. Sitting in the back room, away from the view of the Gatineau forests that greets you in the main reading room, I huddled in a cubicle listening to recordings of radio programs from the 1950s that gave expert advice on how to raise children. In one program, "The Father Who Wouldn't Listen," which was part of *The Way of a Parent* series put on by the Canadian Broadcasting Corporation and the Canadian Home and School and Parent Teacher Federation in 1954, the voice takes us to the suburbs, to warn us about the possible hidden dangers in family life, the kinds of dangers that you needed expert advice to diagnose:

> At the Linden place in the suburbs of the city, the lawn was smooth, the hedge was trim, the rooms were bright and charming. Mrs Linden would never tolerate a speck of dust ... but a kind of dust was collecting in the corners; a dust of bad feeling ... Robert Linden's daughter

was sixteen and unhappy. It wasn't an obvious unhappiness ... It was a submerged unhappiness, for in a model household, Amy was a model daughter.[1]

The narrator's voice creeps and crawls with the hint of looming danger, its tone telling the listeners that they had best pay attention to the advice that follows or risk serious danger. Almost fifty years later, removed from postwar anxieties and social values, the voice seems funny; the response that this kind of voice now usually elicits is laughter. MTV and Much Music splice similar kinds of scenes between videos, putting laugh tracks behind the now humorous voice of former masculine authority. But I sat there that day trying to dispel this response, trying to make sense of the fears and concerns of a time only recently passed, the era of my parent's childhood. Throughout this and other recordings, the voice resonated with authority. How, I wondered, could this voice be so certain?

In this book, I have come up with one important answer to this question: the expert voice spoke with such certainty because it acted as a symbol of a type of male and modern authority that reached its apex in the postwar years. A variety of figures tried to modernize ideas of masculinity, linking the main features of modernity with basic ideals of masculinity and vice versa. In this allegedly more democratic age, men were no longer supposed to be patriarchs in the family, ruling by status and sheer force of will alone. Instead, psychological experts claimed that families were small democracies in which all members had their own roles; a belief in the basic differences between men and women persisted but in slightly altered form. Men maintained their role as final arbiter and disciplinarian, but they were supposed to express this authority in a more reasoned, balanced, and democratic way.[2] In this kind of family, and at this time, men's authority came in large measure from how contemporaries linked masculinity with reasoned expertise. A generation earlier, the voice would have held more religious authority; it might have represented not only a reasoned manhood, but a morally restrained and Christian manhood as well. In the postwar years, secular and technocratic concerns increasingly informed the ideal of the reasonable man. The voice could have belonged to a family expert and psychologist, but it could equally have belonged to any of a number of other experts, including engineers, traffic-safety experts, psychiatrists, government bureaucrats, judges, and lawyers. Many Vancouverites coded these types of expertise and the modernist project more generally as masculine. The "voice" on the recording of "The Father Who Wouldn't Listen" represented the gendered authority of manly modernism.

The logic of manly modernism spread far beyond radio and television; it seeped through the fabric of social relations in postwar Vancouver, colouring everything from Vancouverites' responses to the Second Narrows Bridge collapse to their discussions of driver safety. At its most basic level, the modernist project was about control – control of the physical, social, and psychological environment. Optimism about the modernist project was strong in postwar Vancouver. This optimism revealed itself most clearly at moments when it appeared to be challenged, when the engine of progress stuttered and stalled, eliciting startled cries of disbelief. When the Second Narrows Bridge collapsed, Vancouverites celebrated the risk taking of ironworkers and turned to the expert knowledge of engineers to explain the tragedy; when cars crashed, the consensus was that the technology was not to blame; psychiatrists provided a modern explanation for how seemingly rational men could commit horrible crimes; when the transition from war to peace threatened to bring chaos, the state initiated a host of welfare programs as mechanisms of economic and social control; and even as mountaineers tried to escape suburban existence, they took up their own forms of modernist risk management in the mountains. Even in these situations, when doubts about modernity's benefits or the inherent value of rationality could have been expected, many different Vancouverites instead renewed their faith in the promises, mechanisms, and expertise of the modern.

The connection between masculinity and modernity in postwar Vancouver is especially significant given this strong support for the modernist project. At each of these moments of doubt and uncertainty, Vancouverites coded expertise and modernist schemes of control as inherently masculine. Support for the modernist project was a gendered process: modern women were said to be one thing and modern men another. Yet the relation between the two was hierarchical, not complementary.[3] In these circumstances Vancouverites connected modern masculinity with the establishment of control, with the very basic feature of being modern. This could be control of the physical environment as exhibited by the engineers of the Second Narrows Bridge, of the social environment as demonstrated by the planners of the Veterans Charter, or of the mind and body as in the self-control of the mountaineer and bridge worker. Achieving this kind of control was what made these men masculine; it was also what made them modern. This was the great power of manly modernism at mid-century. In many ways, the social environment had opened up to women; they had gained the vote, a growing number of married women were working, and women were even increasingly invading the previously male sphere of public drinking establishments.[4] But beliefs in the differences between men and women not only persisted, but also expressed themselves in new ways. And the ideology of manly modernism acted as one of the main ways through which some Vancouverites reinscribed men's privilege into the basic social language of postwar life.

Even as manly modernism privileged certain men and particular types of masculine characteristics, it also regulated and disciplined other men and different masculine characteristics. Manly modernism benefited the experts of the modernist project and a rational style of behaviour and social organization. As we saw, a number of postwar men were ambivalent about its legacy. Although veterans benefited from their place at the centre of the state's plans for postwar reconstruction, they simultaneously found themselves the object of the state's and other experts' disciplining strategies. Similarly, Vancouverites may have celebrated the daily risk taking that made building bridges possible, but the state and press eventually turned to middle-class experts and rational risk management – not to the stoic working-class bridge builders – as the ultimate source of authority. As this last example indicates, the inequalities of manly modernism worked along class lines, attributing the privilege of reason to the middle class and assuming that the working class could offer only its brawn. All types of marginalized men, whether for reasons of class, race, or sexuality, found themselves the objects of expert discipline in capital murder cases. In these cases, psychiatrists and psychologists stepped in to redefine masculinity and to outline the parameters of a potential form of men's power: the definition of when and how men could legitimately be violent.

But manly modernism did not discipline only those considered marginal or the working class. Although undoubtedly privileged next to their working-class counterparts, even the middle-class mountaineers experienced a sense of alienation in their relation to the postwar suburban environment and white-collar work, which in turn fuelled their desire to climb. When they embraced a modernist approach to climbing, in their continual emphasis on new peaks and trails and in their approach to risk, they further contributed to the ambiguities of their predicament, reinforcing the very values that they sought to escape. The ironies of manly modernism also expressed themselves clearly in discussions of gender and traffic safety. On the one hand, safety experts presented the ideal driver in a language of rational self-discipline that matched what men were supposed to be more generally. But here, as elsewhere, there were signs of discontent, suggestions that danger was more attractive than safety, that risk taking was more appealing than risk management. Throughout all these cases, there was a sense that the alliance of the modern and the manly delivered less than it promised.

Even as the insistence of men's modernity reached an apex, then, it also seemed to be rotting away from the inside out. Looking over all the various scenarios of manly modernism that we have explored in this book, it is hard not to see these years as also something of a turning point. Yes, stoical and rational restraint were celebrated with great force. But the consequences of bureaucracy and regulation severely tested these manly restraints. In each instance where men's modernity seemed to set them apart, where traditional masculine values were built into the processes of the modern, complaints arose. Manly modernism brought unintended consequences, and several historians have recently traced the ambivalent attitudes of cultural commentators toward modernity in postwar Canada.[5] In this book, we have spread outward, tracing how a much wider range of people responded to the modern, how in Vancouverites' responses to these consequences, we can see one important gendered strain in the more general response to modern life. Ambivalence was not just general, it was gendered.

There is a bigger context. In the 1950s and 1960s, the culture of restraint floundered. Beliefs that had so dominated Canadian cultural life since the nineteenth century – belief in moral responsibility and regulation, self-restraint – came under an unprecedented amount of critique. Canadians' attitudes toward sex, drinking, gambling, and a host of moral issues underwent dramatic change. The general direction of change was away from community and state regulation of all individuals and toward a better targeting of problem individuals. Sex was not bad, only certain sexual predators. Gambling was not always unhealthy, only for problem gamblers. Drinking was bad if you were an alcoholic but acceptable if you were not.

In this more permissive context, the old gender ideal of the responsible and controlled man increasingly chafed. Barbara Ehrenreich has argued that these years saw a "flight from commitment" on the part of men, who desired to run away from domesticity, marriage, and the ideal of the responsible man. It is not a coincidence that Hugh Hefner's *Playboy* emerged in 1953 and became a cultural icon of independent modern manhood in the 1960s. Even if few Vancouverites lived the *Playboy* lifestyle, its dream of sexually liberated and independent men was incredibly popular. This was a very different modern manhood, indeed.[6]

While Ehrenreich focused on family life as the thing that men were fleeing in these years, it is clear that this is not the whole story. The cultural politics of sex and morality were important determinants of masculinity. But there is another story to be told about men, rationality, and risk, which this book has explored. When the responsible father left home, he went into the workplace or had dealings with the state. And he did so in the postwar years in a context in which modern forms of expertise, administration, and regulation had become the norm. Although ostensibly modern himself – supposedly an exemplar of the ideal of the manly modern – he found the experience anything but pleasing. As we have seen, many features of modern life that had built in assumptions of a certain style of masculinity became the very things with which many postwar men found fault. Manly modernism, it seemed, was not so great after all.

Partly based on this sensibility, many contemporaries, and even some historians since that time, suggested that the position of modern men was diminishing in the postwar years. They drew upon a long tradition of criticism that has suggested that modernity hurts men, that masculinity is always about tradition, and that the modern, to the extent that it breaks with tradition, disrupts men's privileges.[7] Yet postwar men were so affected by modernity because masculinity was itself so bound up with the ideas and processes of modernization. At exactly the moments when promises of control and authority came into being – building bridges, giving expertise, and taking risks – Vancouverites defined as masculine the traits and situations that made such promises possible. If men suffered at the hands of modernization, it was because they were so much a part of its powerful whirlwind of forces, because modernity and masculinity were closely entwined, not because they were far apart. Modernity is, as most of its commentators point out, radically contradictory.[8] Modern systems of order, authority, and discipline quite often lead to chaos, rebellion, and transgression. Similarly, schemes to uplift and empower men have often, in practice, involved suppressing certain individuals and groups and have created feelings of alienation and discontent.[9] This is what occurred in postwar Vancouver. By putting masculinity at the centre of the modernist project, many men felt the highs and lows of this tumultuous and transformative process. For men, there seemed to be so many negative consequences of modernity because the logic of manly modernism suggested that the reverse should have been true, that there should have been so many benefits.

Beginning in the 1960s and continuing into the 1970s, a growing number of Vancouverites (and others in North America and the Western world more generally) began radically to question the values of the modernist project. We examined one instance of this historical sea change: Ralph Nader, Jane Jacobs, and the antifreeway activists in Vancouver challenged the idea that vehicles, the people who made them, and those who designed cities around them, were inherently beneficial. They argued that modern technology and expertise could harm as well as help and that, sometimes, the harm outweighed the benefit. Building on the tensions already present in postwar discussions of modernity, they radicalized modernity's contradictions, arguing for a switch in priorities. They were, of course, but a few of the many who made these kinds of arguments in the 1960s. Most prominently, those involved in the youth movement flouted the respectable conventions of their parents by growing their hair long, expanding sexual practices well outside marriage, and denouncing the quest for responsibility that had been the hallmark of the previous generation. A growing environmental consciousness emerged to champion the natural world over scientific and industrial development. Second-wave feminists organized themselves to challenge women's restricted place within the home and workplace and to call for a reordering of social values along different, less patriarchal, principles. In the traditional political sphere and union halls, the New Left called for a new, more democratic style of politics and for radical action on the issue of economic inequality in the country. Collectively, 1960s radicalism represented a break with the style and substance of the social, economic, and political authority of the past.[10]

Manly modernism would seem to be the target of much of this radical activity. This is obvious in the case of feminism, but it could also be true in the case of such things as environmentalism, anti-authoritarianism, and antimodernism more generally. Manly modernism's connection to the modernist project, to its style of authority, its technological determinism, and its emphasis on progress, made the ideal of the reasonable man a significant target for critics of the period. Sixties radicals turned against the authority of the responsible male figure – the bureaucrat, the expert, the patriarch. The popularization of the epithet "The Man" aptly conveys how a certain kind of masculinity was the object of this rebellion. If modernity itself was the problem, so too was the calm and authoritative voice that spoke its expertise.

What is striking about discussions of masculinity before the late 1960s, however, is the extent to which a variety of postwar men had already been speaking about these same kinds of anxieties. As we have seen, many of the men bound up in the politics of risk, restraint, and modernity also found fault with much in manly modernism. Kirchner and his veterans complained of the way that excessive bureaucracy and modern expertise chafed. Bridge workers found the regulations of the workplace to go against their own notions of competence and skill. Psychiatrists and psychologists reined in the language of male deviance, subjecting it to new forms of expertise. Mountaineers struggled to find a balance between expertise and excitement, civilization and wilderness. And driver-safety experts sought to instil in the minds of postwar Vancouverites the ideal of the reasonable man and a wholly modernist subjectivity, even as some began to criticize the limited range of this expert vision. The major debate over modern manhood from the 1940s to the 1960s prefigured the more general criticism of modernity and male authority that emerged in that later decade. It pitted systems against individuals, reason against passion, and expert artifice against lay authenticity. These were the same kinds of concerns that feminists, environmentalists, and other critics of "the system" took up in more radical ways later on. The irony is that even as the approach and tone shifted dramatically, the issues and concerns remained the same.

The main difference between the men of the 1940s and 1950s and those who came later lay in the fact that the earlier men did not turn their concerns into an all-out critique of manly modernism or of the modernist project more generally. Postwar men, even those who felt undermined by manly modernism's contradictory effects, still had much to gain by supporting its ideal of gendered authority. The mountaineers still embraced a type of risk-management expertise even as they sought to escape the downside of what this kind of expertise had done for contemporary urban and suburban existence. The bridge workers played up their role as economic modernizers even as postwar capitalist development took its toll on their bodies. Capital murderers sought out the expert advice of psychiatrists even as this profession rewrote their behaviour in ways that only experts could then interpret. The differences between men were great; manly modernism in no way eliminated inequalities, whether they were based on class, race, or other criteria. But manly modernism provided a source of gendered authority that could reach beyond these categories; it positioned men and masculinity alongside the most dominant social force of these years, the modernist project. This was a privileged position that few were willing to turn their backs on completely.

What happened, then, when the character of the modern experience, the very thing with which dominant ideals of masculinity were associated, changed dramatically in the 1960s and 1970s? The exact nature of these changes, as well as what we might call them, is in dispute; but whether we call this a turn to postmodernity and a post-traditional society or a turn to a fuller, more reflexive modernity, the fact that something did change at this time seems certain.[11] The tensions within the modernist project were radicalized. Running alongside the certainty and optimism of the modernist project came an equally powerful focus on doubt, uncertainty, and pessimism. This focus did not represent a complete rejection of the modernist impulse, but it did mean a growing critique of notions of progress, of technology, and of overarching explanations for truth and meaning. The modernist project emphasized "positivistic, technocentric, and rationalistic" order and was "identified with the belief in linear progress, absolute truths, the rational planning of ideal social orders, and the standardization of knowledge and production." In contrast, the postmodern stance undermined these notions by claiming that the function of such "metanarratives ... was to ground and legitimate the illusion of a 'universal' human history" – and, we might add, a "universal" notion of male authority. Against this backdrop of such overarching explanations, the postmodern privileged diversity, heterogeneity, fragmentation, and uncertainty. In this changed context, the voice of male expert authority – the manly modern – could increasingly appear not as knowledgeable and objective but as authoritarian and domineering.[12]

What, then, happened to masculinity in the process? It would be easy to say that the challenge to modernity represented a challenge to the very idea of masculinity and male power, a challenge to manly modernism. And this is how the story is typically told if it is told at all. This is the commonsense version of contemporary gender history, which posits a general, if slow, movement toward gender equality.[13] The argument goes that as old systems of male authority came under attack, they eventually fell by the wayside. Since the 1960s, the concern over modern man (although usually not using this term) has become even more pronounced than it was in the past. In the 1970s, a men's movement grew up alongside the much larger women's movement. Initially pro-feminist, many elements of the men's movement later splintered off, some continuing in a feminist tradition, while others lamented the decline of primitive manhood and blamed much of this on women or modern society. The men's movement sought to stem a growing uncertainty about what it meant to be masculine, about how to be a man. In the 1990s concern switched to the problem of young boys and how best to train them. Some sociologists and psychologists warned that boys were falling behind girls in education and in the matter of morals and civilized behaviour more generally. Robbed of father figures and proper outlets for aggression, society, experts claimed, faced a real and serious problem because boys were trapped in the past and could not, in essence, adapt to the conditions of modern life. A desire to define masculinity, to achieve a kind of stable masculine identity and role, united all these (and other) disparate concerns over the problem of men in contemporary society.[14]

The content of these concerns suggested that something was uncertain, that masculinity was threatened, that it was endangered. Some saw great potential to reshape masculinity in this situation, while others feared the consequences of a society without strong ideas of manliness and male authority. Yet what is striking about this debate is how it, too, matches debates about modernity (or postmodernity) in contemporary society. The current language of masculinity calls for a more primal manhood, alternately rooted in caveman genetics, pseudo-Jungian claims to a wild-man tradition, or the risk-taking excitement of the corporate world. This matches the current concerns of the modern – the critique of staid, bureaucratic expertise, the quest for primal experience and the heavily advertised possibility of having all desires met through the consumption of new technologies, products, and entertainments. This (at times superficial) commitment to ideals of freedom from restraint, whether sexual, economic, or more usually, governmental, is the modernist orthodoxy of the day. The voice of authority, that singular voice of expertise, is in this context something to be ridiculed. That there could be this one perspective, this one source of rational authority, is presented as humorous. Yet this turn away from the manly modernism of the earlier era has been mirrored not by an abandonment of gendered authority altogether, but by a redefining of the gendered nature of modernity. This turn to a freer, less restricted, less certain postmodernist present also included a similar change in ideals of masculinity. The current ideas of masculinity, with their emphasis on primal experience, risk taking, and the wild-man within, once again define masculinity in line with what we might call the postmodernist project. The difference is that the vision of the modern, or postmodern, has changed, too. Even as women enjoy more political and economic equality, the very meanings of masculinity and femininity continue to be defined in ways that privilege men over women.

The modern man of the 1950s seems old-fashioned now because his style of gendered identity is no longer current. Different notions of gender have come to prominence in the intervening years, based on any number of factors from transformations in the economy to the political battles of men and women who are seeking alternative ways to define what it means to be masculine and feminine. The transformation in these gender ideals, however, seems to have continued in tandem with the fate of the modernist project. Many who today seek out adventure on the mountains in extreme sports or in the stock markets of the global economy still continue to define masculinity in relation to risk.[15] What has changed is the tone of contemporary modernity. Risk taking and risk management are even more prominent features of our current state of modernity. To the extent that masculinity continues to be defined in these areas and that men continue to be the main actors in public fantasies of postmodernist control and self-creation, manly modernism remains with us.

Notes

Chapter 1: Introduction

1 R.W. Connell, *Masculinities* (Berkeley: University of California Press, 1995), 164. See also Victor Seidler, *Rediscovering Masculinity: Reason, Language and Sexuality* (New York: Routledge, 1989).

2 The best earlier work on modernity in Canada is Keith Walden, *Becoming Modern in Toronto: The Industrial Exhibition and the Shaping of a Late Victorian Culture* (Toronto: University of Toronto Press, 1997). Also instructive are Katherine Arnup, *Education for Motherhood: Advice for Mothers in Twentieth-Century Canada* (Toronto: University of Toronto Press, 1994); and Cynthia Comacchio, *Nations Are Built of Babies: Saving Ontario's Mothers and Children, 1900-1940* (Montreal and Kingston: McGill-Queen's University Press, 1993).

3 On the role of expertise in shaping government policy, see Doug Owram, *The Government Generation: Canadian Intellectuals and the State, 1900-1945* (Toronto: University of Toronto Press, 1986). On psychological and psychiatric expertise in the postwar years, see Mona Gleason, *Normalizing the Ideal: Psychology, Schooling and the Family in Postwar Canada* (Toronto: University of Toronto Press, 1999); and Mary Louise Adams, *The Trouble with Normal: Postwar Youth and the Construction of Heterosexuality* (Toronto: University of Toronto Press, 1997). On Keynesianism, see Robert Campbell, *Grand Illusions: The Politics of the Keynesian Experience in Canada, 1945-1975* (Peterborough: Broadview, 1987).

4 Len Kuffert, *A Great Duty: Canadian Responses to Modern Life, 1939-1967* (Montreal and Kingston: McGill-Queen's University Press, 2003); Philip Massolin, *Canadian Intellectuals, the Tory Tradition and the Challenge of Modernity, 1939-1970* (Toronto: University of Toronto Press, 2001).

5 The role of gender in debates about work and unemployment during the Depression is nicely outlined in Ruth Roach Pierson, "Gender and the Unemployment Insurance Debates in Canada, 1934-1940," *Labour/Le Travail* 25 (1990): 77-103. The dilemmas of women workers in this period are perhaps best explored in Joan Sangster, *Earning Respect: The Lives of Working Women in Small-Town Ontario, 1920-1960* (Toronto: University of Toronto Press, 1995). The classic, and still valuable, account of women in the war is Ruth Roach Pierson, *"They're Still Women after All": The Second World War and Canadian Womanhood* (Toronto: McClelland and Stewart, 1986).

6   Although, of course, this view of the family was in fact an ideal that often did not extend to some in the working class or to immigrant groups. See, for example, Franca Iacovetta, *Such Hardworking People: Italian Immigrants in Postwar Toronto* (Toronto: University of Toronto Press, 1993).

7   On the earlier ideal of the Christian gentleman, see Anthony Rotundo, *American Manhood: Transformations in Masculinity from the Revolution to the Modern Era* (New York: Basic Books, 1993). I want to thank Keith Walden for getting me to think about the changing religious meanings of masculinity during the period.

8   Robert Rutherdale's work is key here. See his "Fatherhood, Masculinity and the Good Life during Canada's Baby Boom, 1945-1965," *Journal of Family History* 24, 3 (1999): 351-73; "Fatherhood and Masculine Domesticity during the Baby Boom: Consumption and Leisure in Advertising and Life Stories," in Lori Chambers and Edgar André Montigny, eds., *Family Matters: Papers in Post-Confederation Canadian Family History* (Toronto: Canadian Scholars' Press, 1998), 309-33; "Fatherhood and the Social Construction of Memory: Breadwinning and Male Parenting on a Job Frontier, 1945-1966," in Joy Parr and Mark Rosenfeld, eds., *Gender and History in Canada* (Toronto: Copp Clark, 1996), 357-75. I, too, have worked in this area: Chris Dummitt, "Finding a Place for Father: Selling the Barbecue in Post-War Canada," *Journal of the Canadian Historical Association* 8 (1998): 209-23.

9   On anxiety surrounding postwar manhood, see William Whyte, *The Organization Man* (New York: Simon and Schuster, 1956); Gleason, *Normalizing the Ideal,* 53; Bill Osgerby, *Playboys in Paradise: Masculinity, Youth and Leisure-Style in Modern America* (Oxford: Berg, 2001), 68-75; Michael Kimmel, "'Temporary about Myself': White-Collar Conformists and Suburban Playboys, 1945-1960," in *Manhood in America: A Cultural History* (New York: Free Press, 1996), 223-58.

10   James Rinehart, *The Tyranny of Work: Alienation and the Labour Process,* 4th ed. (Toronto: Harcourt, 2001), 11-13.

11   This is a different kind of argument than that given by one of the leading scholars of masculinity, Michael Kimmel, who argues that it is men's inability to live up to difficult and unattainable ideals that causes constant malaise. Here, I suggest that men's frustrations come from the unintended consequences of privilege. See Kimmel, "Introduction," in *Manhood in America,* 1-10.

12   One could speculate that this was also the case for other social categories, but these haven't been explored in this book.

13   On this more generally, see Martin J. Wiener, *Men of Blood: Violence, Manliness and Criminal Justice in Victorian England* (Cambridge, UK: Cambridge University Press, 2004).

14   On the sources of immigration to postwar British Columbia, see Jean Barman, *The West beyond the West: A History of British Columbia* (Toronto: University of Toronto Press, 1991). See also Gerald Friesen, *The Canadian Prairies: A History* (Lincoln: University of Nebraska Press, 1984).

15   On the overall effects of popular culture in the period, see Doug Owram, *Born at the Right Time: A History of the Baby-Boom Generation* (Toronto: University of Toronto Press, 1996).

16   Defining modernity has always been a tricky concern, although it is perhaps an easier task now than it might have been a few decades ago when discussion of modernization often led one toward ideas of the ideal status of Western societies and economies and the need for other non-Western nations to modernize in

order to become, seemingly, like the United States. The dilemma in defining modernity in this way has frequently been its ethnocentric basis, the assumption that such processes had to (or should) occur in specific ways and that, on a much larger scale, such developments were inherently good, that they represented progress. On this heritage, see S.N. Eisenstadt and Wolfgang Schlucter, "Introduction: Paths to Early Modernities – A Comparative View," *Daedalus* 127 (Summer 1998): 1-18; and S.N. Eisenstadt, "Multiple Modernities," *Daedalus* 129 (Winter 2000): 1-29.

17 On the period as a whole, see Owram, *The Government Generation;* on the social gospel and state planning, Michael Gauvreau and Nancy Christie, *A Full-Orbed Christianity: The Protestant Churches and Social Welfare in Canada, 1900-1940* (Montreal and Kingston: McGill-Queen's University Press, 1996); on science and universities, Massolin, *Canadian Intellectuals,* and Donald A. Wright, *The Professionalization of History in English Canada* (Toronto: University of Toronto Press, 2005); and on state planning and the Depression, James Struthers, *The Limits of Affluence: Welfare in Ontario, 1920-1970* (Toronto: University of Toronto Press, 1994), and Dennis Guest, *The Emergence of Social Security in Canada* (Vancouver: UBC Press, 1980).

18 The modernity of these tactics is discussed in Cynthia Comacchio, "Mechanomorphosis: Science, Management and 'Human Machinery' in Industrial Canada, 1900-1945," *Labour/Le Travail* 41 (1998): 35-67.

19 On exhibitions, see Walden, *Becoming Modern in Toronto;* on urban and suburban planning, Richard Harris, *Creeping Conformity: How Canada Became Suburban, 1900-1960* (Toronto: University of Toronto Press, 2004); on leftist planning, Michiel Horn, *The League for Social Reconstruction: Intellectual Origins of the Democratic Left in Canada, 1930-1942* (Toronto: University of Toronto Press, 1980); and for an innovative discussion of where this type of left thinking fits into left history more generally, Ian McKay, *Rebels, Reds, Radicals: Rethinking Canada's Left History* (Toronto: Between the Lines, 2005), 169-83.

20 On the broader sense in which I use "liberalism" here, I am guided by Ian McKay, "The Liberal Order Framework: A Prospectus for a Reconnaissance of Canadian History," *Canadian Historical Review* 81, 4 (2000): 617-45. The gendered aspects of Cold War containment are covered in Elaine Tyler May, *Homeward Bound: American Families in the Cold War* (New York: Basic Books, 1988). On the Cold War in Canada, see Reginald Whitaker and Gary Marcuse, *Cold War Canada: The Making of a National Insecurity State, 1945-1957* (Toronto: University of Toronto Press, 1994); and Steve Hewitt and Reg Whitaker, *Cold War Canada* (Toronto: Lorimer, 2003).

21 Few historians deal with these developments in the context of a discussion of modernization. For a useful general overview without this discussion, see Alvin Finkel, *Our Lives: Canada after 1945* (Toronto: Lorimer, 1997); and with a focus on political history, Robert Bothwell, Ian Drummond, and John English, *Canada since 1945: Power, Politics and Provincialism,* rev. ed. (Toronto: University of Toronto Press, 1989). On the era's fascination with technology, see Pam Roper, "The Limits of *Laissez-Innover:* Canada's Automation Controversy, 1955-1969," *Journal of Canadian Studies* 34, 3 (1999): 87-105. I owe the connection between the "culture of control" and the welfare state to Jackson Lears, *Something for Nothing: Luck in America* (New York: Viking, 2003), 231.

22   Martin Robin, *Pillars of Profit: The Company Province, 1934-1972* (Toronto: McClelland and Stewart, 1973), 194.

23   Jean Barman, *The West beyond the West: A History of British Columbia* (Toronto: University of Toronto Press, 1991), 280.

24   On changes in Vancouver during these years, see Bruce MacDonald, *Vancouver: A Visual History* (Vancouver: Talon Books, 1992); and Norbert MacDonald, Chapter 8, *Distant Neighbours: A Comparative History of Seattle and Vancouver* (Lincoln: University of Nebraska Press, 1987). Vancouver's population statistics are drawn from MacDonald, *Distant Neighbours,* 156.

25   Rhodri Windsor Liscombe, *The New Spirit: Modern Architecture in Vancouver, 1938-1963* (Montreal and Vancouver: Canadian Centre for Architecture and Douglas and McIntyre, 1997), 33. For a similar critique of Modernist architecture, see James C. Scott, "The High-Modernist City: An Experiment and a Critique," in *Seeing Like a State: How Certain Schemes to Improve the Human Condition Have Failed* (New Haven: Yale University Press, 1998), 103-46.

26   It has become unfashionable of late to say that modernity began in the West and spread outward, although it does still seem an accurate assessment. Nevertheless, for a fascinating discussion of the problems that can result from this approach, see Dipesh Chakrabarty, *Provincializing Europe: Postcolonial Thought and Historical Difference* (Princeton: Princeton University Press, 2000).

27   Marshall Berman, *"All That Is Solid Melts into Air": The Experience of Modernity,* 2nd ed. (New York: Simon and Schuster, 1982), 13-15. Charles Taylor's 1991 Massey Lectures suggested some of the ways that, for the contemporary period, we might think ourselves into a different kind of politics and morality that escapes this dichotomy. See his *The Malaise of Modernity* (Concord, ON: Anansi, 1991).

28   John Jervis, *Exploring the Modern: Patterns in Western Culture and Civilization* (Oxford: Blackwell, 1998).

29   Scott, *Seeing Like a State,* 4.

30   On the similar practices of high modernists on the left and right, see ibid.

31   On modern risk as distinct from earlier types of risk, see Anthony Giddens, *The Consequences of Modernity* (Cambridge, UK: Polity Press, 1990), 100-11; Ulrich Beck, "On the Logic of Wealth Distribution and Risk Distribution," *Risk Society: Towards a New Modernity,* trans. Mark Ritter (London: Sage, 1992), 19-50; Ulrich Beck, *World Risk Society* (Cambridge, UK: Polity Press, 1999).

32   On the "experience" of modernity see Jervis, *Exploring the Modern,* and for a more extensive treatment, his *Transgressing the Modern: Explorations in the Western Experience of Otherness* (Oxford: Blackwell, 1999); Giddens, *The Consequences of Modernity;* and Berman, *"All That Is Solid Melts into Air."*

33   Lears, *Something for Nothing,* 273-320.

34   Dorinda Outram, "Europe's Mirror: The Enlightenment and the Exotic," in *The Enlightenment* (Cambridge, UK: Cambridge University Press, 1995), 63-79; Jervis, *Transgressing the Modern.* The dark history of this history of mirroring is the extent to which being modern has often depended upon defining others – cultures, women, the diseased – as primitive, nonmodern, and uncivilized. See Edward Said, *Culture and Imperialism* (New York: Vintage, 1993).

35   See, for example, George Grant, *Lament for a Nation: The Defeat of Canadian Nationalism* (Toronto: McClelland and Stewart, 1965; reprint, Ottawa: Carleton University Press, 1982). On Canadian criticisms of modernity, see Kuffert, *A Great*

Duty; and Massolin, *Canadian Intellectuals.* For a critique of the snobbery implicit in the postwar Red Tory antimodernism, see Robert Wright's review of Massolin's text in *Canadian Historical Review* 84, 1 (March 2003): 98-101.

36 Paul Litt, "Liberal Humanism" and "Liberal Humanist Nationalism," in *The Muses, the Masses, and the Massey Commission* (Toronto: University of Toronto Press, 1992), 83-120.

37 Kuffert, *A Great Duty,* 236.

38 Arn Keeling and Robert McDonald, "The Profligate Province: Roderick Haig-Brown and the Modernizing of British Columbia," *Journal of Canadian Studies* 36, 3 (Fall 2001): 7-23 at 10.

39 Joan Scott, *Gender and the Politics of History* (New York: Columbia University Press, 1988), 2. The inadequacy of the coat-rack view of the body is discussed in Linda Nicholson, "Interpreting *Gender,*" *Signs* 20, 1 (1994): 79-105. The discussion of gender in this and the following paragraph is based on the above sources as well as on Joy Parr, "Gender History and Historical Practice," in Joy Parr and Mark Rosenfeld, eds., *Gender and History in Canada* (Toronto: Copp Clark, 1996), 8-27; and Kathleen Canning, "Feminist History after the Linguistic Turn: Historicizing Discourse and Experience," *Signs* 19, 2 (1994): 368-404. Scott's use of the term "gender" (and the general poststructuralist slant in gender history) has received a great deal of criticism. See, for example, Laura Lee Downs, "If 'Woman' Is Just an Empty Category Then Why Am I Afraid to Walk Alone at Night? Identity Politics Meets the Postmodern Subject," *Comparative Studies in Society and History* 35, 2 (1993): 414-37; and the exchange between Scott and Downs in the same issue. In Canada, the debate is best represented by Joan Sangster, "Beyond Dichotomies: Re-assessing Gender History and Women's History in Canada," *Left History* 3, 1 (1995): 109-21; and the various responses to that article in *Left History* 3, 2 (1995). In hindsight, these debates seem overly divisive, as much about how arguments were made as about the substantive issues themselves, and, especially, shaped by the need/desire of some academics to present their work as novel and of others to defend the legitimacy of work that had come before and was then under critique.

40 This discussion is also largely indebted to Scott, *Gender and the Politics of History.*

41 Jack Granatstein, *Who Killed Canadian History?* (Toronto: Harper Collins, 1998); Michael Bliss, "Privatizing the Mind: The Sundering of Canadian History, the Sundering of Canada," *Journal of Canadian Studies* 26, 4 (1991-92): 5-17. For a response to Granatstein's critique (although not along the lines of gender), see Bryan Palmer, "Of Silences and Trenches: A Dissident's View of Granatstein's Meaning," *Canadian Historical Review* 80, 4 (1999): 676-86, and A.B. McKillop, "Who Killed Canadian History? A View From the Trenches," *Canadian Historical Review* 80, 2 (1999): 269-99. Joy Parr offers a response to Bliss in "Gender History and Historical Practice," 10.

42 Although historians claiming the authority of "tradition" present gender history (along with other types of social and cultural history) as the irresponsible newcomer, in fact, as Joy Parr notes in "Gender History and Historical Practice," 9, this task of upsetting claims of universality is one of the historical profession's oldest tricks.

43 Christine Stansell, *City of Women: Sex and Class in New York, 1789-1860* (New York: Knopf, 1986); Joanne Meyerowitz, *Women Adrift: Independent Wage Earners in Chicago, 1880-1930* (Chicago: University of Chicago Press, 1988); Kathy Peiss,

Cheap Amusements: Working Women and Leisure in Turn-of-the-Century New York (Philadelphia: Temple University Press, 1986); Judith Walkowitz, *City of Dreadful Delight: Narratives of Sexual Danger in Late-Victorian London* (Chicago: University of Chicago Press, 1992); Carolyn Strange, *Toronto's Girl Problem: The Perils and Pleasures of the City, 1880-1930* (Toronto: University of Toronto Press, 1995); Mary Odem, *Delinquent Daughters: Protecting and Policing Adolescent Female Sexuality in the United States, 1885-1920* (Chapel Hill: University of North Carolina Press, 1995).

44 On women and modernity, see Rita Felski, *The Gender of Modernity* (Cambridge, MA: Harvard University Press, 1995); and Judy Giles, *The Parlour and the Suburb: Domestic Identities, Class, Femininity and Modernity* (Oxford: Berg, 2004).

45 On neurasthenia, see Patricia Jasen, *Wild Things: Nature, Culture and Tourism in Ontario, 1790-1914* (Toronto: University of Toronto Press, 1995); on the Group of Seven, Ross D. Cameron, "Tom Thomson, Antimodernism and the Ideal of Manhood," *Journal of the Canadian Historical Association* 10 (1999): 185-208, and Lynda Jessup, "Prospectors, Bushwhackers, Painters: Antimodernism and the Group of Seven," *International Journal of Canadian Studies* 17 (1998), 193-214; on hunting, Tina Loo, "Of Moose and Men: Hunting for Masculinities in British Columbia, 1880-1939," *Western Historical Quarterly* 32, 3 (2001): 296-319; on muscular Christianity, Gail Bederman, "'The Women Have Had Charge of the Church Long Enough': The Men and Religion Forward Movement of 1911-1912 and the Masculinization of Middle-Class Protestantism," *American Quarterly* 41, 3 (1989): 432-65, and Ralph Connor, *Glengarry School Days* (1902; reprint, Toronto: McClelland and Stewart, 1993); and on Roosevelt, Gail Bederman, *Manliness and Civilization: A Cultural History of Gender and Race in the United States, 1880-1917* (Chicago: University of Chicago Press, 1995). See also Donald A. Wright, "W.D. Lighthall and David Ross McCord: Antimodernism and English Canadian Imperialism, 1880s-1918," *Journal of Canadian Studies* 32, 2 (1997): 134-53; Michael Dawson, "'That Nice Red Coat Goes to My Head Like Champagne': Gender, Antimodernism and the Mountie Image, 1880-1960," *Journal of Canadian Studies* 32, 3 (1997): 119-39; and Mark Moss, *Manliness and Militarism: Educating Young Boys in Ontario for War* (Toronto: Oxford University Press, 2001).

46 Robert Rutherdale noted this theme of resistance to change in his oral histories of fathers in Canada who experienced the 1960s. See Rutherdale, "Fatherhood, Life Stories, and Gendered Responses to Domesticity in Canada during the 1960s," paper presented at the conference "Sixties: Style and Substance," Montreal, November 2003.

47 Kimmel, *Manhood in America*, 6-9; Susan Faludi, "The Son, the Moon, and the Stars: The Promise of Postwar Manhood," in *Stiffed: The Betrayal of the American Man* (New York: William Morrow, 1999), 3-47; and Lynne Segal, "Look Back in Anger: Men in the Fifties," in *Slow Motion: Changing Men, Changing Masculinities* (New Jersey: Rutgers University Press, 1990), 3-26. Recent works on the history of the relationship between masculinity and consumer culture suggest that Faludi's thesis, that the ornamental aspect of manhood developed only recently, is deeply problematic. These works present useful alternative ways of understanding how ideas of masculinity changed over the course of the twentieth century, more often in agreement with changes in consumer capitalism. See

Osgerby, *Playboys in Paradise;* and Tom Pendergast, *Creating the Modern Man: American Magazines and Consumer Culture, 1900-1950* (Columbia, MO: University of Missouri Press, 2000).

48 Much of the initial research into masculinity sought to pinpoint moments of historical crisis in masculinity. The idea was that by showing its crisis moments, we could show the historicity of masculinity, pointing to its contingency and poking holes in the notion of a universal manhood. However, the "discovery" of crises in almost every imaginable time period and circumstance suggests that we need a different tool with which to historicize masculinity. On the psychological and social instability of gender, see Scott, *Gender and the Politics of History*, 38-39.

49 Other case studies could indeed be possible; one anonymous reviewer of the present volume suggested the insurance industry, which would indeed make a fascinating study. On a somewhat related topic, see Michael Roper, *Masculinity and the British Organization Man since 1945* (Oxford: Oxford University Press, 1994).

50 Donald Wright shows how the professionalization of history went hand-in-hand with a process of masculinization. See Wright, "The Importance of Being Sexist: The Masculinization of History," in *The Professionalization of History*, 97-120.

51 For examples of this kind of evolutionary approach to gender see Neil Boyd, *The Beast Within: Why Men Are Violent* (Vancouver: Douglas and McIntyre, 2000); and Charles Crawford and Dennis L. Krebs, *Handbook of Evolutionary Psychology: Ideas, Issues and Applications* (New Jersey: Lawrence Erlbaum Associates, 1998).

Chapter 2: Coming Home

1 Doug Owram, "Canadian Domesticity in the Postwar Era," in Peter Neary and J.L. Granatstein, eds., *The Veterans Charter and Post-World War II Canada* (Montreal and Kingston: McGill-Queen's University Press, 1998), 208.

2 Alvin Finkel notes that by focusing on the collective psychology of the time, Owram is able to overlook the darker aspects of the era's politics. See Alvin Finkel, "Competing Master Narratives on Postwar Canada," *Acadiensis* 29, 2 (2000): 188-204.

3 Nancy Christie, *Engendering the State: Family, Work, and Welfare in Canada* (Toronto: University of Toronto Press, 2000).

4 On the gendered implications of the desire to return to "normal," see Mary Louise Adams, *The Trouble with Normal: Postwar Youth and the Making of Heterosexuality* (Toronto: University of Toronto Press, 1997). Historians in other countries have done a better job of tracing the gendered importance of men's wartime service. See Joanna Bourke, *Dismembering the Male: Men's Bodies, Britain and the Great War* (London: Reaktion, 1996); Marilyn Lake, "Mission Impossible: How Men Gave Birth to the Australian Nation – Nationalism, Gender and Other Seminal Acts," *Gender and History* 4, 3 (1992): 305-22; Daniel J. Sherman, "Monuments, Mourning and Masculinity in France after World War I," *Gender and History* 8, 1 (1996): 82-107; Susan Zeiger, "She Didn't Raise Her Boy to Be a Slacker: Motherhood, Conscription and the Culture of the First World War," *Feminist Studies* 22, 1 (Spring 1996): 7-39.

5 The language of the male veteran's deservedness pervades many popular accounts of the period, including Ben Wicks, *When the Boys Came Marching Home:*

True Stories of the Men Who Went to War and the Women and Children Who Took Them Back (Toronto: Stoddart, 1991); Robert Collins, *You Had to Be There: An Intimate Portrait of the Generation that Survived the Depression, Won the War, and Re-Invented Canada* (Toronto: McClelland and Stewart, 1997). Wartime psychiatrists presented the return to civilian society as an issue of changing from wartime discipline to a new kind of discipline. See J.P.S. Cathcart, "Psychological Problems in Post-War Rehabilitation," *Bulletin of the Canadian Psychological Association*, special issue containing proceedings of the First Annual Meeting of the Canadian Psychological Association (April 1941): 31-32.

6 On plans for postwar reconstruction, see Neary and Granatstein, eds., *The Veterans Charter;* Christie, *Engendering the State;* J.L. Granatstein, *Canada's War: The Politics of the Mackenzie King Government, 1939-1945* (Toronto: Oxford University Press, 1975).

7 See, notably, James Struthers, *The Limits of Affluence: Welfare in Ontario, 1920-1970* (Toronto: University of Toronto Press, 1994); and Christie, *Engendering the State.*

8 See, for example, Walter H. Kirchner, "Widows' Pensions," letter to the editor, *Vancouver Daily Province,* 27 February 1942, 24; "Pensions Act Probe Asked by Veteran," *Vancouver Sun,* 13 December 1944, 13; Walter H. Kirchner, "Letter to the Editor," *Ottawa Citizen,* 6 November 1947; transcripts in Library and Archives Canada (hereafter LAC), *Royal Commission to Investigate Complaints Made by Walter H. Kirchner* (hereafter RCWK), RG 33/85, vol. 1, file 3.

9 On the language of veterans' entitlement as a basis for state action in the interwar years, see Lara Campbell, "'We Who Have Wallowed in the Mud of Flanders': First World War Veterans, Unemployment, and the Development of Social Welfare in Canada, 1929-1939," *Journal of the Canadian Historical Association* 11 (2000): 125-49.

10 On the legacy of the treatment of First World War veterans, see Desmond Morton, "The Canadian Veterans' Heritage from the Great War," in Neary and Granatstein, eds., *The Veterans Charter,* 15-31. The changed relation between the state and citizens created by the war is evident in Jeff Keshen, "Getting It Right the Second Time Around: The Reintegration of Canadian Veterans of World War II," in Neary and Granatstein, eds., *The Veterans Charter,* 62-84, and also evident in the postwar struggle for social housing as outlined in Jill Wade, *Houses for All: The Struggle for Social Housing in Vancouver, 1919-1950* (Vancouver: UBC Press, 1994).

11 The government's desire to use the Royal Commission to silence criticism can be inferred from W.S. Woods to Major General H.F.G. Letson, 5 May 1949; and "Memo Re the Desirability of Appointing Dr. McCann's Committee by Order in Council," 17 November 1947, author unclear [initials indicate that it might be James McCann], LAC, *RCWK,* RG 33/85, vol. 1, file 3.

12 On men and allowable violence, including that of warfare, see Ingeborg Breines, Robert Connell, and Ingrid Eide, eds., *Male Roles, Masculinities and Violence: A Culture of Peace Perspective* (Paris: UNESCO, 2000); Angus McLaren, "Murderers," in *The Trials of Masculinity: Policing Sexual Boundaries, 1870-1930* (Chicago: University of Chicago Press, 1997), 111-31; Robert Nye, *Masculinity and Male Codes of Honor in Modern France* (New York and Oxford: Oxford University Press, 1993); Peter Spierenburg, ed., *Men and Violence: Gender, Honor and Rituals in Modern Europe and America* (Columbus: Ohio State University Press, 1998). For a very

different perspective, based on evolutionary biology, see David Courtwright, *Violent Land: Single Men and Social Disorder from the Frontier to the Inner City* (Cambridge, MA: Harvard University Press, 1996).

13 The connection between masculinity and war is relatively understudied in Canada. Consider, for example, the almost complete absence of this category of analysis from Jonathan Vance's otherwise very fine study of the continuity into the interwar years of pre–First World War ideas about war, *Death So Noble: Memory, Meaning, and the First World War* (Vancouver: UBC Press, 1997). A few good recent works on masculinity and war include Mark Moss, *Manliness and Militarism: Educating Young Boys in Ontario for War* (Toronto: Oxford University Press, 2001); and Mike O'Brien, "Manhood and the Militia Myth: Masculinity, Class, and Militarism in Ontario, 1902-1914," *Labour/Le Travail* 42 (1998): 115-41. Ruth Roach Pierson, *"They're Still Women after All": The Second World War and Canadian Womanhood* (Toronto: McClelland and Stewart, 1986), shows that while service in war represented a challenge to contemporary notions of femininity, the opposite was true for masculinity; war was what made one a man. On Native soldiers, see Robin Brownlie, "Work Hard and Be Grateful: Native Soldier Settlers in Ontario after the First World War," in Franca Iacovetta and Wendy Mitchinson, eds., *On the Case: Explorations in Social History* (Toronto: University of Toronto Press, 1998), 181-203.

14 On breadwinning and social welfare at mid-century, see Christie, *Engendering the State*. On breadwinning as a masculine ideal more generally, see Robert Griswold, *Fatherhood in America: A History* (New York: Basic Books, 1993); and Michael Kimmel, *Manhood in America: A Cultural History* (New York: Free Press, 1996).

15 The quotations are from Barry Broadfoot, *The Veterans' Years: Coming Home from the War* (Vancouver and Toronto: Douglas and McIntyre, 1985), 27; and Pierson, *"They're Still Women after All,"* 140-41. Almost all the veterans whom Broadfoot interviews express some opinion on their relative contempt or resentment for those who did not serve. On veterans and housing, see Wade, *Houses for All*.

16 "Brigadier W.H.S. Macklin's Report on the Mobilization of the 13th Infantry Brigade on an Active Basis," cited in C.P. Stacey, *Arms, Men and Government: The War Policies of Canada, 1939-1945* (Ottawa: Queen's Printer, 1970), 595. The cultural dimensions of conscription, especially its gendered aspects, have hardly been studied. For a discussion of the topic through which this kind of information can be inferred, see J.L. Granatstein, *Broken Promises: A History of Conscription in Canada* (Toronto: University of Toronto Press, 1977); Peter A. Russell, "British Columbia's 'Zombie' Protests against Overseas Conscription, November 1944," paper presented to *BC Studies* conference, Kamloops, BC, 2001; and Stacey, *Arms, Men and Government*, 434-82.

17 Testimony of Walter H. Kirchner, Secretary, Canadian Combat Veterans Association, Transcript of Evidence Taken at Shaughnessy Hospital, 15 January 1948, LAC, *RCWK*, RG 33/85, vol. 2.

18 On the troubled relation in the United States between men as self-sufficient and men as entitled, see Alice Kessler-Harris, "Measures for Masculinity: The American Labor Movement and Welfare State Policy during the Great Depression," in Stefan Dudink, Karen Hagemann, and John Tosh, eds., *Masculinities in Politics and War: Gendering Modern History* (Manchester: Manchester University Press, 2004), 257-75. On the gendered nature of rights-based claims, see Struthers, *The*

Limits of Affluence, 14-16; Linda Gordon, *Pitied but Not Entitled: Single Mothers and the History of Welfare, 1890-1935* (Cambridge, MA: Harvard University Press, 1994), 293-94; Nancy Fraser and Linda Nicholson, "A Genealogy of *Dependency:* Tracing a Keyword of the US Welfare State," *Signs* 19, 2 (1994): 309-36.

19 See, for example, several of the essays in Judith Fingard and Janet Guildford, eds., *Mothers of the Municipality: Women, Work and Social Policy in Post-1945 Halifax* (Toronto: University of Toronto Press, 2005). And Sylvie Murray makes this point in *The Progressive Housewife: Community Activism in Suburban Queens, 1945-1965* (Philadelphia: University of Pennsylvania Press, 2003).

20 Testimony of Ernest Maxwell, Transcript of Evidence Taken at Shaughnessy Hospital, 15 January 1948, LAC, *RCWK,* RG 33/85, vol. 2.

21 See Dennis Guest, *The Emergence of Social Security in Canada* (Vancouver: UBC Press, 1980), 95-97.

22 Testimony of John T., Transcript of Evidence Taken at Shaughnessy Hospital, 15 January 1948, LAC, *RCWK,* RG 33/85, vol. 2. Only a first name and last initial will be used to identify veterans who appeared before the Royal Commission. I have decided to do this because the names themselves are not essential to an understanding of the story and out of respect for the sensitivity of some of the issues brought up at the commission and the possibility that some of the veterans and/or their immediate family may wish to have such matters kept private.

23 Christie, *Engendering the State,* 316. On the growing critique of the poorhouse, see James Snell, *The Citizen's Wage: The State and the Elderly in Canada* (Toronto: University of Toronto Press, 1996).

24 Testimony of John B., Transcript of Evidence Taken at Shaughnessy Hospital, 14 January 1948, LAC, *RCWK,* RG 33/85, vol. 1.

25 Walter S. Woods, *Rehabilitation, a Combined Operation* (Ottawa: Queen's Printer, 1953), 3; Don Ives, "The Veterans Charter: The Compensation Principle and the Principle of Recognition for Service," in Neary and Granatstein, eds., *The Veterans Charter,* 88-89. See also the essays by Jeff Keshen and Peter Neary in the same collection.

26 Robert England, *Discharged: A Commentary on Civil Re-Establishment of Veterans in Canada* (Toronto: Macmillan, 1943), xv-xviii.

27 See Desmond Morton and Glenn Wright, *Winning the Second Battle: Canadian Veterans and the Return to Civilian Life, 1915-1930* (Toronto: University of Toronto Press, 1987).

28 See Morton, "The Canadian Veterans' Heritage," 28.

29 The quotations are from Walter H. Kirchner, "Need for Enquiry," letter to the editor, *Vancouver Daily Province,* 22 August 1944, 4; and Walter H. Kirchner, "Thousand Cases," letter to the editor, *Vancouver Daily Province,* 31 October 1942, 32. See also "Pensions Act Probe Asked by Veteran," *Vancouver Sun,* 13 December 1944, 13; J.V. Thom, "Cheating the Disabled," letter to the editor, *Vancouver Daily Province,* 30 August 1946, 4.

30 Testimony of Dr. Laing, Pension Medical Examiner, Shaughnessy Hospital, Transcript of Evidence Taken at Shaughnessy Hospital, 14 January 1948, LAC, *RCWK,* RG 33/85, vol. 1.

31 Ibid.

32 On this process as characteristic of state simplification schemes more generally, see James C. Scott, *Seeing Like a State: How Certain Schemes to Improve the Human Condition Have Failed* (New Haven: Yale University Press, 1998), 76-83.

33 Major J.S.A. Bois, "The Morale of the Fighting Soldier," *Bulletin of the Canadian Psychological Association* 3, 2 (April 1943): 17-20 at 18. See also Major B.H. McNeel and Major T.E. Dancey, "The Personality of the Successful Soldier," *The American Journal of Psychiatry* 102, 3 (November 1945): 337-42.

34 England, *Discharged*, 10-11.

35 Ibid., 10-11. See also Cathcart, "Psychological Problems."

36 Rehabilitation Information Committee, Wartime Information Board, *The Common-Sense of Re-Establishment* (Ottawa: Edmond Cloutier, King's Printer, 1945), 34.

37 This is certainly the conclusion of Christie, *Engendering the State*, and of James Struthers, "Family Allowances, Old Age Security and the Construction of Entitlement in the Canadian Welfare State, 1943-1951," in Neary and Granatstein, eds., *The Veterans Charter*, at 183. For other perspectives, see Granatstein, "Public Welfare and Party Benefit," in *Canada's War*, 249-93; and Keshen, "Getting it Right," 66-67.

38 Here, I am somewhat guided by the provocative work of Ian McKay, especially his *Rebels, Reds, Radicals: Rethinking Canada's Left History* (Toronto: Between the Lines, 2005), and "The Liberal Order Framework: A Prospectus for a Reconnaissance of Canadian History," *Canadian Historical Review* 81, 4 (2000): 617-45. My use of this work is tempered, however, by the fact that it would likely lead to an interpretation that described veterans' responses to these liberalizing tendencies as "resistance." As noted in the Introduction, the gendered nature of veterans' responses – that the men are feeling alienated from the prerogatives of male power – makes this characterization, in my perspective, inaccurate.

39 Ministry of Veterans Affairs, *Back to Civil Life*, 3rd ed. (Ottawa: King's Printer, 1946), reprinted in Neary and Granatstein, eds., *The Veterans Charter*, 246-90 at 247 and 249; Rehabilitation Information Committee, *The Common-Sense of Re-Establishment*, 3.

40 Ministry of Veterans Affairs, *Back to Civil Life*, in Neary and Granatstein, eds, *The Veterans Charter*, 276. Similar sentiments can be seen in England, *Discharged*, esp. ch. 7.

41 On Sholto M.'s case, see Testimony of S.D. McClellan, Transcript of Evidence Taken at Shaughnessy Hospital, 15 January 1948, LAC, *RCWK*, RG 33/85, vol. 1; and House of Commons Debates, Hansard, 8 June 1948, 4903-4906, copy in LAC, *RCWK*, RG 33/85, vol. 1, file 3. On old-age-pension legislation in Canada, see James Snell, *The Citizen's Wage: The State and the Elderly in Canada, 1900-1951* (Toronto: University of Toronto Press, 1996); and Struthers, "Family Allowances."

42 On this trend in Canadian psychiatric thought, see "Minutes," 1 December 1947, LAC, *RCWK*, RG 33/85, vol. 1, file 4; Terry Copp, "From Neurasthenia to Post-Traumatic Stress Disorder: Canadian Veterans and the Problem of Persistent Emotional Disabilities," in Neary and Granatstein, eds., *The Veterans Charter*, 152; and Terry Copp and Bill McAndrew, *Battle Exhaustion: Soldiers and Psychiatrists in the Canadian Army, 1939-1945* (Montreal and Kingston: McGill-Queen's University Press, 1990). For trends in psychological thought, see also Mona Gleason, *Normalizing the Ideal: Psychology, Schooling and the Family in Postwar Canada* (Toronto: University of Toronto Press, 1999).

43 Travis E. Dancey, "Treatment in the Absence of Pensioning for Psychoneurotic Veterans," *The American Journal of Psychiatry* 107 (November 1950): 347-49;

Kenneth Cragg, "Pensions Aggravate Neurotics," *Globe and Mail,* 31 January 1948, 1, copy in LAC, *RCWK,* RG 33/85, vol. 1, file 3.

44 On manhood and responsibility in the postwar years, see Robert Rutherdale, "Fatherhood and Masculine Domesticity during the Baby Boom: Consumption and Leisure in Advertising and Life Stories," in Lori Chambers and Edgar André Montigny, eds., *Family Matters: Papers in Post-Confederation Canadian Family History* (Toronto: Canada Scholars' Press, 1998), 309-33, and "Fatherhood and the Social Construction of Memory: Breadwinning and Male Parenting on a Job Frontier, 1945-1966," in Joy Parr and Mark Rosenfeld, eds., *Gender and History in Canada* (Toronto: Copp Clark, 1996), 357-75; Robert Griswold, *Fatherhood in America;* Barbara Ehrenreich, *The Hearts of Men: American Dreams and the Flight from Commitment* (New York: Doubleday, 1983).

45 Dancey, "Treatment in the Absence of Pensioning," 347.

46 Copp, "From Neurasthenia"; and Copp and McAndrew, *Battle Exhaustion.* On the emergence of Freudian ideas in North America, see Edward Shorter, "The Psychoanalytic Hiatus," *A History of Psychiatry: From the Era of the Asylum to the Age of Prozac* (New York: John Wiley, 1997).

47 See, for example, Testimony of Frank C., Transcript of Evidence Taken at Shaughnessy Hospital, 15 January 1948, LAC, *RCWK,* RG 33/85, vol. 2.

48 Walter H. Kirchner, "Psychiatry and Moral Law," letter to the editor, *Vancouver Sun,* 8 November 1945, 4.

49 "MP Would Banish Psychiatrists from Veterans' Dept.," *Ottawa Morning Journal,* 9 June 1948, copy in LAC, *RCWK,* RG 33/85, vol. 1, file 3.

50 House of Commons Debates, *Hansard,* 8 June 1948, 4903-4906, copy in LAC, *RCWK,* RG 33/85, vol. 1, file 3.

51 Information on John B.'s case in this and the next paragraph is taken from Testimony of John B., Transcript of Evidence Taken at Shaughnessy Hospital, 14 January 1948, LAC, *RCWK,* RG 33/85, vol. 1.

52 Given the sexual nature of Margetts' questioning and his junior status, it seems possible that Margetts was following Freudian psychoanalytic procedures, which perhaps explains the commissioners' willingness to dwell on this line of questioning.

53 "Report of the Commission Appointed under the Provisions of Part I of the Inquiries Act by Order in Council PC 4980," LAC, *RCWK,* RG 33/85, vol. 2; Testimony of Walter H. Kirchner, Transcript of Evidence Taken at Shaughnessy Hospital, 16 January 1948, LAC, *RCWK,* RG 33/85, vol. 2.

54 On the dilemmas of high modernist schemes for social improvement, albeit in less democratic contexts, see Scott, *Seeing Like a State.*

Chapter 3: At Work

1 Eric Hobsbawm, *The Age of Extremes: A History of the World, 1914-1991* (New York: Pantheon, 1994), 257-59. Joy Parr, *Domestic Goods: The Material, the Moral and the Economic in the Postwar Years* (Toronto: University of Toronto Press, 1999), has recently complicated this optimistic vision of postwar abundance, noting the extent to which depression and wartime anxieties continued and provided a legacy of consumer conservatism.

2 The selection here is of my own making and matches the tone of most reporting on the disaster. Aside from newspaper accounts, see also T.W. Paterson, *Disaster: Tales of Heroism and Hardship in the Face of Catastrophe* (Victoria: Solitaire, 1973);

and the Canadian Broadcasting Corporation news feature commemorating the fortieth anniversary of the collapse, which aired in 1998.

3 Immediate media response was filled with these images. These examples are taken from Bill Fletcher, "Crash 'Impossible' Engineers Thought," *Vancouver Sun,* 18 June 1958, D1; "Testimony of Alfred Engelman," 23 July 1958, British Columbia Archives (hereafter BCA), British Columbia Royal Commission: Second Narrows Bridge Inquiry (hereafter SNB), GR-1250, box 1, file 4; "Span Disaster Still Mystery: Divers Hunt for Missing Workers," *Vancouver Sun,* 18 June 1958, 1.

4 The topsy-turvy language pervades much of the initial reporting; quotations here are from "Fear 18 Dead in Bridge Tragedy," *Vancouver Daily Province,* 18 June 1958, 32; "Fifty Feet from the Bridge as It Went," *Vancouver Daily Province,* 18 June 1958, 3; "Span Disaster Still Mystery: Divers Hunt for Missing Workers," *Vancouver Sun,* 18 June 1958, 1.

5 See, for example, "Towboat Men Harvested Grisly Sheaves of Death," *Vancouver Sun,* 18 June 1958, D1; Jerry Brown, "Hurtling-Span Ride 'Nightmare,'" *Vancouver Sun,* 18 June 1958, C1. On masculinity in Canada in the postwar years, see Robert Rutherdale, "Fatherhood and Masculine Domesticity during the Baby Boom: Consumption and Leisure in Advertising and Life Stories," in Lori Chambers and Edgar André Montigny, eds., *Family Matters: Papers in Post-Confederation Canadian Family History* (Toronto: Canada Scholars' Press, 1998), 309-33; Robert Rutherdale, "Fatherhood and the Social Construction of Memory: Breadwinning and Male Parenting on a Job Frontier, 1945-1966," in Joy Parr and Mark Rosenfeld, eds., *Gender and History in Canada* (Toronto: Copp Clark, 1996), 357-75; Doug Owram, *Born at the Right Time: A History of the Baby-Boom Generation* (Toronto: University of Toronto Press, 1996); and Chris Dummitt, "Finding a Place for Father: Selling the Barbecue in Post-War Canada," *Journal of the Canadian Historical Association* 8 (1998): 209-23.

6 In using this kind of linguistic and literary-genre approach to the historical past, I have been guided by key works in cultural history, including Natalie Zemon Davis, *Fiction in the Archives: Pardon Tales and Their Tellers in Sixteenth-Century France* (Stanford: Stanford University Press, 1987); Robert Darnton, *The Great Cat Massacre and Other Episodes in French Cultural History* (New York: Basic Books, 1984); Lynn Hunt, ed., *The New Cultural History* (Berkeley: University of California Press, 1989); and in Canada, by Keith Walden, *Becoming Modern in Toronto: The Industrial Exhibition and the Shaping of a Late Victorian Culture* (Toronto: University of Toronto Press, 1997).

7 David Nye, *American Technological Sublime* (Cambridge, MA: MIT Press, 1994), notes the importance of bridges as features of a modern notion of the technological sublime. Although Nye positions bridges in a chronological order in the late nineteenth century, moving on to skyscrapers and other later technologies, the response to the building of the Second Narrows Bridge in Vancouver in the late 1950s suggests that bridges remained an impressive sight for many Vancouverites until well after the Second World War.

8 On the timing of bridge building in Vancouver, see Bruce MacDonald, *Vancouver: A Visual History* (Vancouver: Talon, 1992). On the politics of postwar infrastructure development in British Columbia, see Martin Robin, *Pillars of Profit: The Company Province, 1934-1972* (Toronto: McClelland and Stewart, 1973), esp. ch. 7; Jean Barman, *The West beyond the West: A History of British Columbia* (Toronto: University of Toronto Press, 1996); David J. Mitchell, *W.A.C. Bennett and*

the Rise of British Columbia (Vancouver and Toronto: Douglas and McIntyre, 1983), esp. ch. 8; Mel Rothenburger, *Friend o' Mine: The Story of Flyin' Phil Gaglardi* (Victoria: Orca, 1991); John R. Wedley, "A Development Tool: W.A.C. Bennett and the PGE Railway," *BC Studies* 117 (1998): 29-50; and Stephen G. Tomblin, "W.A.C. Bennett and Province-Building in British Columbia," *BC Studies* 85 (1990): 45-61. The moves of the British Columbia government in the area of highways followed developments south of the border in the creation of highways policy. See Kenneth Jackson, *Crabgrass Frontier: The Suburbanization of the United States* (New York: Oxford University Press, 1985); and Norbert MacDonald, *Distant Neighbours: A Comparative History of Seattle and Vancouver* (Lincoln: University of Nebraska Press, 1987).

9   Nye, *American Technological Sublime,* xiii-xiv, ch. 4.
10 See, for example, "95-Ton Girders Fixed to Bridge," *Vancouver Sun,* 18 September 1959, 27; "Bridge Completed in 4 1/2 Years," *Vancouver Sun,* 25 August 1960, 23; "Blast to Destroy 2nd Narrows Pier," *Vancouver Sun,* 3 March 1959, 2; "20 Begin Work to Salvage Span," *Vancouver Daily Province,* 7 August 1958, 8; "Underwater TV to Aid Span Salvage," *Vancouver Sun,* 12 July 1958, 21; "Bridge Salvage Work Shifts to High Gear," *Daily Province,* 13 August 1958, 28; "Second Narrows Bridge," *Public Works in Canada,* vol. 6, no. 6, pp. 12-16, BCA, Association of Professional Engineers of the Province of British Columbia (hereafter APEBC), MS-2832, box 3, file 8; "Second Narrows Bridge Is Biggest Yet for Vancouver," *The Span* 4, 5 (January-February 1958), 1, BCA, Dominion Bridge Company (hereafter DBC), MS-0521, box 16, file 2.
11 On murder rates, see *Murder Statistics, 1961-1970* (Ottawa: Statistics Canada, 1973). Murder statistics in Canada come from two sources: those collected by Health Canada from coroner's reports and those provided to Statistics Canada from police departments. I have chosen the larger number provided by Health Canada. Statistics Canada reported only 153 murders in 1958, so the discrepancy between workplace death and murder could be even more significant. On workplace deaths, see Workmen's Compensation Board [of BC], *Annual Report* (Victoria: Queen's Printer, 1958 and 1959).
12 Some sense of this history can be garnered from Robert H. Babcock, "Blood on the Factory Floor: The Workers' Compensation Movement in Canada and the United States," in Raymond Blake and Jeff Keshen, eds., *Social Welfare Policy in Canada: Historical Readings* (Toronto: Copp Clark, 1995), 107-21. For British Columbia, see Ian Tom Coneybeer, "The Origins of Workmen's Compensation in British Columbia: State Theory and Law" (MA thesis, Simon Fraser University, 1990); John Thomas Keelor, "The Price of Lives and Limbs Lost at Work: The Development of No-Fault Workers' Compensation Legislation in British Columbia, 1910-1916" (MA thesis, University of Victoria, 1996); Allen Specht, "Workers' Compensation Board of British Columbia History Project" (introduction to program in BCA, Allen Specht, 1979). On the British example, see P.W.J. Bartrip, *Workmen's Compensation in Twentieth Century Britain: Law, History and Social Policy* (Aldershot: Gower, 1987); and P.W.J. Bartrip and S.B. Burman, *The Wounded Soldiers of Industry: Industrial Compensation Policy, 1833-1897* (Oxford: Oxford University Press, 1983).
13 David Rosner and Gerald Markowitz, "The Early Movement for Occupational Safety and Health, 1900-1917," in Judith Walzer Leavitt and Ronald L. Numbers,

eds., *Sickness and Health in America: Readings in the History of Medicine and Public Health* (Madison: University of Wisconsin, 1997), at 480.

14 Karl Figlio, "What Is an Accident?" in P. Weidling, ed., *The Social History of Occupational Health* (London: Croom Helm, 1986),180-206 at 180-81, emphasis in original. See also, Bill Luckin, "Accidents, Disasters and Cities," *Urban History* 20, 2 (October 1993): 177-90.

15 Ulrich Beck makes this point about industrial society more broadly, noting how issues of production always take precedence over the detriments of modernization; see "The Politics of Knowledge in the Risk Society," *The Risk Society: Towards a New Modernity,* trans. Mark Ritter (London: Sage, 1992), 51-84.

16 Interviews with Jim Paton and Art Francis, February 1978, BCA, WCBOHP, transcripts.

17 Safety campaign image from Dominion Bridge's company paper, *The Span,* January-February 1959, BCA, DBC, box 16, file 2.

18 WCB inspector Jim Paton recalled that in the 1960s unions became much more active on the issue of workplace safety. This matches the approach of the province's main union, the International Woodworkers of America, as noted in Andrew Neufeld and Andrew Parnaby, *The IWA in Canada: The Life and Times of an Industrial Union* (Vancouver: New Star, 2000). The period before the collapse saw two different Royal Commissions into workmen's compensation, and in both cases, labour organizations focused almost exclusivley on the financial implications of the program, not on improving safety in the workplace. See Brief on Workmen's Compensation Act, Vancouver and District Labor Council, British Columbia Federation of Labour, and the Brotherhood of Railway Trainmen, 17 September 1957, University of British Columbia Archives (hereafter UBC), Vancouver and District Labour Council Records (hereafter VDLC), series C, box 4, file 12; Brief by Vancouver, New Westminster and District Trades and Lab Council, November 1949, BCA, British Columbia Commission on Workmen's Compensation, 1949-52, GR-0384, box 46, file 10; Brief Submitted by British Columbia Federation of Labour, 7 November 1949, BCA, GR-0384, box 43, file 5; Testimony of H.E. Winch, 7 November 1949, BCA, GR-0384, Proceedings, vol. 1; Testimony of G.C. Home, 9 November 1949, BCA, GR-0384, Proceedings, vol. 1; Testimony of J.C. Bury, BCA, GR-0384, Proceedings, vol. 12.

19 Quoted in Jean Howarth, "Families Fund Grows Steadily," *Vancouver Daily Province,* 23 June 1958, 1.

20 Jean Howarth, "'Sight of Boots Was What Hurt,'" *Vancouver Daily Province,* 18 June 1958, 3; Jack McCaugherty, "'Men Didn't Have a Chance,'" *Vancouver Daily Province,* 18 June 1958, 3.

21 Robert Griswold, *Fatherhood in America: A History* (New York: Basic Books, 1993), 2.

22 For articles on Crusch and other widows, see William McCarthy, "'Bridge of Hope' Road to Despair," *Vancouver Sun,* 18 June 1958, C1; Denny Boyd, "Widows Rebuilding Lives," *Vancouver Sun,* 19 December 1958, 29; "These Are Dead in Bridge Tragedy," *Vancouver Daily Province,* 18 June 1958, 6; Jean Howarth, "It's Looking ... and Not Seeing Him," *Vancouver Daily Province,* 19 June 1958, 1; Jean Howarth, "Province Opens Fund for Bereaved Families," *Vancouver Daily Province,* 20 June 1958, 1; Jean Howarth, "Her World Ended When Bridge Fell," *Vancouver Daily Province,* 25 June 1958, 1; "Donations Sought for 'Bridge' Families," *Labor Statesman,* 28 June 1958, 6; Regular Minutes of VDLC, 15 July 1958,

UBC, *Vancouver and District Labour Council* (hereafter *VDLC*), series A, box 16. On the gendering of "need," see Linda Gordon, *Pities but Not Entitled: Single Mothers and the History of Welfare* (Cambridge, MA: Harvard University Press, 1994); James Struthers, *The Limits of Affluence: Welfare in Ontario, 1920-1970* (Toronto: University of Toronto Press, 1994); and Margaret Jane Little, *No Car, No Radio, No Liquor Permit: The Moral Regulation of Single Mothers in Ontario, 1920-1997* (Toronto: Oxford University Press, 1998).

23 Cited in Jean Howarth, "City Rallies to Aid of Stricken Families," *Vancouver Daily Province*, 21 June 1958, 1.

24 Tom Ardies, "'It Happened Like This ... ': Blood, Tears, People," *Vancouver Sun*, 18 June 1958, 1.

25 On the memorial service, see "Nineteen Red Roses Cast on Water at Bridge Tragedy Memorial Service," *Vancouver Daily Province*, 7 July 1958, 3; "Memorial Service for Span Victims," *Vancouver Sun*, 3 July 1958, 9; Jack Lee, "Long Roll-Call of the Dead Sounded as the Roses Fall," *Vancouver Sun*, 7 July 1958, 37.

26 Letter to the editor, *Vancouver Province*, 25 June 1958.

27 Interview with Art Francis, February 1978, BCA, WCBOHP. See also Safety Committee Reports, November 1957-June 1958, BCA, SNB, GR-1250, box 5, file 12; and WCB Inspection Report, 7 February 1958, BCA, SNB, GR-1250, box 5, file 13.

28 "This Month's Question," *The Span* 4, 1 (May-June 1957): 2; "This Month's Question," *The Span* 5, 3 (September-October 1958): 2, BCA, MS-0521, box 16, file 2.

29 On the Western fascination with the "other" more generally, see John Jervis, "Exotic Encounters: Savagery, Civilization and the Imperial Other," *Transgressing the Modern: Explorations in the Western Experience of Otherness* (Oxford: Blackwell, 1999), 57-82.

30 Peter Stearns, *American Cool: Constructing a Twentieth-Century Emotional Style* (New York: New York University Press, 1994); Michael Barton, "Journalistic Gore: Disaster Reporting and Emotional Discourse in the *New York Times*, 1852-1956," in Peter N. Stearns and Jan Lewis, eds., *An Emotional History of the United States* (New York and London: New York University Press, 1998), 155-72. Stearns slightly deviates from an older literature on the history of emotions that I have also found useful in interpreting modern responses to violence resulting from ostensibly rational processes; see Norbert Elias, *The Civilizing Process*, trans. Edmund Jephcott (Oxford and Cambridge, MA: Blackwell, 1994), esp. 156-68. For a critique of this approach to the history of emotions, see Barbara H. Rosenswein, "Worrying about Emotions in History," *American Historical Review* 107, 3 (2002): 821-45.

31 "Span Disaster Still Mystery: Divers Hunt for Missing Workers," *Vancouver Sun*, 18 June 1958, 1.

32 "Investigate All Crossings," editorial, *Vancouver Sun*, 18 June 1958, 1.

33 "Probe Opens into Disaster," *Vancouver Daily Province*, 19 June 1958, 1; "Facts, Not Emotionalism," editorial, *Vancouver Province*, 19 June 1958, 4.

34 Pratley later had to withdraw for medical reasons. Lett called on the advice of two Canadian engineers: A.B. Sanderson and Professor Alexander Hrennikof of the University of British Columbia.

35 The actual names of the unions are longer, but I am using these two popular shortened forms for ease of reading. The ironworkers union represented most of those who were actually killed in the collapse (fourteen because they were those

who were on the outermost spans), while one painter was killed and two company engineers. The eighteenth death to come out of the collapse was of a "frogman" (underwater diver) who drowned in the rescue operation.

36 N.S. Edison to Sherwood Lett, 30 June 1958, BCA, GR-1250, box 10, file 1; Taft [of the BTC] to W.A.C. Bennett, 23 June 1958, BCA, SNB, GR-1250, box 10, file 1; Regular Minutes of VDLC, 15 July 1958, UBC, VDLC, series A, box 16.

37 On safety at the Second Narrows Bridge work site, see "Testimony of Walter Miller," WCB safety inspector, 23 July 1958; and "Testimony of Arthur Francis," WCB director of Accident Prevention, 23 July 1958, BCA, SNB, GR-1250, box 1, file 4.

38 See entries in "Commissioner's Diary," various dates, City of Vancouver Archives (hereafter CVA), Sherwood Lett Fonds, Add Ms 361, vol. 6, file 6.

39 See the Proceedings of the Commission, various dates, BCA, SNB, GR-1250, box 1, file 2.

40 "Testimony of W.J. Stroud," 21 July 1958, BCA, SNB, GR-1250, box 1, file 2.

41 These matters were the subject of much discussion among Lett and the consulting engineers. See Pratley to Lett, 18 July 1958, BCA, SNB, GR-1250, box 10, file 1; Lett to Freeman, 7 November 1958, and Farris to Masters, 10 November 1958, BCA, SNB, GR-1250, box 10, file 2.

42 Information for this paragraph is taken from "Testimony of H. Minshall," 2 October 1958, BCA, SNB, GR-1250, box 1, file 9.

43 Sherwood Lett, *Report of the BC Royal Commission, Second Narrows Bridge Inquiry*, vol. 1 (Victoria: Queen's Printer, 1958), 9.

44 A.H. Finlay to Lett, 9 March 1959, BCA, SNB, GR-1250, box 10, file 3. See also Ralph Freeman and Joseph Otter, "The Collapse of the SNB, Van, June 1958," *Civil Engineering*, February 1959, transcripts; Freeman to Lett, 6 May 1959; Excerpt from Proceedings – The Institution of Civil Engineers, vol. 14, sessions 1958-59, N8; and J.A. Merchant [Association of Professional Engineers of British Columbia] to Lett, 29 December 1959, BCA, SNB, GR-1250, box 10, file 3.

45 Lett to Mrs. McDonald, 29 December 1958, BCA, SNB, GR-1250, box 10, file 2. See also Mary McDonald and Barbara McKibb[i]n to Lett, 15 December 1958, BCA, SNB, GR-1250, box 10, file 2.

46 "Steel Men Halt $90 Million Jobs," *Vancouver Sun*, 23 June 1959, 1; "'Prove Bridge Safe' Demand of Strikers," *Vancouver Sun*, 24 June 1959, 1; "Ironworkers Going Back on Bridge," *Vancouver Sun*, 27 June 1959, 1; "Bridge Crew Defies Second Court Order," *Vancouver Sun*, 29 June 1959, 1. On the fallout of these tactics for the union leadership, see "Proceedings of Trial of Thomas E. McGrath," 30 November 1959, UBC, Tom McGrath Fonds, box 2, file 16.

47 Brief on ironworkers' wages, circa 1959, UBC, *Trade Union Research Bureau* (hereafter *TURB*), box 41, file 2.

48 Seventeen men died in the collapse proper and one in the clean-up, but the union seems to have focused only on the number of dead ironworkers in its appeal.

49 Brief in support of Ironworkers L-97 contract demands, 1962, UBC, *TURB*, box 18, file 17. Even when other labour groups criticized the special treatment afforded the collapse victims, they still emphasized the financial as opposed to the safety aspects of workplace danger, arguing for more money for all widows and injured workers rather than calling for improved safety measures. See Rae Eddie (IWA l-357) to E.A. Jamieson (VDLC), 20 July 1958, UBC, *VDLC*, series C, box 2, file 31.

50 "New Bridge Open amid Subdued Air," *Vancouver Daily Province,* 26 August 1960, 1; "Bennett's $2 Riding on Border Highway," *Vancouver Sun,* 26 August 1960, 1; "Everyone Straight Man in Phil's Show," *Vancouver Sun,* 26 August 1960, 1.

51 Income differences from table in *The Canadian Encyclopedia,* 2nd ed., vol. 2 (Edmonton: Hurtig, 1988), 1051. See also John Porter, *The Vertical Mosaic: An Analysis of Social Class and Power in Canada* (Toronto: University of Toronto Press, 1965); and Bryan Palmer, *Working-Class Experience: The Rise and Reconstitution of Canadian Labour, 1800-1980* (Toronto: Butterworth, 1983), 229-31.

52 On the postwar compromise, see Craig Heron, *The Canadian Labour Movement: A Brief History* (Toronto: James Lorimer, 1996), 75-84; Bryan Palmer, *Working-Class Experience: Re-Thinking the History of Canadian Labour, 1800-1991,* 2nd ed. (Toronto: McClelland and Stewart, 1992). On the American example, see Mike Davis, *Prisoners of the American Dream: Politics and Economy in the History of the US Working Class* (London: Verso, 1986).

53 On the importance of breadwinning to nineteenth- and early-twentieth-century unionism, see Steven Penfold, "'Have You No Manhood in You?': Gender and Class in the Cape Breton Coal Towns, 1920-1926," *Acadiensis* 23, 2 (1994), 21-44; also in Parr and Rosenfeld, eds., *Gender and History in Canada,* 270-93; Christina Burr, *Spreading the Light: Work and Labour Reform in Late Nineteenth-Century Toronto* (Toronto: University of Toronto Press, 1999); Ava Baron, ed., *Work Engendered: Toward a New History of American Labor* (Ithaca: Cornell University Press, 1991).

Chapter 4: In the Mountains
This chapter was originally published in *BC Studies* and is reprinted with permission.

1 Mountaineering is an iconic modern activity. Although its historians like to begin their books by citing premodern climbers, these are exceptions; its actual history begins in the latter half of the eighteenth century. Along with developments such as the expansion of mercantile capitalism and overseas exploration, mountaineering was one of the activities that helped to lend a positive connotation to the word "risk" in the English language, framing it as something dynamic and stimulating. See Anthony Giddens and Christopher Pierson, *Conversations with Anthony Giddens: Making Sense of Modernity* (Stanford, CA: Stanford University Press, 1998). Mountaineering historians who cite premodern examples include Walt Unsworth, *Hold the Heights: The Foundations of Mountaineering* (London: Hodder and Stoughton, 1993); and Chris Jones, *Climbing in North America* (Berkeley: University of California Press, 1976).

2 On criticism of suburbanization, see Doug Owram, "Safe in the Hands of Mother Suburbia: Home and Community, 1950-1965," in *Born at the Right Time: A History of the Baby-Boom Generation* (Toronto: University of Toronto Press, 1996); and Veronica Strong-Boag, "Home Dreams: Women and the Suburban Experiment in Canada, 1945-1960," *Canadian Historical Review* 72, 4 (1991): 471-504.

3 Mona Gleason, *Normalizing the Ideal: Psychology, Schooling, and the Family in Postwar Canada* (Toronto: University of Toronto Press, 1999), 53.

4 On a similar process at work in early-twentieth-century conservation efforts, see Tina Loo, "Making a Modern Wilderness: Conserving Wildlife in Twentieth-Century Canada," *Canadian Historical Review* 82, 1 (2001): 92-121. On this process as related to modernity more generally, see John Jervis, *Transgressing the*

Modern: Explorations in the Western Experience of Otherness (Oxford: Blackwell, 1999), 134-56.

5 See Patricia Jasen, *Wild Things: Nature, Culture and Tourism in Ontario, 1790-1914* (Toronto: University of Toronto Press, 1995), 105-32; and Gail Bederman, *Manliness and Civilization: A Cultural History of Gender and Race in the United States, 1880-1917* (Chicago: University of Chicago Press, 1995), 170-215.

6 On the role of gender and national identity in creating an interest in mountaineering, see Peter H. Hansen, "Albert Smith, the Alpine Club, and the Invention of Mountaineering in Mid-Victorian Britain," *Journal of British Studies* 34 (July 1995): 300-24; Peter H. Hansen, "Confetti of Empire: The Conquest of Everest in Nepal, India, Britain and New Zealand," *Comparative Studies in Society and History* 42, 2 (2000): 207-32; and Raymond Huel, "The Creation of the Alpine Club of Canada: An Early Manifestation of Canadian Nationalism," *Prairie Forum* 15, 1 (1990): 25-43.

7 Huel, "The Creation"; Susan Leslie, "In the Western Mountains: Early Mountaineering in British Columbia," *Sound Heritage* 8, 4 (1980); Hansen, "Albert Smith"; Peter H. Hansen, "Vertical Boundaries, National Identities: British Mountaineering on the Frontiers of Europe and the Empire, 1868-1914," *Journal of Imperial and Commonwealth History* 24, 1 (January 1996): 48-71.

8 The BCMC first went by this name in 1909 after initially being called the Vancouver Mountaineering Club.

9 Interview with Esther and Martin Kafer, Oral History Project (hereafter OHP), 1997, in *British Columbia Mountaineering Club Archives* (hereafter BCMC), box 9, vol. 10.

10 Statistics are culled from information published regularly in the postwar years in *The BC Mountaineer.*

11 Leslie, "In the Western Mountains."

12 The statistics on BCMC members' class positions are based on the divisions outlined in Michael Zweig, *The Working-Class Majority: America's Best Kept Secret* (New York: Cornell University Press, 2000). Zweig assesses class position based on power over production rather than on income. When BCMC members' names are checked against city directories for three different years (1949, 1959, and 1969, respectively), the following class positions emerge: in 1949, 35 middle-class and 22 working-class positions (of which 11 involved skilled workers); in 1959, 42 middle-class and 21 working-class positions (of which 17 involved skilled workers); and in 1969, 58 middle-class and 38 working-class positions (of which 31 involved skilled workers). In each of these years, the number of members for whom I could determine class position is less than the overall membership. Other historians of mountaineering note the upper- and middle-class status of its participants; see Sherry B. Ortner, *Life and Death on Mount Everest: Sherpas and Himalayan Mountaineering* (Princeton: Princeton University Press, 1999); Hansen, "Albert Smith"; and Unsworth, *Hold the Heights.*

13 BCMC members' residence information is based on comparisons between membership lists published in *The BC Mountaineer* and city directories.

14 Jean Barman, *The West beyond the West: A History of British Columbia* (Toronto: University of Toronto Press, 1991), 271. On earlier processes of transportation development that broke down barriers of time and space in the region, see Cole Harris, *The Resettlement of British Columbia: Essays on Colonialism and Geographical Change* (Vancouver: UBC Press, 1998), 161-93.

15 See Barman, *The West beyond the West;* John R. Wedley, "A Development Tool: W.A.C. Bennett and the PGE Railway," *BC Studies* 117 (1998): 29-50; Stephen G. Tomblin, "W.A.C. Bennett and Province-Building in British Columbia," *BC Studies* 85 (1990): 45-61.

16 On the general acceptance of the forty-hour work week as standard, see *Hours of Work in Canada: An Historical Series* (Ottawa: Canada Department of Labour, Economics and Research Branch, 1971).

17 Strong-Boag, "Home Dreams"; Robert Rutherdale, "Fatherhood and Masculine Domesticity during the Baby Boom: Consumption and Leisure in Advertising and Life Stories," in Lori Chambers and Edgar André Montigny, eds., *Family Matters: Papers in Post-Confederation Canadian Family History* (Toronto: Canadian Scholars' Press, 1998), 309-33; Robert Rutherdale, "Fatherhood and the Social Construction of Memory: Breadwinning and Male Parenting on a Job Frontier, 1945-1966," in Joy Parr and Mark Rosenfeld, eds., *Gender and History in Canada* (Toronto: Copp Clark, 1996), 357-75; Chris Dummitt, "Finding a Place for Father: Selling the Barbecue in Post-War Canada," *Journal of the Canadian Historical Association* 8 (1998): 209-23.

18 On modernity's contradictions in this regard, see John Jervis, *Exploring the Modern: Patterns of Western Culture and Civilization* (Oxford: Blackwell, 1998); and Marshall Berman, *"All That Is Solid Melts into Air": The Experience of Modernity,* 2nd ed. (New York: Penguin, 1982).

19 Quotations from Tim Kendrick, ed., *Get Back Alive! Safety in the BC Coast Mountains* (Vancouver: Federation of Mountain Clubs of British Columbia, 1973), 4.

20 R.A.M.[Pilkington], "A Personal Opinion," *The BC Mountaineer* (May 1951).

21 As a promoter of wildlife conservation, the BCMC seems typical of other mountaineering organizations. See PearlAnn Reichwein, "'Hands Off Our National Parks': The Alpine Club of Canada and Hydro-Development Controversies in the Canadian Rockies, 1922-1930," *Journal of the Canadian Historical Association* 6 (1995): 129-55.

22 On the cabins and huts, see Minutes of the British Columbia Mountaineering Club for appropriate years, in *BCMC,* box 8, files 1-3; interviews with Dick Chambers, Esther and Martin Kafer, and Irene and Jack Apps, in OHP, *BCMC,* box 9, vol. 10.

23 Interview with Ralph Hutchinson, in OHP, *BCMC,* box 9, vol. 9; and interview with Esther and Martin Kafer, in OHP, *BCMC,* box 9, vol. 10.

24 For some American climbers' thoughts about British Columbia climbers, see Chris Jones, *Climbing in North America* (Berkeley: University of California Press, 1976).

25 Interview with Ralph Hutchinson, in OHP, *BCMC,* box 9, vol. 9.

26 Dick Culbert, *A Climber's Guide to the Coastal Ranges of British Columbia,* 2nd ed. (Vancouver: Alpine Club of Canada, 1969).

27 Interview with Esther and Martin Kafer, in OHP, *BCMC,* box 9, vol. 10.

28 "Turkey Dinner," *The BC Mountaineer* ([month unknown] 1970).

29 E. Joyce Davies [secretary of BCMC] to Hon. W.K. Kiernan, Minister of Recreation and Conservation, 27 November 1970, in *BCMC,* box 1, file 30.

30 For the club's involvement in trail construction, see various entries in "Hut and Trail Construction," in *BCMC,* box 9, vol. 45.

31 "Mt. Shuksan, September 1, 2, 3, 1956," in *BCMC,* box 3, file 27. See also "Editorial," *The BC Mountaineer* (August 1956); and "The Mountaineer's Ten Commandments," *The BC Mountaineer* (March 1960).

32 "Snowcraft Lecture and Practice Climb," *The BC Mountaineer* (April 1950).
33 "Quick Tricks for Mountain Popularity (or How to Get Pushed Off Devil's Leap)," *The BC Mountaineer* (October 1945).
34 When commenting on BCMC trips in recent years, both Martin and Esther Kafer cited the lack of leadership as a serious problem. Interview with Esther and Martin Kafer, in OHP, *BCMC*, box 9, vol. 10.
35 Michael Kimmel, *Manhood in America: A Cultural History* (New York: Free Press, 1996), 236, 251-52; William Whyte, *The Organization Man* (New York: Simon and Schuster, 1956). This dilemma is also addressed in Barbara Ehrenreich, *The Hearts of Men: American Dreams and the Flight from Commitment* (New York: Doubleday, 1983).
36 Statistics on sex ratios in the BCMC are culled from membership lists published in *The BC Mountaineer*.
37 On trips breaking up, see, for example, "Mount Arrowsmith Trip, May 22-24, 1954," in *BCMC*, box 3, file 27; and "Interview with Jim Woodfield," in OHP, *BCMC*, box 9, vol. 12. On the experience of a woman climber in the ACC during a slightly earlier period, which also provides evidence of the gendering of skill, see PearlAnn Reichwein and Karen Fox, "Margaret Fleming and the Alpine Club of Canada: A Woman's Place in Mountain Leisure and Literature, 1932-1952," *Journal of Canadian Studies* 36, 3 (Fall 2001): 35-60.
38 Women's role as social organizers is apparent in the minutes of the Executive for most years and is commented upon in an interview with Joan Ford, in OHP, *BCMC*, box 9, vol. 8. Information on committee members and chairs was published annually in *The BC Mountaineer*. On Kafer, see the interview with Esther and Martin Kafer, in OHP, *BCMC*, box 9, vol. 10.
39 "Snowcraft and Icecraft in Mountaineering," by Eric C. Brooks, Lecture Course in Mountaincraft [lecture transcripts], 22 March to 26 April 1956, in *BCMC*, box 8, file 7.
40 Tim Kendrick, ed., *Get Back Alive! Safety in the BC Coast Mountains* (Vancouver: Federation of Mountain Clubs of British Columbia, 1973).
41 "Safety in the Mountains," by Ian Kay, Lecture Course in Mountaincraft [lecture transcripts], 22 March to 26 April 1956, in *BCMC*, box 8, file 7.
42 On manly responsibility and ethics of citizenship in the Cold War, see Elaine Tyler May, *Homeward Bound: American Families in the Cold War* (New York: Basic Books, 1988); and Robert Griswold, *Fatherhood in America: A History* (New York: Basic Books, 1993).
43 "The First Canadian Ascent of Mount McKinley," *The BC Mountaineer* (July 1961). See also [press release from Paddy Sherman], 4 May 1944 [incorrectly dated; accurate date appears to be 1958], in *BCMC*, box 4, file 11.
44 "Lost on Seymour," *The BC Mountaineer* (October 1956).
45 "The Mountaineer's Ten Commandments," *The BC Mountaineer* (March 1960).
46 "The Climbing Code," partially reprinted from the Seattle Mountaineers' monthly paper *The Mountaineer*, in *The BC Mountaineer* (August 1953).
47 "Mount McKinley," *The BC Mountaineer* (July 1960).
48 Dorothy Hodgson, ed., *Gendered Modernities: Ethnographic Perspectives* (New York: Palgrove, 2001); Jervis, *Exploring the Modern*. Gendering of the instrumental-ornamental divide is also something that appeared frequently in the late 1960s reporting on the Royal Commission on the Status of Women. See Barbara Freeman, "Framing Feminine/Feminist: English-Language Press Coverage of the Royal

Commission on the Status of Women in Canada, 1968," in *Women in Canadian Society – les femmes de la société Canadienne* (Ottawa: International Council of Canadian Studies, 1995), 11-31.

49 On the Taylor accident, see Minutes of the British Columbia Mountaineering Club for 1952, in *BCMC*, box 8, files 1-3; "Holy Cross, June 28-29th," *The BC Mountaineer* (July 1952); "City Woman Injured in Mountain Plunge," *Vancouver Province*, 2 July 1952, 17; "Mountaineers Rescue Girl," *Vancouver Sun*, 2 July 1952, 1.

50 R.A.P., "Mountain Literature," *The BC Mountaineer* (September 1951).

51 "April 18th – Rock Slide," *The BC Mountaineer* (May 1948).

52 On the McKinley expedition, see "McKinley Climb Worth the Pain of Frostbite," *Vancouver Sun*, 8 June 1961, in *BCMC*, box 4, file 29; "The First Canadian Ascent of Mount McKinley," *The BC Mountaineer* (July 1961); and interviews with Ralph Hutchinson and Jim Woodfield, in OHP, *BCMC*, box 9, vols. 9 and 12.

53 See Owram, *Born at the Right Time*, 204-10. Although Owram notes the romanticist and experiential critiques of the 1960s, he, too, readily downplays its connection to earlier movements (such as the beat movement and existentialism); he fails to see how such criticisms are structured into the very process of modernity itself.

54 On the frustration of mountaineers having to face questions about why they climb, see Leslie, "In the Western Mountains"; and Ortner, *Life and Death on Mount Everest*.

55 "So You Climb, Do You?" *The BC Mountaineer* (March 1959).

56 [Report of Speech by Dr. Norman McKenzie] *The BC Mountaineer* (May 1951).

57 "Brief to the Royal Commission on Forests for the Province of British Columbia, 1955," in *BCMC*, box 1, file 8.

58 "Mount Shuksan, August 31, September 1-2," *The BC Mountaineer* (December 1946).

59 "Paul Binkert," in *BCMC*, box 4, files 36-37.

60 Minutes of the British Columbia Mountaineering Club, 1967, in *BCMC*, box 8, files 1-3.

61 This conflict between specialization and totality is one that Freud put at the beginning of his discussion of the effect of civilization on the individual. See Sigmund Freud, *Civilization and its Discontents*, trans. by James Strachey (New York: Norton, 1961).

62 Leslie, "In the Western Mountains." On the German search for a more authentic climbing experience, see Unsworth, "'They Have Picked Out the Plums and Left Us the Stones," in *Hold the Heights*, 102-4.

63 Kimmel, *Manhood in America*, 236. For an enlightening discussion of how these same kinds of tensions were exhibited in Canadians' attitudes toward men and gambling, see Susanne Morton, *At Odds: Gambling and Canadians, 1919-1969* (Toronto: University of Toronto Press, 2003). Although this debate between rough and respectable is usually discussed in terms of class – see Roger Horowitz, ed., *Boys and Their Toys: Masculinity, Technology and Class in America* (London and New York: Routledge, 2001) – the presence of this debate in a relatively homogenous middle-class organization suggests that we need to look beyond the material relations of production for an adequate explanation.

64 Wolfgang Gerson, in the *Journal of the Royal Architectural Institute of Canada* 38, 4 (April 1961): 71, cited in Rhodri Windsor Liscombe, *The New Spirit: Modern Ar-*

chitecture in Vancouver, 1938-1963 (Montreal and Vancouver: Canadian Centre for Architecture and Douglas and McIntyre, 1997), 19-20.

Chapter 5: Before the Courts and on the Couch

1 Robertson Davies, *Leaven of Malice* (1954; reprint, New York: Penguin, 1981), 195.
2 On the history of murder in Canada, see Neil Boyd, *The Last Dance: Murder in Canada* (Scarborough: Prentice-Hall, 1988). Psychiatrists and psychologists also involved themselves in many areas of Vancouver life, including the school system, as shown in Gerald E. Thomson, "'Not an Attempt to Coddle Children': Dr. Charles Hegler Gundry and the Mental Hygiene Division of the Vancouver School Board, 1939-1969," *Historical Studies in Education/Revue d'histoire de l'éducation* 14, 2 (2002): 247-78.
3 The more common gendered approach to capital cases involves the study of women sentenced to death. See F. Murray Greenwood and Beverley Boissery, *Uncertain Justice: Canadian Women and Capital Punishment, 1754-1953* (Toronto: Dundurn Press, [2000]); Franca Iacovetta and Karen Dubinsky, "Murder, Womanly Virtue and Motherhood: The Case of Angelina Napolitano, 1911-1922," *Canadian Historical Review* 72, 4 (1991): 505-31.
4 This fits in with a long history of men's allowed violence. See, for example, Ingeborg Breines, Robert Connell, and Ingrid Eide, eds., *Male Roles, Masculinities and Violence: A Culture of Peace Perspective* (Paris: UNESCO, 2000); Angus McLaren, "Murderers," *The Trials of Masculinity: Policing Sexual Boundaries, 1870-1930* (Chicago: University of Chicago Press, 1997), 111-31; Robert Nye, *Masculinity and Male Codes of Honor in Modern France* (New York and Oxford: Oxford University Press, 1993); Peter Spierenburg, ed., *Men and Violence: Gender, Honor and Rituals in Modern Europe and America* (Columbus: Ohio State University Press, 1998).
5 Katherine Arnup, *Education for Motherhood: Advice for Mothers in Twentieth-Century Canada* (Toronto: University of Toronto Press, 1994); Cynthia Comacchio, *Nations are Built of Babies: Saving Ontario's Mothers and Children, 1900-1940* (Montreal and Kingston: McGill-Queen's University Press, 1993).
6 This type of process, which occurred earlier in the century, is nicely captured in McLaren, *Trials of Masculinity,* although it does seem that the extent of medical involvement had grown significantly by the postwar years.
7 On the involvement of psychiatrists in defining manhood in the postwar years, see Elise Chenier, "The Criminal Sexual Psychopath in Canada: Sex, Psychiatry and the Law at Mid-Century," *Canadian Bulletin of Medical History* 20, 1 (2003): 75-101. This medicalization of manhood in these years is also noted in Edward Shorter, *A History of Psychiatry: From the Era of Asylum to the Age of Prozac* (New York: John Wiley, 1997), 289-90.
8 D. Owen Carrigan, *Crime and Punishment in Canada: A History* (Toronto: McClelland and Stewart, 1991), 398-99.
9 Diana Doherty and John W. Ekstedt, *Conflict, Control and Supervision: The History of the Corrections Branch in British Columbia* (Burnaby, BC: Simon Fraser University Institute for Studies in Criminal Justice Policy, 1990), 69-80.
10 On psychology at mid-century, see Mona Gleason, "Prelude to the Postwar Agenda," *Normalizing the Ideal: Psychology, Schooling and the Family in Postwar Canada* (Toronto: University of Toronto Press, 1999), 19-36.
11 For trends in the history of Canadian psychiatry in the early and mid-twentieth century, see Geoffrey Reaume, *Remembrance of Patients Past: Patient Life at the*

Toronto Hospital for the Insane, 1870-1940 (Toronto: Oxford University Press, 2000), 15-20; Harley D. Dickinson, *The Two Psychiatries: The Transformation of Psychiatric Work in Saskatchewan, 1905-1984* (Regina: Canadian Plains Research Centre, 1989). On the use of electric-shock therapy at Oakalla, see Doherty and Edstedt, *Conflict, Care and Control,* 80. Earlier twentieth-century psychiatry had been more inclined, like psychology, to align itself with eugenics; see Ian Dowbiggin, "'Keeping This Young Country Sane': C.K. Clarke, Immigration Restriction, and Canadian Psychiatry, 1890-1925," *Canadian Historical Review* 76, 4 (1995): 598-627. Useful American books include: Gerald Grob, *From Asylum to Community: Mental Health Policy in Modern America* (New Jersey: Princeton University Press, 1991); Robert Castel, Françoise Castel, and Anne Lovell, *The Psychiatric Society,* trans. Arthur Goldhammer (New York: Columbia University Press, 1982).

12 On the promises and perils of this kind of case-file research, see the essays in Franca Iacovetta and Wendy Mitchinson, eds., *On the Case: Explorations in Social History* (Toronto: University of Toronto Press, 1998), especially the "Introduction" by the editors, 3-21, and Karen Dubinsky, "Telling Stories about Dead People," 359-66.

13 The seven cases in which psychiatrists appeared were those of Hainen, Ducharme, Matthews, Hoodley, McKenna, Casagrande, and Fulton.

14 "Condensed Summary," *R. v. Henderson,* Library and Archives Canada (hereafter LAC), Capital Case Files, RG 13, 1664, CC 630, part 2; "Condensed Summary," *R. v. Lifton,* LAC, Capital Case Files, RG 13, 1837, CC 901, vol. 3.

15 "Condensed Summary," *R. v. Hainen,* LAC, Capital Case Files, RG 13, 1650, CC 583, part 1.

16 A.M. Manson to Gordon F. Bradley, Secretary of State, 4 April 1953, LAC, Capital Case Files, RG 13, 1715, CC 764, part 1.

17 A.M. Manson to Hon. E. Davie Fulton, Minister of Justice, 29 September 1958, LAC, Capital Case Files, RG 13, 1771, CC 850, vol. 1, part 1.

18 Karen Halttunen, *Murder Most Foul: The Killer and the American Gothic Imagination* (Cambridge, MA: Harvard University Press, 1998), 4, 210, also notes this tendency toward the medicalization of murder and the construction of the murderer as a "mental alien."

19 "Condensed Summary," *R. v. McKenna,* LAC, Capital Case Files, RG 13, 1762, CC 833, vol. 1, part 2.

20 W.J. Graham to [Prime Minister], [early April 1956], LAC, Capital Case Files, RG 13, 1750, CC 812, vol. 1, part 1.

21 Testimony of G. Casagrande, *R. v. Casagrande,* LAC, Capital Case Files, RG 13, 1771, CC 850, vol. 2, part 1.

22 "Condensed Summary," *R. v. Casagrande,* LAC, Capital Case Files, RG 13, 1771, CC 850, vol. 1, part 2.

23 A.M. Manson to Hon. E. Davie Fulton, Minister of Justice, 29 September 1958, LAC, Capital Case Files, RG 13, 1771, CC 850, vol. 1, part 1.

24 "Condensed Summary," *R. v. McKenna,* LAC, Capital Case Files, RG 13, 1762, CC 833, vol. 1, part 2.

25 On the behaviourist turn in postwar psychology, see Gleason, *Normalizing the Ideal.*

26 J.M. Coady to Secretary of State, 20 December 1952, LAC, Capital Case Files, RG 13, 1709, CC 750, part 1.

27 J.M. Coady to Secretary, 3 February 1955, LAC, Capital Case Files, RG 13, 1740, CC 800, vol. 1, part 1.
28 A.M Manson to Hon. Colin Gibson, Secretary of State, 20 June 1947, LAC, Capital Case Files, RG 13, 1664, CC 629, part 1.
29 On overmothering, see Gleason, *Normalizing the Ideal*, 64; Michael Kimmel, *Manhood in America: A Cultural History* (New York: Free Press, 1996), 229; Mary Louise Adams, *The Trouble with Normal: Postwar Youth and the Making of Heterosexuality* (Toronto: University of Toronto Press, 1997).
30 Joseph Carlin to Minister of Justice, 15 October 1945, LAC, Capital Case Files, RG 13, 1650, CC583, part 1.
31 B.M. Isman to Minister of Justice, 11 September 1947, LAC, Capital Case Files, RG 13, 1664, CC 629, part 1. Justice Manson also brought up this possibility of the negative effect of the mother's mental illness in his letter to Ottawa, A.M. Manson to Hon. Colin Gibson, Secretary of State, 20 June 1947, LAC, Capital Case Files, RG 13, 1664, CC 629, part 1.
32 John S. Burton to J.O. Wilson, 7 December 1955, LAC, Capital Case Files, RG 13, 1750, CC 812, vol. 1, part 1.
33 Ibid.
34 R.G.E. Richmond to MacLeod, 5 May 1956, LAC, Capital Case Files, RG 13, 1750, CC 812, vol. 1, part 1.
35 Mark Moss, *Manliness and Militarism: Educating Young Boys in Ontario for War* (Toronto: Oxford University Press, 2001); Colin Howell, *Northern Sandlots: A Social History of Maritime Baseball* (Toronto: University of Toronto Press, 1995).
36 "Report of the Provincial Probation Officer re: Harry Medos," LAC, Capital Case Files, RG 13, 1664, CC 629, part 1.
37 "Condensed Summary," *R. v. Fulton*, LAC, Capital Case Files, RG 13, 1821, CC 941, vol. 2, part 3.
38 C.F. Stephens to Minister of Justice, 8 April 1954, LAC, Capital Case Files, RG 13, 1726, CC 783, vol. 1, part 1.
39 S. Jenkins, Pastor, Pender Christian Mission, to Hon. Stuart S. Garson, Minister of Justice, 23 March 1954; Reverend Donald D. Macqueen, Vicar of St. Peter's Anglican Church, to Minister of Justice, 15 April 1954, LAC, Capital Case Files, RG 13, 1726, CC 783, vol. 1, part 1.
40 Jack O'Reilly to Hon. E. Davie Fulton, Minister of Justice, 20 November 1957, LAC, Capital Case Files, RG 13, 1763, CC 834, vol. 1, part 1.
41 W. Braden to Director of Remissions, 8 October 1957, LAC, Capital Case Files, RG 13, 1763, CC 834, vol. 1, part 1.
42 On postwar manhood and breadwinning, see Robert Rutherdale, "Fatherhood and the Social Construction of Memory: Breadwinning and Male Parenting on a Job Frontier, 1945-1966," in Joy Parr and Mark Rosenfeld, eds., *Gender and History in Canada* (Toronto: Copp Clark, 1996), 357-75; Robert Rutherdale, "Fatherhood and Masculine Domesticity during the Baby Boom: Consumption and Leisure in Advertising and Life Stories," in Lori Chambers and Edgar André Montigny, eds., *Family Matters: Papers in Post-Confederation Canadian Family History* (Toronto: Canada Scholars' Press, 1998), 309-33. Useful counterpoints in the American literature include: Elaine Tyler May, *Homeward Bound: American Families in the Cold War Era* (New York: Basic Books, 1988); Robert Griswold, *Fatherhood in America: A History* (New York: Basic Books, 1993); Kimmel, *Manhood in America*.

43   "Gunman Bargained for Freedom," *Vancouver Sun,* 10 February 1962, 1, 2C.
44   Testimony of M.M. Peterson, *R. v. Medos,* LAC, Capital Case Files, RG 13, 1664, CC 629, part 3.
45   Testimony of M.M. Peterson, *R. v. Henderson,* 2 June 1947, LAC, Capital Case Files, RG 13, 1664, CC 630, part 3.
46   See the large number of letters in LAC, Capital Case Files, RG 13, 1664, CC 630, part 1.
47   Adams, *The Trouble With Normal;* Franca Iacovetta, "Gossip, Contest, and Power in the Making of Suburban Bad Girls: Toronto, 1945-1960," *Canadian Historical Review* 80, 4 (1999): 585-623.
48   S. Jenkins, Pastor, Pender Christian Mission, to Hon. Stuart S. Garson, Minister of Justice, 23 March 1954, LAC, Capital Case Files, RG 13, 1726, CC 783, vol. 1, part 1.
49   A.M. Manson to Colin Gibson, 20 June 1947, LAC, Capital Case Files, RG 13, 1664, CC 630, part 1.
50   Condensed Summary, *R. v. Fulton,* LAC, Capital Case Files, RG 13, 1821, CC 941, vol. 2, part 3; Testimony of G.H. Fulton, *R. v. Fulton,* LAC, Capital Case Files, RG 13, 1821, CC 941, vol. 1, part 2; "Jury against clemency as killer found guilty," *Vancouver Daily Province,* 21 October 1965, 1-2.
51   A.M. Manson to Hon. Senator W. Ross Macdonald, Solicitor General, 27 April 1956, LAC, Capital Case Files, RG 13, 1753, CC 820, vol. 2, part 1.
52   (Mrs.) Iris E. Lorntzsen to Norman D. Mullins, 22 February 1957, LAC, Capital Case Files, RG 13, 1753, CC 820, vol. 7, part 2.
53   Arnold Wennberg to Minister of Justice, 11 November 1947, LAC, Capital Case Files, RG 13, 1664, CC 630, part 1.
54   Ellen Watson to Minister of Justice, 11 November 1947, LAC, Capital Case Files, RG 13, 1664, CC 630, part 1.
55   John S. Burton to Hon. Stuart Garson, Minister of Justice, 18 April 1956, LAC, Capital Case Files, RG 13, 1750, CC 812, vol. 1, part 1.
56   "Another Grandma" to Minister of Justice, 11 November 1947, LAC, Capital Case Files, RG 13, 1664, CC 630, part 1.
57   Doris Boynes to Minister of Justice, 10 November 1947, LAC, Capital Case Files, RG 13, 1664, CC 630, part 1.
58   "Deliberate Act of Innocence Hid Intention of Murder, Says Hoare," *Vancouver Daily Province,* 27 February 1947, 1, 9.
59   "Two Policemen Die in Gun Fight," *Vancouver Daily Province,* 26 February 1947, 1.
60   Estelle B. Freedman, "Uncontrolled Desires: The Response to the Sexual Psychopath, 1920-1960," in Kathy Peiss and Christina Simmons, eds., *Passion and Power: Sexuality in History* (Philadelphia: Temple University Press, 1989), 199-225. On the cultural history of concern over criminal sexual psychopaths in Canada, see Chenier, "The Criminal Sexual Psychopath"; Adams, *The Trouble with Normal,* 122-23.
61   "$250 Reward Posted in Woman's Mystery Death," *Vancouver Sun,* 10 November 1949, 1-2.
62   "Body of Woman in False Creek," *Vancouver Sun,* 9 November 1949, 1-2.
63   "$250 Reward Posted in Woman's Mystery Death," *Vancouver Sun,* 10 November 1949, 1-2.

64 British Columbia Police Crime Report on Rex Ducharme, M.T. Phipps, Vancouver Detachment, 23 March 1950, LAC, Capital Case Files, RG 13, 1688, CC 701, vol. 1, part 1.

65 J.P.S. Cathcart to M.F. Gallagher, 21 June 1950, LAC, Capital Case Files, RG 13, 1688, CC 701, vol. 1, part 1.

66 J.P.S. Cathcart to F.W. Thompson, 11 July 1950, LAC, Capital Case Files, RG 13, 1688, CC 701, vol. 1, part 1.

67 A.M. Manson to Secretary of State, LAC, Capital Case Files, RG 13, 1688, CC 701, vol. 1, part 1.

68 Jack Webster, "Ducharme Letter Court Sensation," *Vancouver Sun*, 14 March 1950, 1-2; Frederick Rodger Ducharme to Stuart Garson, Minister of Justice, 22 June 1950, LAC, Capital Case Files, RG 13, 1688, CC 701, vol. 1, part 1; Frederick Graham Farnsworth, "The Ducharme Murder Case: The Evidence of the Death of Miss Blanche Verne Fisher by Frederick Rodger Ducharme," 30 March 1950, LAC, Capital Case Files, RG 13, 1688, CC 701, vol. 1, part 1.

69 Jack Webster, "Fred Ducharme 'Just Fool' His Lawyer Pleads in Court," *Vancouver Sun*, 21 March 1950, 1-2.

70 That Wallberg, the woman whom Matthews beat but did not kill, was white drew attention, too. In fact, the popular link between aggressive black sexuality and vulnerable white womanhood tainted memories of the trial. A year later, the director of the federal government's Remissions Office, A.J. MacLeod, referred back to the Matthews case as one in which a twenty-year-old murderer had been executed. But MacLeod misremembered the racial details of the case. He claimed that it had been a "very bad case" in which the African American Matthews had killed a black woman for getting in the way of his relationship with a white girlfriend. But Matthews' girlfriend had been black, and Wallberg had been the white neighbour. Nevertheless, the racial anxiety around black men's sexuality and especially the threat of black men's relations with white women seem to have distorted McLeod's recollections. See "Memorandum to the Solicitor General," 5 April 1955, LAC, Capital Case Files, RG 13, 1740, CC 800, vol. 2, part 1.

71 See Gail Bederman's comments on the image of the "Negro rapist" in "'The White Man's Civilization on Trial': Ida B. Wells, Representations of Lynching, and Northern Middle-Class Manhood," in *Manliness and Civilization: A Cultural History of Gender and Race in the United States, 1880-1917* (Chicago: University of Chicago Press, 1995), 45-76.

72 See, for example, "'I Love You' Says Slayer from Dock," *Vancouver Sun*, 16 June 1953, 1-2.

73 J.V. Clyne to Secretary of State, LAC, Capital Case Files, RG 13, 1717, CC 768, vol. 1, part 1.

74 J.P.S. Cathcart to A.J. McLeod, Director of Justice, 19 September 1953, LAC, Capital Case Files, RG 13, 1717, CC 768, vol. 1, part 1.

75 R.G.E. Richmond to Dr. E.A. Campbell, 15 October 1953, LAC, Capital Case Files, RG 13, 1717, CC 768, vol. 1, part 1.

76 On the postwar history of capital punishment, see Carrigan, *Crime and Punishment*, 379-80; C.H.S. Jayewardene, "The Canadian Movement against the Death Penalty," *Canadian Journal of Criminology and Corrections*, 14-15 (1972-73): 367-82;

Carolyn Strange, "The Politics of Punishment: The Death Penalty in Canada, 1867-1976," *Manitoba Law Journal* 23, 3 (1996): 594-619; and Carolyn Strange, "The Undercurrents of Penal Culture: Punishment of the Body in Mid-Twentieth-Century Canada," *Law and History Review* 19, 2 (2001): 343-85.

77 Carolyn Strange, "Discretionary Justice: Political Culture and the Death Penalty in New South Wales and Ontario, 1890-1920," in Carolyn Strange, ed., *Qualities of Mercy: Justice, Punishment, and Discretion* (Vancouver: UBC Press, 1996), 130-65. On the rationalization of punishment in the modern era more generally, see Pieter Spierenburg, *The Spectacle of Suffering: Executions and the Evolution of Repression, from a Preindustrial Metropolis to the European Experience* (Cambridge, UK: Cambridge University Press, 1984); David Garland, *Punishment and Modern Society: A Study in Social Theory* (Chicago: University of Chicago Press, 1990); Michel Foucault, *Discipline and Punish: The Birth of the Prison,* 2nd ed. (New York: Vantage, 1995); Greg Smith, "Civilized People Don't Want to See That Sort of Thing: The Decline of Capital Punishment in London, 1760-1840," in Strange, ed., *Qualities of Mercy,* 21-51.

78 On the importance of a murderer's masculinity to his murder trial in early-twentieth-century British Columbia, see McLaren, *The Trials of Masculinity,* 111.

79 Dr. J.P.S. Cathcart, "Every Physician a Psychiatrist," *National Health Review* 7, 4 (January 1939): 1-11; J.P.S. Cathcart, "Mental Illness and War," *National Health Review* (July 1940): 149-51; J.P.S. Cathcart, "Psychological Problems in Post-War Rehabilitation," *Bulletin of the Canadian Psychological Association,* special issue containing proceedings of the First Annual Meeting of the Canadian Psychological Association (April 1941): 31-32. See also Terry Copp, "From Neurasthenia to Post-Traumatic Stress Disorder: Canadian Veterans and the Problem of Persistent Emotional Disabilities," in Peter Neary and J.L. Granatstein, eds., *The Veterans Charter and Post-World War II Canada* (Montreal and Kingston: McGill-Queen's University Press, 1998), 149-59. An interesting coincidence: Cathcart shares a name with the character Colonel Cathcart in Joseph Heller's *Catch-22,* the officer who continually devises new means to get his air men to fly more and more missions.

Chapter 6: On the Road

1 W.A. Bryce, "Luck or Calculated Risk?" *Vancouver Traffic and Safety Council Annual Report* (hereafter VTSC Annual Report), 1960, Vancouver City Archives (hereafter VCA), Mayor's Office fond, 36-E-2, file 129.

2 Most notably, this same approach to risk showed up in the work of the British Columbia Mountaineering Club and in the Workmen's Compensation Board.

3 Bryce, "Luck or Calculated Risk?"

4 The modern version of the reasonable man dates from the rise of the capitalist middle class during the Industrial Revolution. This class insisted on its own superior ability to be sober financial leaders, and they demonstrated these traits in their style of masculine and feminine comportment. See Leonore Davidoff and Catherine Hall, *Family Fortunes: Men and Women of the English Middle Class, 1780-1850* (Chicago: University of Chicago Press, 1987).

5 Ralph Nader, *Unsafe at Any Speed: The Designed-in Dangers of the American Automobile* (New York: Grossman, 1965); Jane Jacobs, *The Death and Life of Great American Cities* (New York: Random House, 1961).

6 Pam Roper, "The Limits of *Laissez-innover:* Canada's Automation Controversy, 1955-1969," *Journal of Canadian Studies* 34, 3 (Autumn 1999): 87-105 at 88.

7 On how this distinction between processed/modern and natural/traditional affected immigrant families, see Franca Iacovetta, "Recipes for Democracy? Gender, Family and Making Female Citizens in Cold War Canada," in Veronica Strong-Boag et al., eds., *Rethinking Canada: The Promise of Women's History,* 4th ed. (Toronto: Oxford University Press, 2002), 299-312.

8 American historians frequently refer to the period after the Second World War and before the late 1960s as the "golden age" of the automobile. See David Thoms, Len Holden, and Tim Claydon, eds., *The Motor Car and Popular Culture in the 20th Century* (Aldershot: Ashgate, 1998); James J. Flink, *The Automobile Age* (Cambridge, MA: MIT Press, 1988); John Jerome, *The Death of the Automobile: The Fatal Effect of the Golden Era, 1955-1970* (New York: Norton, 1972); James E. Vance Jr., *Capturing the Horizon: The Historical Geography of Transportation since the Sixteenth Century* (Baltimore and London: Johns Hopkins University Press, 1986).

9 For statistics on car registrations, see *Annual Report of the Department of Motor Vehicles* (Victoria: King's Printer, 1945-49); and *Annual Report of the Motor Vehicle Branch* (Victoria: King's Printer, 1950-70). On Vancouver's growing population in the postwar years, see Jean Barman, *The West beyond the West: A History of British Columbia* (Toronto: University of Toronto Press, 1991), 273; and Joy Parr, *Domestic Goods: The Material, the Moral and the Economic in the Postwar Years* (Toronto: University of Toronto Press, 1999).

10 "Protecting the Motorist," *Vancouver Province,* 17 January 1952, 4.

11 The filling in of Vancouver is nicely visualized in Bruce MacDonald, *Vancouver: A Visual History* (Vancouver: Talon, 1992). On suburbanization, see Richard Harris and Peter J. Larkham, eds., *Changing Suburbs: Foundation, Form, and Function* (New York: Routledge, 1999). On the gender dynamics of this suburbanization, see Veronica Strong-Boag, "Home Dreams: Women and the Suburban Experiment in Canada, 1945-1960," *Canadian Historical Review* 72, 4 (1991): 471-504. On the relation between automobiles and suburbanization, see Kenneth T. Jackson, *Crabgrass Frontier: The Suburbanization of the United States* (New York: Oxford University Press, 1985). On urban transportation changes in Vancouver, see Henry Ewert, *The Story of the B.C. Electric Railway Company* (North Vancouver: Whitecap Books, 1986).

12 On the family orientation of the era, see Doug Owram, *Born at the Right Time: A History of the Baby-Boom Generation* (Toronto: University of Toronto Press, 1996). Standard Motor Company advertisement in *Vancouver Sun,* 6 May 1950, 50.

13 Advertisements cited here are from *Vancouver Sun,* 5 May 1948, 13; 2 October 1952, 9; and 4 October 1954, 17. On the link between modernity and the automobile, see Wolfgang Sachs, *For Love of the Automobile: Looking Back into the History of Our Desires,* trans. Don Reneau (Berkeley: University of California Press, 1992).

14 Virginia Scharff, "Gender, Electricity, and Automobility," in Martin Wachs and Margaret Crawford, eds., *The Car and the City: The Automobile, the Built Environment, and Daily Urban Life* (Ann Arbor: University of Michigan Press, 1992), 75-85.

15 Clay McShane, *Down the Asphalt Path: The Automobile and the American City* (New York: Columbia University Press, 1994), 152-53.

16 The number of car accidents in Vancouver during this period are drawn from *Annual Report of the Department of Motor Vehicles;* and *Annual Report of the Motor Vehicle Branch.*

17 Sean O'Connell, *The Car in British Society: Class, Gender and Motoring, 1896-1939* (Manchester: Manchester University Press, 1998), 143-44. See also, McShane, "Red Light, Green Light," in *Down the Asphalt Path,* 173-202.

18 My assessment of Vancouver's safety advocates in these paragraphs is based on the minutes of the city's Official Traffic Commission, annual reports, select records of the Vancouver Traffic and Safety Council, and articles published in local, provincial, and national publications by traffic-safety advocates, all of which are quoted from directly to prove more specific points below.

19 Ethel McLellan, "A Lion in the Streets," *Canadian Motorist* (November 1958): 5-6; J.C. Furnas, "And Sudden Death," *Readers' Digest,* reprinted in *Trades and Labor Congress Journal* 25, 9 (September 1946): 42-44.

20 "Automation and the Human Approach," *Canadian Motorist,* October-November 1959, 3.

21 George Hood, in *Annual Report of the Department of Motor Vehicles,* 19; S.C. Kershaw, "Driver Education – Essence of Road Safety," *BC Motorist* 3, 5 (September-October 1964).

22 "Automation and the Human Approach," *Canadian Motorist* (October-November 1959): 3; George R. Jackson, "Don't Overdrive Your Car," *Canadian Motorist* (November 1958): 8.

23 See minutes of the Vancouver OTC for this period. For more on the role of traffic engineers in automobile safety, see McShane, "The Motor Boys Rebuild Cities," in *Down the Asphalt Path,* 203-28.

24 "Drivers Blamed for 99 Pct. of Crashes," *Vancouver Sun,* 5 January 1949; Bill Fletcher, *Vancouver Sun,* 28 October 1958. This is the irony in discussions of engineering car safety during the period: the car companies created the very standards against which they could be judged. So long as cars matched up with how safe the companies said that cars could be, the technology was deemed to be safe. See Jerry L. Mashaw and David L. Harfst, "The Law of a Mobile Society," in *The Struggle for Auto Safety* (Cambridge, MA: Harvard University Press, 1990), 27-46.

25 Fred Bodsworth, "How to Live through a Crash," *Maclean's,* 1 October 1952, 10-11, 55, 57-59.

26 Marcus Van Steen, "Slogans Won't Stop the Highway Slaughter," *Canadian Business* (September 1957): 138-48 at 140.

27 *VTSC Annual Report, 1962,* VCA, Office of the City Clerk, Series 40, 120-C-2, file 148; Robert Johnston, "Temperature Plays Tricks on Your Car," *Canadian Motorist* (June 1958): 4; Jackson, "Don't Overdrive Your Car."

28 Sidney Katz, "8 Ways to Cut Traffic Deaths," *Maclean's,* 28 February 1959, 13-14, 53-55.

29 "Corvair Monza," *Canadian Motorist* (June 1964): 20.

30 On the safety advocates' education plans, see, for example, VTSC, various documents, VCA, City Clerk's Dept., Series 20, 19-D-4, file 6; comments during the period by each superintendent of Motor Vehicles for British Columbia in *Annual Report of the Department of Motor Vehicles* and *Annual Report of the Motor Vehicle Branch;* and *British Columbia Automobile Association Annual Report,* 1958, BCAA Archives, box A-19, file 1.

31 *VTSC Annual Report,* 1956, VCA, Mayor's Office fonds, 35-F-3, file 16.

32 On advice to men, see Mona Gleason, *Normalizing the Ideal: Psychology, Schooling and the Family in Postwar Canada* (Toronto: University of Toronto Press, 1999), 66-71; Robert Griswold, *Fatherhood in America: A History* (New York: Basic Books, 1993).

33 *Annual Report of the Motor Vehicle Branch, 1953* (Victoria: King's Printer, 1954).

34 *VTSC Annual Report, 1956,* VCA, Mayor's Office fond, 35-F-3, file 16.

35 On the transformation of one Canadian police force as a result of the automobile, see John Weaver, *Crimes, Constables and Courts: Order and Transgression in a Canadian City, 1816-1970* (Montreal and Kingston: McGill Queen's University Press, 1995).

36 "City Police Begin Drunkometer Use," *Vancouver Sun,* 28 October 1953; "The Cup That Kills," *Canadian Motorist* (January-February 1967): 12-14; the debates on 22 April 1947 and at various points in February and April of 1954, Canada, Parliament, House of Commons, *House of Commons Debates: Official Report (Hansard)* (Ottawa: Queen's Printers, 1947, 1954). See also Joseph R. Gusfield, *The Culture of Public Problems: Drinking-Driving and the Symbolic Order* (Chicago: University of Chicago Press, 1981).

37 "Alcohol and Driving – A Renewed Appeal for Action," *British Columbia Medical Journal* 6, 3 (March 1964). On gender and drinking in other contexts, see Robert Campbell, *"Sit Down and Drink Your Beer": Regulating Vancouver's Beer Parlours, 1925-1954* (Toronto: University of Toronto Press, 2001); Jan Noel, *Canada Dry: Temperance Crusades before Confederation* (Toronto: University of Toronto Press, 1995); Mariana Valverde, *The Age of Light, Soap and Water: Moral Reform in English Canada, 1885-1925* (Toronto: McClelland and Stewart, 1991).

38 Hal Tennant, "The Public Crime," *Maclean's,* 10 February 1962, 16-17.

39 "1,508 Hit-Run Accidents in 1959," *Vancouver Province,* 4 June 1960, 1.

40 On juvenile delinquency, see Mary Louise Adams, *The Trouble with Normal: Postwar Youth and the Making of Heterosexuality* (Toronto: University of Toronto Press, 1997); and Franca Iacovetta, "Gossip, Contest, and Power in the Making of Suburban Bad Girls: Toronto, 1945-1960," *Canadian Historical Review* 80, 4 (1999): 585-623.

41 D.G. Dainton, "Concerning Automobile Accidents," *Saturday Night,* 18 March 1961, 54.

42 Benjamin Spock, "Some Differences between the Sexes," in *Problems of Parents* (New York: Houghton Mifflin, 1960), 121-28. Elsewhere in the article, Spock railed against feminists who were "resentful of men's advantages," 121. On the advice of Canadian parenting experts for the same period, see Gleason, *Normalizing the Ideal.*

43 M. Prados, "On Promoting Mental Health," *Canadian Psychiatric Association Journal* 2 (January 1957): 36-51, cited in Gleason, *Normalizing the Ideal,* 69.

44 Margot A. Henrickson, *Dr. Strangelove's America: Society and Culture in the Atomic Age* (Berkeley and Los Angeles: University of California Press, 1997). See also Alan Nadel, *Containment Culture: American Narratives, Postmodernism and the Atomic Age* (Durham: Duke University Press, 1995).

45 Arn Keeling and Robert McDonald, "The Profligate Province: Roderick Haig-Brown and the Modernizing of British Columbia," *Journal of Canadian Studies* 36, 3 (Fall 2001): 7-23; Catherine Cartstairs, "The Natural High? Health Food and the 1960s," paper presented at the conference "Sixties – Style and Substance," McCord Museum, Montreal, November 2003.

46 Stephen S. Conroy, "Popular Technology and Youth Rebellion in America," *Journal of Popular Culture* 16, 4 (Spring 1983): 123-33; Leerom Medovoi, "Democracy, Capitalism and American Literature: The Cold War Construction of J.D. Salinger's Paperback Hero," in Joel Foreman, ed., *The Other Fifties: Interrogating Mid-Century American Icons* (Urbana and Chicago: University of Illinois Press, 1997), 255-87.

47 The 1965 United States Senate subcommittee hearings into traffic accidents under the leadership of Senators Ribicoff and Robert Kennedy provided a friendly context for Nader and no doubt contributed to the media's willingness to listen to him. See Mashaw and Harfst, *The Struggle for Auto Safety*.

48 Nader, *Unsafe at Any Speed*.

49 Ibid., 232. See also, William Whyte, *The Organization Man* (New York: Simon and Schuster, 1956). 172.

50 "Traffic and Safety Committee Annual Report to the BCMA," reprinted in *British Columbia Medical Journal* 8, 5 (May 1966): 199-202.

51 Annual Report of the Traffic and Safety Committee, 1961-62, of the BC Division, Canadian Medical Association, printed in *British Columbia Medical Journal* 4, 9 (September 1962); Annual Report of the Traffic and Safety Committee, 1962-63, of the BC Division, Canadian Medical Association, printed in *British Columbia Medical Journal* 5, 9 (September 1963).

52 "A Word with You," editorial, *Canadian Motorist* (August-September 1965).

53 "Nader's a Nut, Says Gaglardi," *Vancouver Sun*, 8 June 1966, 13.

54 Kim Livingston, "Urban Social Movements: Urban Renewal and Neighbourhood Mobilization in Vancouver during the 1960s and '70s" (MA thesis, Simon Fraser University, 1999), 56. On the freeway debates, see Norbert MacDonald, *Distant Neighbours: A Comparative History of Seattle and Vancouver* (Lincoln: University of Nebraska Press, 1987), 160-62; Ken McKenzie, "Freeway Planning and Protests in Vancouver, 1954-1972" (MA Thesis, Simon Fraser University, 1984).

55 V. Setty Pendakur, *Cities, Citizens, and Freeways* (Vancouver, 1972). Walter Hardwick, another of the critics of the freeway plan, made the same kind of critique. See, for example, his assessment of Vancouver's municipal governance in *Vancouver* (Don Mills, ON: Collier-Macmillan, 1974).

56 Jacobs, *The Death and Life of Great American Cities*. For an insightful discussion of Jacobs' challenge to modernist urban planning, see James C. Scott, *Seeing Like a State: How Certain Schemes to Improve the Human Condition Have Failed* (New Haven: Yale University Press, 1998), 132-46.

57 The transformations of the 1960s have so far only begun to be studied in Canada. For a general overview focusing on, but not limited to, youth culture, see Owram, *Born at the Right Time*.

Chapter 7: Conclusion

1 George Salverson, "The Father Who Wouldn't Listen," in the radio series *The Way of a Parent*, produced by the Canadian Broadcasting Corporation and the Canadian Home and School and Parent Teacher Federation, 17 January 1954, Library and Archives Canada, 1989-0415, ISN 137469.

2 On changing ideals of fatherhood and family relations, see Cynthia Comacchio, "'A Postscript for Father: Defining a New Fatherhood in Interwar Canada," *Canadian Historical Review* 78, 3 (1997): 385-408; Robert Griswold, *Fatherhood in America: A History* (New York: Basic Books, 1993); Mona Gleason, "Disciplining

Children, Disciplining Parents: The Nature and Meaning of Advice to Canadian Parents, 1945-1955," *Histoire Sociale/Social History* 29, 57 (1996): 187-209.

3 The development of sex-role theory in this period, although allowing for significant insights into the social construction of gender, nevertheless tended to overlook the hierarchical nature of what were allegedly complementary relations between the sexes. See Robert Connell, *Masculinities* (Berkeley: University of California Press, 1995), 21-27.

4 On the changing attitudes toward women, especially working women, in this period, see Veronica Strong-Boag, "Canada's Wage-Earning Wives and the Construction of the Middle-Class, 1945-1960," *Journal of Canadian Studies* 29, 3 (1994): 5-25; Joan Sangster, *Earning Respect: The Lives of Working-Women in Small-Town Ontario, 1920-1960* (Toronto: University of Toronto Press, 1995); Valerie Korinek, *Roughing It in the Suburbs: Reading* Chatelaine *Magazine in the Fifties and Sixties* (Toronto: University of Toronto Press, 2000). On women's "invasion" of public drinking establishments, see Robert Campbell, *"Sit Down and Drink Your Beer": Regulating Vancouver's Beer Parlours, 1925-1954* (Toronto: University of Toronto Press, 2001); and Craig Heron, *Booze: A Distilled History* (Toronto: Between the Lines, 2003).

5 Len Kuffert, *A Great Duty: Canadian Responses to Modern Life and Mass Culture in Canada, 1939-1967* (Montreal and Kingston: McGill-Queen's University Press, 2003); Philip Massolin, *Canadian Intellectuals, the Tory Tradition and the Challenge of Modernity, 1939-1970* (Toronto: University of Toronto Press, 2001).

6 Barbara Ehrenreich, *The Hearts of Men: American Dreams and the Flight from Commitment* (New York: Doubleday, 1983). See also Bill Osgerby, *Playboys in Paradise: Masculinity, Youth and Leisure-Style in Modern America* (Oxford: Berg, 2001).

7 The most obvious case is William Whyte, *The Organization Man* (New York: Simon and Schuster, 1956).

8 Marshall Berman, *"All That Is Solid Melts into Air": The Experience of Modernity*, 2nd ed. (New York: Penguin, 1982), 15.

9 The doubled nature of the modern experience is nicely outlined in Keith Walden, *Becoming Modern in Toronto: The Industrial Exhibition and the Shaping of a Late Victorian Culture* (Toronto: University of Toronto Press, 1997), especially the chapters on order and confidence and their attendant problems of disorder and uncertainty.

10 For a general survey of these trends, see Doug Owram, *Born at the Right Time: A History of the Baby-Boom Generation* (Toronto: University of Toronto Press, 1996).

11 While the changes of the 1960s and 1970s are commonly referred to as postmodernity, both Ulrich Beck and Anthony Giddens see key continuities with the past and therefore argue for the notion of a fuller, more reflexive modernity. See Giddens, *The Consequences of Modernity* (Cambridge, UK: Polity Press, 1990); and Ulrich Beck, Anthony Giddens, and Scott Lasch, *Reflexive Modernization: Politics, Tradition and Aesthetics in the Modern Social Order* (Cambridge, UK: Polity Press, 1994).

12 Quotations here are from PRECIS 6, *The Culture of Fragments* (New York: Columbia University Graduate School of Architecture, 1987) and Terry Eagleton, "Awakening from Modernity," *Times Literary Supplement*, 20 February 1987, both cited in David Harvey, *The Condition of Postmodernity: An Enquiry into the Origins of Cultural Change* (Oxford: Basil Blackwell, 1989), 9. See also J. David Hoeveler Jr.,

The Postmodern Turn: American Thought and Culture in the 1970s (New York: Twayne, 1996).

13   This is the story almost universally told to me by undergraduate students who take my course on gender and history.

14   On the men's movement, see Michael Kimmel, ed., *The Politics of Manhood: Profeminist Men Respond to the Mythopoetic Men's Movement (and Mythopoetic Leaders Answer)* (Philadelphia: Temple University Press, 1995). Concern over young boys and the absence of an appropriate male role has been discussed in many areas, but see, for example, the best-selling work by James Garbarino, *Lost Boys: Why Our Sons Turn Violent and How We Can Save Them* (New York: Free Press, 1999).

15   The changed tone of contemporary capitalism is nicely captured in Thomas Frank, *One Market under God: Extreme Capitalism, Market Populism and the End of Economic Democracy* (New York: Doubleday, 2000).

Bibliography

Archival Records

British Columbia Archives
British Columbia Commission on Workmen's Compensation, 1949-52
Second Narrows Bridge Inquiry Records
Workers' Compensation Board of British Columbia Oral History Project

British Columbia Automobile Association Archives (Private)
British Columbia Automobile Association Annual Reports

British Columbia Mountaineering Club Archives (Private)
The BC Mountaineer, 1945-70
British Columbia Mountaineering Club Fonds
British Columbia Mountaineering Club Oral History Project

City of Vancouver Archives
Official Traffic Commission, City Council and Office of the City Clerk Fonds, 1945-70
Sherwood Lett Fonds
"Vancouver Traffic and Safety Council," City Clerk's Department
Vancouver Traffic and Safety Council Annual Report, City Clerk's Department
Vancouver Traffic and Safety Council Annual Report, Mayor's Office Fonds
Vancouver Traffic and Safety Council Annual Report, Office of the City Clerk
Vancouver Traffic and Safety Council Programme, City Clerk's Department

Library and Archives Canada
Capital Case Files, RG13
Royal Commission to Investigate Complaints Made by Walter H. Kirchner, RG 33/85

University of British Columbia Archives
Tom McGrath Fonds
Trade Union Research Bureau
Vancouver and District Labour Council

Other Sources

Adams, Mary Louise. *The Trouble with Normal: Postwar Youth and the Making of Heterosexuality.* Toronto: University of Toronto Press, 1997.

"Alcohol and Driving – A Renewed Appeal for Action." *British Columbia Medical Journal* 6, 3 (March 1964).

Anderson, Kay. *Vancouver's Chinatown: Racial Discourse in Canada, 1875-1980.* Montreal and Kingston: McGill-Queen's University Press, 1991.

Annual Report of the Department of Motor Vehicles. Victoria: King's Printer, 1945-49.

Annual Report of the Motor Vehicle Branch. Victoria: King's Printer, 1950-70.

"Annual Report of the Traffic and Safety Committee." Canadian Medical Association, BC Division. *British Columbia Medical Journal* (1960-68).

Arnup, Katherine. *Education for Motherhood: Advice for Mothers in Twentieth-Century Canada.* Toronto: University of Toronto Press, 1994.

Babcock, Robert H. "Blood on the Factory Floor: The Workers' Compensation Movement in Canada and the United States." In Raymond Blake and Jeff Keshen, eds., *Social Welfare Policy in Canada: Historical Readings,* 107-21. Toronto: Copp Clark, 1995.

Bacchi, Carol Lee. *Liberation Deferred? The Ideas of the English Canadian Suffragists, 1877-1918.* Toronto: University of Toronto Press, 1983.

Barman, Jean. *The West beyond the West: A History of British Columbia.* Toronto: University of Toronto Press, 1991.

Baron, Ava, ed. *Work Engendered: Toward a New History of American Labor.* Ithaca: Cornell University Press, 1991.

Barton, Michael. "Journalistic Gore: Disaster Reporting and Emotional Discourse in the *New York Times,* 1852-1956." In Peter N. Stearns and Jan Lewis, eds., *An Emotional History of the United States,* 155-72. New York and London: New York University Press, 1998.

Bartrip, P.W.J. *Workmen's Compensation in Twentieth Century Britain: Law, History and Social Policy.* Aldershot: Gower, 1987.

Bartrip, P.W.J., and S.B. Burman. *The Wounded Soldiers of Industry: Industrial Compensation Policy, 1833-1897.* Oxford: Oxford University Press, 1983.

Beck, Ulrich. *The Risk Society: Towards a New Modernity.* Trans. Mark Ritter. London: Sage, 1992.

–. *World Risk Society.* Cambridge, UK: Polity Press, 1999.

Beck, Ulrich, Anthony Giddens, and Scott Lasch. *Reflexive Modernization: Politics, Tradition and Aesthetics in the Modern Social Order.* Cambridge, UK: Polity Press, 1994.

Bederman, Gail. *Manliness and Civilization: A Cultural History of Gender and Race in the United States, 1880-1917.* Chicago: University of Chicago Press, 1995.

–. "'The Women Have Had Charge of the Church Long Enough': The Men and Religion Forward Movement of 1911-1912 and the Masculinization of Middle-Class Protestantism." *American Quarterly* 41, 3 (1989): 432-65.

Berman, Marshall. *"All That Is Solid Melts into Air": The Experience of Modernity.* 2nd ed. New York: Simon and Schuster, 1982.

Bliss, Michael. "Privatizing the Mind: The Sundering of Canadian History, the Sundering of Canada." *Journal of Canadian Studies* 26, 4 (1991-92): 5-17.

Bois, J.S.A., Major. "The Morale of the Fighting Soldier." *Bulletin of the Canadian Psychological Association* 3, 2 (April 1943): 17-20.

Bothwell, Robert, Ian Drummond, and John English. *Canada since 1945: Power, Politics and Provincialism.* Rev. ed. Toronto: University of Toronto Press, 1989.

Bourke, Joanna. *Dismembering the Male: Men's Bodies, Britain and the Great War.* London: Reaktion, 1996.

Boyd, Neil. *The Beast Within: Why Men Are Violent.* Vancouver: Douglas and McIntyre, 2000.

–. *The Last Dance: Murder in Canada.* Scarborough: Prentice-Hall, 1988.

Bradbury, Bettina. *Working Families: Age, Gender and Daily Survival in Montreal.* Toronto: McClelland and Stewart, 1993.

Breines, Ingeborg, Robert Connell, and Ingrid Eide, eds. *Male Roles, Masculinities and Violence: A Culture of Peace Perspective.* Paris: UNESCO, 2000.

Broadfoot, Barry. *The Veterans' Years: Coming Home from the War.* Vancouver and Toronto: Douglas and McIntyre, 1985.

Brownlie, Robin. "Work Hard and Be Grateful: Native Soldier Settlers in Ontario after the First World War." In Franca Iacovetta and Wendy Mitchinson, eds., *On the Case: Explorations in Social History,* 181-203. Toronto: University of Toronto Press, 1998.

Burr, Christina. *Spreading the Light: Work and Labour Reform in Late Nineteenth-Century Toronto.* Toronto: University of Toronto Press, 1999.

Cameron, Ross D. "Tom Thomson, Antimodernism and the Ideal of Manhood." *Journal of the Canadian Historical Association* 10 (1999): 185-208.

Campbell, Lara. "'We Who Have Wallowed in the Mud of Flanders': First World War Veterans, Unemployment, and the Development of Social Welfare in Canada, 1929-1939." *Journal of the Canadian Historical Association* 11 (2000): 125-49.

Campbell, Robert. *Grand Illusions: The Politics of the Keynesian Experience in Canada, 1945-1975.* Peterborough: Broadview, 1987.

–. *"Sit Down and Drink Your Beer": Regulating Vancouver's Beer Parlours, 1925-1954.* Toronto: University of Toronto Press, 2001.

Canning, Kathleen. "Feminist History after the Linguistic Turn: Historicizing Discourse and Experience." *Signs* 19, 2 (1994): 368-404.

Carnes, Mark, and Clyde Griffen, eds. *Meanings for Manhood: Construction of Masculinity in Victorian America.* Chicago: University of Chicago Press, 1990.

Carrigan, D. Owen. *Crime and Punishment in Canada: A History.* Toronto: McClelland and Stewart, 1991.

Carter, Sarah. *Capturing Women: The Manipulation of Cultural Imagery in Canada's Prairie West.* Montreal and Kingston: McGill-Queen's University Press, 1997.

Carstairs, Catherine. "The Natural High? Health Food and the 1960s." Paper presented at the conference "Sixties – Style and Substance," McCord Museum, Montreal, November 2003.

Castel, Robert, Françoise Castel, and Anne Lovell. *The Psychiatric Society.* Trans. Arthur Goldhammer. New York: Columbia University Press, 1982.

Cathcart, J.P.S. "Every Physician a Psychiatrist." *National Health Review* 7, 4 (January 1939): 1-11.

–. "Mental Illness and War." *National Health Review* (July 1940): 149-51.

–. "Psychological Problems in Post-War Rehabilitation." *Bulletin of the Canadian Psychological Association,* special issue containing proceedings of the First Annual Meeting of the Canadian Psychological Association (April 1941): 31-32.

Chakrabarty, Dipesh. *Provincializing Europe: Postcolonial Thought and Historical Difference.* Princeton: Princeton University Press, 2000.

Chambers, Lori, and Edgar André Montigny, eds. *Family Matters: Papers in Post-Confederation Canadian Family History.* Toronto: Canada Scholars' Press, 1998.

Chenier, Elise. "The Criminal Sexual Psychopath in Canada: Sex, Psychiatry and the Law at Mid-Century." *Canadian Bulletin of Medical History* 20, 1 (2003): 75-101.

Christie, Nancy. *Engendering the State: Family, Work and Welfare in Canada.* Toronto: University of Toronto Press, 2000.

Collins, Robert. *You Had to Be There: An Intimate Portrait of the Generation that Survived the Depression, Won the War, and Re-Invented Canada.* Toronto: McClelland and Stewart, 1997.

Comacchio, Cynthia. "Mechanomorphosis: Science, Management and 'Human Machinery' in Industrial Canada, 1900-1945." *Labour/Le Travail* 41 (1998): 35-67.

–. *Nations Are Built of Babies: Saving Ontario's Mothers and Children, 1900-1940.* Montreal and Kingston: McGill-Queen's University Press, 1993.

–. "'A Postscript for Father': Defining a New Fatherhood in Interwar Canada." *Canadian Historical Review* 78, 3 (1997): 385-408.

Coneybeer, Ian Tom. "The Origins of Workmen's Compensation in British Columbia: State Theory and Law." MA thesis, Simon Fraser University, 1990.

Connell, Robert. *Masculinities.* Berkeley: University of California Press, 1995.

Connor, Ralph. *Glengarry School Days.* 1902. Reprint, Toronto: McClelland and Stewart, 1993.

Conroy, Stephen S. "Popular Technology and Youth Rebellion in America." *Journal of Popular Culture* 16, 4 (Spring 1983): 123-33.

Copp, Terry. "From Neurasthenia to Post-Traumatic Stress Disorder: Canadian Veterans and the Problem of Persistent Emotional Disabilities." In Peter Neary and J.L. Granatstein, eds., *The Veterans Charter and Post-World War II Canada.* Montreal and Kingston: McGill-Queen's University Press, 1998.

Copp, Terry, and Bill McAndrew. *Battle Exhaustion: Soldiers and Psychiatrists in the Canadian Army, 1939-1945.* Montreal and Kingston: McGill-Queen's University Press, 1990.

Courtwright, David. *Violent Land: Single Men and Social Disorder from the Frontier to the Inner City.* Cambridge, MA: Harvard University Press, 1996.

Crawford, Charles, and Dennis L. Krebs. *Handbook of Evolutionary Psychology: Ideas, Issues and Applications.* New Jersey: Lawrence Erlbaum Associates, 1998.

Culbert, Dick. *A Climber's Guide to the Coastal Ranges of British Columbia.* 2nd ed. Vancouver: Alpine Club of Canada, 1969.

Dancey, Travis E. "Treatment in the Absence of Pensioning for Psychoneurotic Veterans." *The American Journal of Psychiatry* 107 (November 1950): 347-49.

Darnton, Robert. *The Great Cat Massacre and Other Episodes in French Cultural History.* New York: Basic Books, 1984.

Davidoff, Leonore, and Catherine Hall. *Family Fortunes: Men and Women of the English Middle Class, 1780-1850.* Chicago: University of Chicago Press, 1987.

Davies, Robertson. *Leaven of Malice.* 1954. Reprint, New York: Penguin, 1981.

Davis, Mike. *Prisoners of the American Dream: Politics and Economy in the History of the US Working Class.* London: Verso, 1986.

Davis, Natalie Zemon. *Fiction in the Archives: Pardon Tales and Their Tellers in Sixteenth-Century France.* Stanford: Stanford University Press, 1987.

Dawson, Michael. "'That Nice Red Coat Goes Right to My Head Like Champagne': Gender, Antimodernism and the Mountie Image, 1880-1960." *Journal of Canadian Studies* 32, 3 (1997): 119-39.

Dickinson, Harley D. *The Two Psychiatries: The Transformation of Psychiatric Work in Saskatchewan, 1905-1984.* Regina: Canadian Plains Research Centre, 1989.

Doherty, Diana, and John W. Ekstedt. *Conflict, Control and Supervision: The History of the Corrections Branch in British Columbia.* Burnaby: Simon Fraser University Institute for Studies in Criminal Justice Policy, 1990.

Dowbiggin, Ian. "'Keeping This Young Country Sane': C.K. Clarke, Immigration Restriction, and Canadian Psychiatry, 1890-1925." *Canadian Historical Review* 76, 4 (1995): 598-627.

Downs, Laura Lee. "If 'Woman' Is Just an Empty Category Then Why Am I Afraid to Walk Alone at Night? Identity Politics Meets the Postmodern Subject." *Comparative Studies in Society and History* 35, 2 (1993): 414-37.

Dummitt, Chris. "Finding a Place for Father: Selling the Barbecue in Post-War Canada." *Journal of the Canadian Historical Association* 8 (1998): 209-23.

Echols, Alice. *Daring to Be Bad: Radical Feminism in America, 1967-1975.* Minneapolis: University of Minnesota Press, 1989.

Ehrenreich, Barbara. *The Hearts of Men: American Dreams and the Flight from Commitment.* New York: Doubleday, 1983.

Eisenstadt,S.N. "Multiple Modernities." *Daedalus* 129 (Winter 2000): 1-29.

Eisenstadt, S.N., and Wolfgang Schlucter. "Introduction: Paths to Early Modernities – A Comparative View." *Daedalus* 127 (Summer 1998): 1-18.

Elias, Norbert. *The Civilizing Process.* Trans. Edmund Jephcott. Oxford and Cambridge, MA: Blackwell, 1994.

England, Robert. *Discharged: A Commentary on Civil Re-Establishment of Veterans in Canada.* Toronto: Macmillan, 1943.

Ewert, Henry. *The Story of the B.C. Electric Railway Company.* North Vancouver: Whitecap Books, 1986.

Faludi, Susan. *Stiffed: The Betrayal of the American Man.* New York: William Morrow, 1999.

Felski, Rita. *The Gender of Modernity.* Cambridge, MA: Harvard University Press, 1995.

Figlio, Karl. "What Is an Accident?" In P. Weindling, ed., *The Social History of Occupational Health.* London: Croom Helm, 1986.

Fingard, Judith, and Janet Guildford, eds. *Mothers of the Municipality: Women, Work and Social Policy in Post-1945 Halifax.* Toronto: University of Toronto Press, 2005.

Finkel, Alvin. "Competing Master Narratives on Postwar Canada." *Acadiensis* 29, 2 (2000): 188-204.

–. *Our Lives: Canada after 1945.* Toronto: Lorimer, 1997.

Fletcher, Anthony. *Gender, Sex, and Subordination in England, 1500-1800.* New Haven: Yale University Press, 1995.

Flink, James J. *The Automobile Age.* Cambridge, MA: MIT Press, 1988.

Foucault, Michel. *Discipline and Punish: The Birth of the Prison.* 2nd ed. New York: Vantage, 1995.

Frank, Thomas. *One Market under God: Extreme Capitalism, Market Populism and the End of Economic Democracy.* New York: Doubleday, 2000.

Fraser, Nancy, and Linda Nicholson. "A Genealogy of *Dependency:* Tracing a Keyword of the US Welfare State." *Signs* 19, 2 (1994): 309-36.

Freedman, Estelle B. "Uncontrolled Desires: The Response to the Sexual Psychopath, 1920-1960." In Kathy Peiss and Christina Simmons, eds., *Passion and Power: Sexuality in History,* 199-225. Philadelphia: Temple University Press, 1989.

Freeman, Barbara. "Framing Feminine/Feminist: English-Language Press Coverage of the Royal Commission on the Status of Women in Canada, 1968." In *Women in Canadian Society – les femmes de la société Canadienne,* 11-31. Ottawa: International Council of Canadian Studies, 1995.

Freeman, Ralph, and Joseph Otter. "The Collapse of the SNB, Van, June 1958." *Civil Engineering,* February 1959.

Freud, Sigmund. *Civilization and Its Discontents.* Trans. James Strachey. New York: Norton, 1961.

Friesen, Gerald. *The Canadian Prairies: A History.* Lincoln: University of Nebraska Press, 1984.

Furnas, J.C. "And Sudden Death." *Readers' Digest.* Reprinted in *Trades and Labor Congress Journal* 25, 9 (September 1946): 42-44.

Garbarino, James. *Lost Boys: Why Our Sons Turn Violent and How We Can Save Them.* New York: Free Press, 1999.

Garland, David. *Punishment and Modern Society: A Study in Social Theory.* Chicago: University of Chicago Press, 1990.

Gauvreau, Michael, and Nancy Christie. *A Full-Orbed Christianity: The Protestant Churches and Social Welfare in Canada, 1900-1940.* Montreal and Kingston: McGill-Queen's University Press, 1996.

Giddens, Anthony. *The Consequences of Modernity.* Cambridge, UK: Polity Press, 1990.

Giddens, Anthony, and Christopher Pierson. *Conversations with Anthony Giddens: Making Sense of Modernity.* Stanford, CA: Stanford University Press, 1998.

Giles, Judy. *The Parlour and the Suburb: Domestic Identities, Class, Femininity and Modernity.* Oxford: Berg, 2004.

Gleason, Mona. "Disciplining Children, Disciplining Parents: The Nature and Meaning of Advice to Canadian Parents, 1945-1955." *Histoire Sociale/Social History* 29, 57 (1996): 187-209.

–. *Normalizing the Ideal: Psychology, Schooling and the Family in Postwar Canada.* Toronto: University of Toronto Press, 1999.

Gordon, Linda. *Pitied but Not Entitled: Single Mothers and the History of Welfare.* Cambridge, MA: Harvard University Press, 1994.

Granatstein, J.L. *Broken Promises: A History of Conscription in Canada.* Toronto: University of Toronto Press, 1977.

–. *Canada's War: The Politics of the Mackenzie King Government, 1939-1945.* Toronto: Oxford University Press, 1975.

–. *Who Killed Canadian History?* Toronto: Harper Collins, 1998.

Grant, George. *Lament for a Nation: The Defeat of Canadian Nationalism.* Toronto: McClelland and Stewart, 1965; reprint, Ottawa: Carleton University Press, 1982.

Greenwood, F. Murray, and Beverley Boissery. *Uncertain Justice: Canadian Women and Capital Punishment, 1754-1953.* Toronto: Dundurn Press, [2000].

Griswold, Robert. *Fatherhood in America: A History.* New York: Basic Books, 1993.

Grob, Gerald. *From Asylum to Community: Mental Health Policy in Modern America.* New Jersey: Princeton University Press, 1991.

Guest, Dennis. *The Emergence of Social Security in Canada.* Vancouver: UBC Press, 1980.

Gusfield, Joseph R. *The Culture of Public Problems: Drinking-Driving and the Symbolic Order.* Chicago: University of Chicago Press, 1981.

Halttunen, Karen. *Murder Most Foul: The Killer and the American Gothic Imagination.* Cambridge, MA: Harvard University Press, 1998.

Hansen, Peter H. "Albert Smith, the Alpine Club, and the Invention of Mountaineering in Mid-Victorian Britain." *Journal of British Studies* 34 (July 1995): 300-24.

–. "Confetti of Empire: The Conquest of Everest in Nepal, India, Britain and New Zealand." *Comparative Studies in Society and History* 42, 2 (2000): 207-32.

–. "Vertical Boundaries, National Identities: British Mountaineering on the Frontiers of Europe and the Empire, 1868-1914." *Journal of Imperial and Commonwealth History* 24, 1 (January 1996): 48-71.

Hardwick, Walter. *Vancouver.* Don Mills, ON: Collier-Macmillan, 1974.

Harris, Cole. *The Resettlement of British Columbia: Essays on Colonialism and Geographical Change.* Vancouver: UBC Press, 1998.

Harris, Richard. *Creeping Conformity: How Canada Became Suburban, 1900-1960.* Toronto: University of Toronto Press, 2004.

Harris, Richard, and Peter J. Larkham, eds. *Changing Suburbs: Foundation, Form, and Function.* New York: Routledge, 1999.

Harvey, David. *The Condition of Postmodernity: An Enquiry into the Origins of Cultural Change.* Oxford: Basil Blackwell, 1989.

Henrickson, Margot A. *Dr. Strangelove's America: Society and Culture in the Atomic Age.* Berkeley and Los Angeles: University of California Press, 1997.

Heron, Craig. *Booze: A Distilled History.* Toronto: Between the Lines, 2003.

–. *The Canadian Labour Movement: A Brief History.* Toronto: James Lorimer, 1996.

Hewitt, Steve, and Reg Whitaker. *Cold War Canada.* Toronto: Lorimer, 2003.

Hobsbawm, Eric. *The Age of Extremes: A History of the World, 1914-1991.* New York: Pantheon, 1994.

Hodgson, Dorothy, ed. *Gendered Modernities: Ethnographic Perspectives.* New York: Palgrove, 2001.

Hoeveler, J. David Jr. *The Postmodern Turn: American Thought and Culture in the 1970s.* New York: Twayne, 1996.

Hooper, Charlotte. *Manly States: Masculinities, International Relations and Gender Politics.* New York: Columbia University Press, 2001.

Horn, Michiel. *The League for Social Reconstruction: Intellectual Origins of the Democratic Left in Canada, 1930-1942.* Toronto: University of Toronto Press, 1980.

Horowitz, Roger, ed. *Boys and Their Toys: Masculinity, Technology and Class in America.* London and New York: Routledge, 2001.

Hours of Work in Canada: An Historical Series. Ottawa: Canada Department of Labour, Economics and Research Branch, 1971.

Howell, Colin. *Northern Sandlots: A Social History of Maritime Baseball.* Toronto: University of Toronto Press, 1995.

Huel, Raymond. "The Creation of the Alpine Club of Canada: An Early Manifestation of Canadian Nationalism." *Prairie Forum* 15, 1 (1990): 25-43.

Hunt, Lynn, ed. *The New Cultural History*. Berkeley: University of California Press, 1989.

Iacovetta, Franca. "Gossip, Contest, and Power in the Making of Suburban Bad Girls: Toronto, 1945-1960." *Canadian Historical Review* 80, 4 (1999): 585-623.

–. "Recipes for Democracy? Gender, Family and Making Female Citizens in Cold War Canada." In Veronica Strong-Boag et al., eds., *Rethinking Canada: The Promise of Women's History*, 4th ed., 299-312. Toronto: Oxford University Press, 2002.

–. *Such Hardworking People: Italian Immigrants in Postwar Toronto*. Toronto: University of Toronto Press, 1993.

Iacovetta, Franca, and Karen Dubinsky. "Murder, Womanly Virtue and Motherhood: The Case of Angelina Napolitano, 1911-1922." *Canadian Historical Review* 72, 4 (1991): 505-31.

Iacovetta, Franca, and Wendy Mitchinson, eds. *On the Case: Explorations in Social History*. Toronto: University of Toronto Press, 1998.

Ives, Don. "The Veterans Charter: The Compensation Principle and the Principle of Recognition for Service." In Peter Neary and J.L. Granatstein, eds., *The Veterans Charter and Post-World War II Canada*. Montreal and Kingston: McGill-Queen's University Press, 1998.

Jackson, Kenneth T. *Crabgrass Frontier: The Suburbanization of the United States*. New York: Oxford University Press, 1985.

Jacobs, Jane. *The Death and Life of Great American Cities*. New York: Random House, 1961.

Jasen, Patricia. *Wild Things: Nature, Culture and Tourism in Ontario, 1790-1914*. Toronto: University of Toronto Press, 1995.

Jayewardene, C.H.S. "The Canadian Movement against the Death Penalty." *Canadian Journal of Criminology and Corrections*, 14-15 (1972-73): 367-82.

Jeffords, Susan. *The Remasculinization of America: Gender and the Vietnam War*. Bloomington: Indiana University Press, 1989.

Jerome, John. *The Death of the Automobile: The Fatal Effect of the Golden Era, 1955-1970*. New York: Norton, 1972.

Jervis, John. *Exploring the Modern: Patterns in Western Culture and Civilization*. Oxford: Blackwell, 1998.

–. *Transgressing the Modern: Explorations in the Western Experience of Otherness*. Oxford: Blackwell, 1999.

Jessup, Lynda. "Prospectors, Bushwhackers, Painters: Antimodernism and the Group of Seven." *International Journal of Canadian Studies* 17 (1998): 193-214.

Jones, Chris. *Climbing in North America*. Berkeley: University of California Press, 1976.

Keeling, Arn, and Robert McDonald. "The Profligate Province: Roderick Haig-Brown and the Modernizing of British Columbia." *Journal of Canadian Studies* 36, 3 (Fall 2001): 7-23.

Keelor, John Thomas. "The Price of Lives and Limbs Lost at Work: The Development of No-Fault Workers' Compensation Legislation in British Columbia, 1910-1916." MA thesis, University of Victoria, 1996.

Kendrick, Tim, ed. *Get Back Alive! Safety in the BC Coast Mountains*. Vancouver: Federation of Mountain Clubs of British Columbia, 1973.

Keshen, Jeff. "Getting It Right the Second Time Around: The Reintegration of Canadian Veterans of World War II." In Peter Neary and J.L. Granatstein, eds.,

The Veterans Charter and Post-World War II Canada, 62-84. Montreal and Kingston: McGill-Queen's University Press, 1998.

Kessler-Harris. "Measures for Masculinity: The American Labor Movement and Welfare State Policy during the Great Depression." In Stefan Dudink, Karen Hagemann, and John Tosh, eds., *Masculinities in Politics and War: Gendering Modern History,* 257-75. Manchester: Manchester University Press, 2004.

Kimmel, Michael. *Manhood in America: A Cultural History.* New York: Free Press, 1996.

–, ed. *The Politics of Manhood: Profeminist Men Respond to the Mythopoetic Men's Movement (and the Mythopoetic Leaders Answer).* Philadelphia: Temple University Press, 1995.

Korinek, Valerie. *Roughing It in the Suburbs: Reading* Chatelaine Magazine *in the Fifties and Sixties.* Toronto: University of Toronto Press, 2000.

Krakauer, Jon. *Into Thin Air: A Personal Account of the Mount Everest Disaster.* London: Macmillan, 1997.

Kuffert, Len. *A Great Duty: Canadian Responses to Modern Life and Mass Culture in Canada, 1939-1967.* Montreal and Kingston: McGill-Queen's University Press, 2003.

Lake, Marilyn. "Mission Impossible: How Men Gave Birth to the Australian Nation – Nationalism, Gender and Other Seminal Acts." *Gender and History* 4, 3 (1992): 305-22.

Laqueur, Thomas. *Making Sex: The Body and Gender from the Greeks to Freud.* Cambridge, MA: Harvard University Press, 1990.

Lears, Jackson. *Something for Nothing: Luck in America.* New York: Viking, 2003.

Leslie, Susan. "In the Western Mountains: Early Mountaineering in British Columbia." *Sound Heritage* 8, 4 (1980).

Lett, Sherwood. *Report of the BC Royal Commission, Second Narrows Bridge Inquiry.* Vol. 1. Victoria: Queen's Printer's, 1958.

Liscombe, Rhodri Windsor. *The New Spirit: Modern Architecture in Vancouver, 1938-1963.* Montreal and Vancouver: Canadian Centre for Architecture and Doublas and McIntyre, 1997.

Litt, Paul. *The Muses, the Masses, and the Massey Commission.* Toronto: University of Toronto Press, 1992.

Little, Margaret Jane. *No Car, No Radio, No Liquor Permit: The Moral Regulation of Single Mothers in Ontario, 1920-1997.* Toronto: Oxford University Press, 1998.

Livingston, Kim. "Urban Social Movements: Urban Renewal and Neighbourhood Mobilization in Vancouver during the 1960s and '70s." MA thesis, Simon Fraser University, 1999.

Loo, Tina. "Making a Modern Wilderness: Conserving Wildlife in Twentieth-Century Canada." *Canadian Historical Review* 82, 1 (2001): 92-121.

–. "Of Moose and Men: Hunting for Masculinities in British Columbia, 1880-1939." *Western Historical Quarterly* 32, 3 (2001): 296-319.

Luckin, Bill. "Accidents, Disasters and Cities." *Urban History* 20, 2 (October 1993): 177-90.

MacDonald, Bruce. *Vancouver: A Visual History.* Vancouver: Talon, 1992.

MacDonald, Norbert. *Distant Neighbours: A Comparative History of Seattle and Vancouver.* Lincoln: University of Nebraska Press, 1987.

Marsh, Leonard. *Rebuilding a Neighbourhood: Report on a Demonstration Slum-Clearance and Urban Rehabilitation Project in a Key Central Area in Vancouver.* Vancouver: University of British Columbia, 1950.

—. *Report on Social Security for Canada.* Ottawa: King's Printer, 1943.

Mashaw, Jerry L., and David L. Harfst. *The Struggle for Auto Safety.* Cambridge, MA: Harvard University Press, 1990.

Massolin, Phillip A. *Canadian Intellectuals, the Tory Tradition and the Challenge of Modernity, 1939-1970.* Toronto: University of Toronto Press, 2001.

May, Elaine Tyler. *Homeward Bound: American Families in the Cold War.* New York: Basic Books, 1988.

McKay, Ian. "The Liberal Order Framework: A Prospectus for a Reconnaissance of Canadian History." *Canadian Historical Review* 81, 4 (2000): 617-45.

—. *Rebels, Reds, Radicals: Rethinking Canada's Left History.* Toronto: Between the Lines, 2005.

McKenzie, Ken. "Freeway Planning and Protests in Vancouver, 1954-1972." MA thesis, Simon Fraser University, 1984.

McKillop, A.B. "Who Killed Canadian History? A View from the Trenches." *Canadian Historical Review* 80, 2 (1999): 269-99.

McLaren, Angus. *The Trials of Masculinity: Policing Sexual Boundaries, 1870-1930.* Chicago: University of Chicago Press, 1997.

McNeel, Major B.H., and Major T.E. Dancey. "The Personality of the Successful Soldier." *The American Journal of Psychiatry* 102, 3 (November 1945): 337-42.

McPherson, Kathryn, Cecilia Morgan, and Nancy M. Forestell, eds. *Gendered Pasts: Historical Essays in Femininity and Masculinity in Canada.* Don Mills, ON: Oxford University Press, 1999.

McShane, Clay. *Down the Asphalt Path: The Automobile and the American City.* New York: Columbia University Press, 1994.

Medovoi, Leerom. "Democracy, Capitalism and American Literature: The Cold War Construction of J.D. Salinger's Paperback Hero." In Joel Foreman, ed., *The Other Fifties: Interrogating Mid-Century American Icons,* 255-87. Urbana and Chicago: University of Illinois Press, 1997.

Meyerowitz, Joanne. *Women Adrift: Independent Wage Earners in Chicago, 1880-1930.* Chicago: University of Chicago Press, 1988.

Ministry of Veterans Affairs. *Back to Civil Life.* 3rd ed. Ottawa: King's Printer, 1946. Reprinted in Peter Neary and J.L. Granatstein, eds., *The Veterans Charter and Post-World War II Canada.* Montreal and Kingston: McGill-Queen's University Press, 1998.

Mitchell, David J. *W.A.C. Bennett and the Rise of British Columbia.* Vancouver and Toronto: Douglas and McIntyre, 1983.

Morton, Desmond. "The Canadian Veterans' Heritage from the Great War." In Peter Neary and J.L. Granatstein, eds., *The Veterans Charter and Post-World War II Canada,* 15-31. Montreal and Kingston: McGill-Queen's University Press, 1998.

Morton, Desmond, and Glenn Wright. *Winning the Second Battle: Canadian Veterans and the Return to Civilian Life, 1915-1930.* Toronto: University of Toronto Press, 1987.

Morton, Susanne. *At Odds: Gambling and Canadians, 1919-1969.* Toronto: University of Toronto Press, 2003.

Moss, Mark. *Manliness and Militarism: Educating Young Boys in Ontario for War.* Toronto: Oxford University Press, 2001.

Murder Statistics, 1961-1970. Ottawa: Statistics Canada, 1973.

Murray, Sylvie. *The Progressive Housewife: Community Activism in Suburban Queens, 1945-1965.* Philadelphia: University of Pennsylvania Press, 2003.

Nadel, Alan. *Containment Culture: American Narratives, Postmodernism and the Atomic Age.* Durham: Duke University Press, 1995.

Nader, Ralph. *Unsafe at Any Speed: The Designed-in Dangers of the American Automobile.* New York: Grossman, 1965.

Neary, Peter, and J.L. Granatstein, eds. *The Veterans Charter and Post-World War II Canada.* Montreal and Kingston: McGill-Queen's University Press, 1998.

Neufeld, Andrew, and Andrew Parnaby. *The IWA in Canada: The Life and Times of an Industrial Union.* Vancouver: New Star, 2000.

Nicholson, Linda. "Interpreting *Gender.*" *Signs* 20, 1 (1994): 79-105.

Noel, Janet. *Canada Dry: Temperance Crusades before Confederation.* Toronto: University of Toronto Press, 1995.

Nye, David. *American Technological Sublime.* Cambridge, MA: MIT Press, 1994.

Nye, Robert. *Masculinity and Male Codes of Honor in Modern France.* New York and Oxford: Oxford University Press, 1993.

O'Brien, Mike. "Manhood and the Militia Myth: Masculinity, Class and Militarism in Ontario, 1902-1914." *Labour/Le Travail* 42 (1998): 115-41.

O'Connell, Sean. *The Car in British Society: Class, Gender and Motoring, 1896-1939.* Manchester: Manchester University Press, 1998.

Odem, Mary. *Delinquent Daughters: Protecting and Policing Adolescent Female Sexuality in the United States, 1885-1920.* Chapel Hill: University of North Carolina Press, 1995.

Oldenziel, Ruth. *Making Technology Masculine: Men, Women, and Modern Machines in America, 1870-1945.* Amsterdam: Amsterdam University Press, 1999.

Ortner, Sherry B. *Life and Death on Mount Everest: Sherpas and Himalayan Mountaineering.* Princeton: Princeton University Press, 1999.

Osgerby, Bill. *Playboys in Paradise: Masculinity, Youth and Leisure-Style in Modern America.* Oxford: Berg, 2001.

Outram, Dorinda. *The Enlightenment.* Cambridge, UK: Cambridge University Press, 1995.

Owram, Doug. *Born at the Right Time: A History of the Baby-Boom Generation.* Toronto: University of Toronto Press, 1996.

–. "Canadian Domesticity in the Postwar Era." In Peter Neary and J.L. Granatstein, eds., *The Veterans Charter and Post-World War II Canada.* Montreal and Kingston: McGill-Queen's University Press, 1998.

–. *The Government Generation: Canadian Intellectuals and the State, 1900-1945.* Toronto: University of Toronto Press, 1986.

Palmer, Bryan. "Of Silences and Trenches: A Dissident's View of Granatstein's Meaning." *Canadian Historical Review* 80, 4 (1999): 676-86.

–. *Working-Class Experience: Re-Thinking the History of Canadian Labour, 1800-1991.* 2nd ed. Toronto: McClelland and Stewart, 1992.

–. *Working-Class Experience: The Rise and Reconstitution of Canadian Labour, 1800-1980.* Toronto: Butterworth, 1983.

Parr, Joy. *Domestic Goods: The Material, the Moral and the Economic in the Postwar Years.* Toronto: University of Toronto Press, 1999.

–. "Gender History and Historical Practice." In Joy Parr and Mark Rosenfeld, eds., *Gender and History in Canada,* 8-27. Toronto: Copp Clark, 1996.

–. *The Gender of Breadwinners: Women, Men, and Change in Two Industrial Towns, 1880-1950.* Toronto: University of Toronto Press, 1990.

Parr, Joy, and Mark Rosenfeld, eds. *Gender and History in Canada.* Toronto: Copp Clark, 1996.

Paterson, T.W. *Disaster: Tales of Heroism and Hardship in the Face of Catastrophe.* Victoria: Solitaire, 1973.

Peiss, Kathy. *Cheap Amusements: Working Women and Leisure in Turn-of-the-Century New York.* Philadelphia: Temple University Press, 1986.

Pendakur, V. Setty. *Cities, Citizens, and Freeways.* Vancouver, 1972.

Pendergast, Tom. *Creating the Modern Man: American Magazines and Consumer Culture, 1900-1950.* Columbia: University of Missouri Press, 2000.

Penfold, Steven. "'Have You No Manhood in You?' Gender and Class in the Cape Breton Coal Towns, 1920-1926." *Acadiensis* 23, 2 (1994): 21-44. Reprinted in Joy Parr and Mark Rosenfeld, eds., *Gender and History in Canada,* 270-93. Toronto: Copp Clark, 1996.

Pierson, Ruth Roach. "Gender and the Unemployment Insurance Debates in Canada, 1934-1940." *Labour/Le Travail* 25 (1990): 77-103.

–. *"They're Still Women after All": The Second World War and Canadian Womanhood.* Toronto: McClelland and Stewart, 1986.

Porter, John. *The Vertical Mosaic: An Analysis of Social Class and Power in Canada.* Toronto: University of Toronto Press, 1965.

Reaume, Geoffrey. *Remembrance of Patients Past: Patient Life at the Toronto Hospital for the Insane, 1870-1940.* Toronto: Oxford University Press, 2000.

Rehabilitation Information Committee, Wartime Information Board. *The Common-Sense of Re-Establishment.* Ottawa: Edmond Cloutier, King's Printer, 1945.

Reichwein, PearlAnn. "'Hands Off Our National Parks': The Alpine Club of Canada and Hydro-Development Controversies in the Canadian Rockies, 1922-1930." *Journal of the Canadian Historical Association* 6 (1995): 129-55.

Reichwein, PearlAnn, and Karen Fox. "Margaret Fleming and the Alpine Club of Canada: A Woman's Place in Mountain Leisure and Literature, 1932-1952." *Journal of Canadian Studies* 36, 3 (Fall 2001): 35-60.

Rinehart, James. *The Tyranny of Work: Alienation and the Labour Process.* 4th ed. Toronto: Harcourt, 2001.

Robin, Martin. *Pillars of Profit: The Company Province, 1934-1972.* Toronto: McClelland and Stewart, 1973.

Roper, Michael. *Masculinity and the British Organization Man since 1945.* Oxford: Oxford University Press, 1994.

Roper, Michael, and John Tosh, eds. *Manful Assertions: Masculinities in Britain since 1800.* London: Routledge, 1991.

Roper, Pam. "The Limits of *Laissez-innover:* Canada's Automation Controversy, 1955-1969." *Journal of Canadian Studies* 34, 3 (Autumn 1999): 87-105.

Rosenswein, Barbara H. "Worrying about Emotions in History." *American Historical Review* 107, 3 (2002): 821-45.

Rosner, David, and Gerald Markowitz. "The Early Movement for Occupational Safety and Health, 1900-1917." In Judith Walzer Leavitt and Ronald L. Numbers, eds., *Sickness and Health in America: Readings in the History of Medicine and Public Health.* Madison: University of Wisconsin, 1997.

Rothenburger, Mel. *Friend o' Mine: The Story of Flyin' Phil Gaglardi.* Victoria: Orca, 1991.

Rotundo, Anthony. *American Manhood: Transformations in Masculinity from the Revolution to the Modern Era.* New York: Basic Books, 1993.

Russell, Peter A. "British Columbia's 'Zombie' Protests against Overseas Conscription, November 1944." Paper delivered to *BC Studies* conference, Kamloops, BC, 2001.

Rutherdale, Robert. "Fatherhood and Masculine Domesticity during the Baby Boom: Consumption and Leisure in Advertising and Life Stories." In Lori Chambers and Edgar André Montigny, eds., *Family Matters: Papers in Post-Confederation Canadian Family History,* 309-33. Toronto: Canadian Scholars' Press, 1998.

–. "Fatherhood and the Social Construction of Memory: Breadwinning and Male Parenting on a Job Frontier, 1945-1966." In Joy Parr and Mark Rosenfeld, eds., *Gender and History in Canada,* 357-75. Toronto: Copp Clark, 1996.

–. "Fatherhood, Life Stories, and Gendered Responses to Domesticity in Canada during the 1960s." Paper presented at the conference "Sixties: Style and Substance," Montreal, November 2003.

–. "Fatherhood, Masculinity and the Good Life during Canada's Baby Boom, 1945-1965." *Journal of Family History* 24, 3 (1999): 351-73.

Sachs, Wolfgang. *For Love of the Automobile: Looking Back into the History of Our Desires.* Trans. Don Reneau. Berkeley: University of California Press, 1992.

Said, Edward. *Culture and Imperialism.* New York: Vintage, 1993.

Sangster, Joan. "Beyond Dichotomies: Re-assessing Gender History and Women's History in Canada." *Left History* 3, 1 (1995): 109-21.

–. *Earning Respect: The Lives of Working Women in Small-Town Ontario, 1920-1960.* Toronto: University of Toronto Press, 1995.

Scharff, Virginia. "Gender, Electricity, and Automobility." In Martin Wachs and Margaret Crawford, eds., *The Car and the City: The Automobile, the Built Environment, and Daily Urban Life,* 75-85. Ann Arbor: University of Michigan Press, 1992.

Scott, James C. *Seeing Like a State: How Certain Schemes to Improve the Human Condition Have Failed.* New Haven: Yale University Press, 1998.

Scott, Joan. *Gender and the Politics of History.* New York: Columbia University Press, 1998.

Segal, Lynne. *Slow Motion: Changing Men, Changing Masculinities.* New Jersey: Rutgers University Press, 1990.

Seidler, Victor. *Rediscovering Masculinity: Reason, Language and Sexuality.* New York: Routledge, 1989.

Sherman, Daniel J. "Monuments, Mourning and Masculinity in France after World War I." *Gender and History* 8, 1 (1996): 82-107.

Shorter, Edward. *A History of Psychiatry: From the Era of Asylum to the Age of Prozac.* New York: John Wiley, 1997.

Smith, Greg. "Civilized People Don't Want to See That Sort of Thing: The Decline of Capital Punishment in London, 1760-1840." In Carolyn Strange, ed., *Qualities of Mercy: Justice, Punishment and Discretion,* 21-51. Vancouver: UBC Press, 1996.

Snell, James. *The Citizen's Wage: The State and the Elderly in Canada, 1900-1951.* Toronto: University of Toronto Press, 1996.

Spierenburg, Pieter, ed. *Men and Violence: Gender, Honor and Rituals in Modern Europe and America.* Columbus: Ohio State University Press, 1998.

–. *The Spectacle of Suffering: Executions and the Evolution of Repression, from a Preindustrial Metropolis to the European Experience*. Cambridge, UK: Cambridge University Press, 1984.

Spock, Benjamin. *Problems of Parents*. New York: Houghton Mifflin, 1960.

Stacey, C.P. *Arms, Men and Government: The War Policies of Canada, 1939-1945*. Ottawa: Queen's Printer, 1970.

Stansell, Christine. *City of Women: Sex and Class in New York, 1789-1860*. New York: Knopf, 1986.

Stearns, Peter. *American Cool: Constructing a Twentieth-Century Emotional Style*. New York: New York University Press, 1994.

Strange, Carolyn. "Discretionary Justice: Political Culture and the Death Penalty in New South Wales and Ontario, 1890-1920." In Carolyn Strange, ed., *Qualities of Mercy: Justice, Punishment, and Discretion*, 130-65. Vancouver: UBC Press, 1996.

–. "The Politics of Punishment: The Death Penalty in Canada, 1867-1976." *Manitoba Law Journal* 23, 3 (1996): 594-619.

–. *Toronto's Girl Problem: The Perils and Pleasures of the City, 1880-1930*. Toronto: University of Toronto Press, 1995.

–. "The Undercurrents of Penal Culture: Punishment of the Body in Mid-Twentieth-Century Canada." *Law and History Review* 19, 2 (2001): 343-85.

Strange, Carolyn, and Tina Loo. *Making Good: Law and Moral Regulation in Canada, 1867-1939*. Toronto: University of Toronto Press, 1997.

Strong-Boag, Veronica. "Canada's Wage-Earning Wives and the Construction of the Middle Class, 1945-1960." *Journal of Canadian Studies* 29, 3 (1994): 5-25.

–. "Home Dreams: Women and the Suburban Experiment in Canada, 1945-1960." *Canadian Historical Review* 72, 4 (1991): 471-504.

Strong-Boag, Veronica, et al., eds. *Rethinking Canada: The Promise of Women's History*. 4th ed. Toronto: Oxford University Press, 2002.

Struthers, James. "Family Allowances, Old Age Security and the Construction of Entitlement in the Canadian Welfare State, 1943-1951." In Peter Neary and J.L. Granatstein, eds., *The Veterans Charter and Post-World War II Canada*. Montreal and Kingston: McGill-Queen's University Press, 1998.

–. *The Limits of Affluence: Welfare in Ontario, 1920-1970*. Toronto: University of Toronto Press, 1994.

Taylor, Charles. *The Malaise of Modernity*. Concord, ON: Anansi, 1991.

Thoms, David, Len Holden, and Tim Claydon, eds. *The Motor Car and Popular Culture in the 20th Century*. Aldershot: Ashgate, 1998.

Thomson, Gerald E. "'Not an Attempt to Coddle Children': Dr. Charles Hegler Gundry and the Mental Hygiene Division of the Vancouver School Board, 1939-1969." *Historical Studies in Education/Revue d'histoire de l'éducation* 14, 2 (2002): 247-78.

Tomblin, Stephen G. "W.A.C. Bennett and Province-Building in British Columbia." *BC Studies* 85 (1990): 45-61.

Unsworth, Walt. *Hold the Heights: The Foundations of Mountaineering*. London: Hodder and Stoughton, 1993.

Valverde, Mariana. *The Age of Light, Soap and Water: Moral Reform in English Canada, 1885-1925*. Toronto: McClelland and Stewart, 1991.

Vance, James E. Jr. *Capturing the Horizon: The Historical Geography of Transportation since the Sixteenth Century*. Baltimore and London: Johns Hopkins University Press, 1986.

Vance, Jonathan. *Death So Noble: Memory, Meaning, and the First World War.* Vancouver: UBC Press, 1997.

Vancouver Planning Department. *Vancouver Redevelopment Study.* Vancouver, 1957.

Wade, Jill. *Houses for All: The Struggle for Social Housing in Vancouver, 1919-1950.* Vancouver: UBC Press, 1994.

Walden, Keith. *Becoming Modern in Toronto: The Industrial Exhibition and the Shaping of a Late Victorian Culture.* Toronto: University of Toronto Press, 1997.

Walkowitz, Judith. *City of Dreadful Delight: Narratives of Sexual Danger in Late-Victorian London.* Chicago: University of Chicago Press, 1992.

Weaver, John. *Crimes, Constables and Courts: Order and Transgression in a Canadian City, 1816-1970.* Montreal and Kingston: McGill Queen's University Press, 1995.

Wedley, John R. "A Development Tool: W.A.C. Bennett and the PGE Railway." *BC Studies* 117 (1998): 29-50.

Whitaker, Reginald, and Gary Marcuse. *Cold War Canada: The Making of a National Insecurity State, 1945-1957.* Toronto: University of Toronto Press, 1994.

Whyte, William. *The Organization Man.* New York: Simon and Schuster, 1956.

Wicks, Ben. *When the Boys Came Marching Home: True Stories of the Men Who Went to War and the Women and Children Who Took Them Back.* Toronto: Stoddart, 1991.

Wiener, Martin J. *Men of Blood: Violence, Manliness and Criminal Justice in Victorian England.* Cambridge, UK: Cambridge University Press, 2004.

Woods, Walter S. *Rehabilitation, a Combined Operation.* Ottawa: Queen's Printer, 1953.

Workmen's Compensation Board [of BC]. *Annual Report.* Victoria: Queen's Printer, 1950-60.

Wright, Donald A. *The Professionalization of History in English Canada.* Toronto: University of Toronto Press, 2005.

–. "W.D. Lighthall and David Ross McCord: Antimodernism and English Canadian Imperialism, 1880s-1918." *Journal of Canadian Studies* 32, 2 (1997): 134-53.

Wylie, Philip. *Generation of Vipers.* New York: Rinehart, 1946.

Zeiger, Susan. "She Didn't Raise Her Boy to Be a Slacker: Motherhood, Conscription and the Culture of the First World War." *Feminist Studies* 22, 1 (Spring 1996): 7-39.

Zweig, Michael. *The Working-Class Majority: America's Best Kept Secret.* New York: Cornell University Press, 2000.

Index

Note: "CPC" stands for Canadian Pension Commission; "DVA" for Department of Veterans' Affairs; "WCB" for Workmen's Compensation Board

alienation, 6-7, 75
Alpine Club of Canada (ACC), 79, 91
antimodernism, 7, 13, 14-15, 18, 19, 157
anxiety
  antimodernist, 18-19
  culture of, 142
  gender, 4
  and modernism, 20, 141
  and modernist project, 15
  nuclear, 141
  and technology, 141
  of Vancouverites, 15
automobile
  accidents (see traffic accidents)
  associations, 133-34
  and automophilia, 128-31
  and controversy, 128
  Corvair, 137, 143, 144-45
  critics of, 142
  critique of, 144-45
  driving, 127, 130, 138-40, 140-41, 144
  and gender, 130-31
  golden age of, 131, 191n8
  Highway Safety Program, 145
  and hot rodders, 142
  manufacturers, 130, 137, 143, 145
  Motor Vehicle Safety Act, 145
  North American, 144-45
  organizations, 129

  ownership, 132
  and radicalism, 141-50
  and risk taking, 142
  safety, 135-37, 135-40, 144, 145
  and suburbanization, 129
  as symbol of modernity, 128, 130
  and threatened manhood, 131

Barman, Jean, 10, 81
BC Mountaineer, 80, 86-87, 88, 91, 92
Beck, Ulrich, 177n15, 195n11
Bennett, W.A.C.
  and bridge collapse, 55, 65, 67
  and infrastructure development, 72, 81, 82, 129
  modernist project of, 10-11, 72
Berman, Marshall, 12, 18
Binkert, Paul, 92, 96
British Columbia
  BC Safety Council, 134
  car ownership, 128
  Department of Motor Vehicles, 137, 138
  economy, 45
  employment, 37
  Gaol Commission, 104
  and geographical isolation, 81
  and high modernist optimism, 72-73
  infrastructure development, 81
  Ministry of Highways, 10, 129

modernist project of, 9-11
postwar expansion, 57, 73, 82
workers' mortality, 57-58
British Columbia Automobile
   Association (BCAA), 129, 133,
   137
British Columbia Medical Association (BCMA), 134, 139, 144-45
British Columbia Mountaineering
   Club (BCMC)
   activities, 81, 84
   amateurism of, 85
   and civilization vs wilderness, 83-
      84
   and class, 80-81
   and control, 86
   and danger, 93-94
   establishment of, 79
   firsts, 84-85, 94
   and Goldilocks dilemma, 89
   grading system of, 96
   and manly modernism, 23
   membership of, 80-81, 89-90,
      181nn12-13
   Mountain Access Committee, 87
   Mountain Rescue Group, 86, 91,
      93
   name, 181n8
   regulations of, 77, 87
   sexism of, 89-90, 92-93
   and trail building, 87
   view of highway expansion, 82-83
   See also mountaineering
Bryce, W.A., 125, 126, 149
bureaucracy
   consequences of, 155, 158
   of CPC, 40-41
   of DVA, 40-41, 48-49
   and high modernism, 40
   and modernist project, 6
   problems of, 22
   of psychiatric expertise, 142
   and threatened man, 40
   and veterans, 40-41, 49, 50-51
   of Workmen's Compensation
      Board (WCB), 59
   and workplace safety, 13
   See also experts, bureaucrats

bureaucratic
   desires, 138
   expertise, 160
   logic, 22
   mentality, 40, 41
   practice, 148
   processes, 7
   rationality, 5, 64
   state, 22, 146
   suburban life, 23, 144
   unionism, 73
   world, 131

Campbell, Ernest A., 104, 105, 120
Canadian Combat Veterans' Association (CCVA), 31, 32, 35
Canadian Highway Safety Conference (CHSC), 133
Canadian Highway Safety Council,
   125, 136
Canadian Motorist, 134, 141, 145
Canadian Pension Commission
   (CPC), 31-33, 36, 40-41
Canadian Psychological Association,
   47, 104
capitalism
   and alienation, 6
   consumer, 168n47
   and contract-based relations, 59
   corporate, 7
   effects of, 6
   industrial, 9, 59
   liberal, 42, 59
   liberal bias of, 7
   mercantile, 180n1
   and the reasonable man, 190n4
   and the state, 10
   welfare, 60, 64
   worldwide, 12
car accidents. *See* traffic accidents
Carey, James, 114-15
Casagrande, Gino, 108, 186n13
Cathcart, J.P.S., 117, 119, 122
Christie, Nancy, 29-30, 37
citizenship
   benefits of, 7
   disciplined, 91, 140
   entitlement of, 43

gendered nature of, 39
male, 42
military, 39, 42
privileged, 39
traits of, 17
veterans', 39
women's, 36
class
and alienation, 6
antagonism, 58
and automobile ownership, 132
conflict, 59
and expertise, 24
and gender, 190n4
and income gap, 73
inequalities, 154
and liberal self-sufficiency, 45
and modernist project, 74
and mountaineering, 77, 80-81,
181nn12-13
and power, 39
and radicalism, 58
and risk, 74, 77
and status, 63
Cold War, 9, 73, 141
commutation, 102-3, 106, 112-13,
115, 119-20, 122
control
of the automobile, 135
of emotions, 62
of environment, 12, 153
of natural world, 1, 2
of the self, 153
of technology, 134
Cooperative Commonwealth
Federation (CCF), 26, 43, 65
counterculture, 142, 146, 157
criminal justice system
capital cases, 102-23
and the death penalty, 120-23, 121
and mental health, 103-6
and mental health experts, 104-23
and newspaper coverage, 115-16
postwar initiatives of, 103-9
and reformers, 111
and rehabilitation, 105-6
Remissions Office, 106, 117, 119,
120, 122, 189n70

Royal Commission on the Law
Relating to Sexual Psychopaths, 116
Royal Commission on the Penal
System of Canada, 103-4
See also murderers
culture
of anxiety, 142
and beliefs, 56
car, 24, 141-50
of control, 14
of domestic goods, 128
of planning, 8
popular, 5, 20, 141-42
postwar, 34
of restraint, 155
youth, 142-43, 157

Department of Veterans' Affairs
(DVA), 22, 31-33, 40-41, 46-47
development
consequences of, 86, 157
critics of, 14
economic, 10, 12, 22, 81, 108
and the environment, 86
expert-led, 146, 148
industrial, 58
infrastructure, 56, 65, 81-82, 86
and male workers, 74, 158
scientific, 3
technological, 10
urban, 10, 129, 146-47
See also modernist project
discipline
and automobile safety, 137
consequences of, 149
and drinking cycle, 139-40
and driving, 140-41
and liberal individualism, 42-43
and manly modernism, 154
as preparedness, 91
of safety, 54-60
and the Self-Made Man, 19
and violence, 115
and workplace accidents, 56
and workplace safety, 60, 63
discourse
of deservedness, 30

gendered, 74-75
of manly heroism, 39
of militaristic nationalism, 38
psychological, 110, 113-14, 121
public, 116
of risk management, 24
on threatened manhood, 21
of traffic safety, 140-41
See also language
Dominion Bridge, 60, 63, 65, 66, 69,
    70, 71
Ducharme, Frederick Roger, 116-18,
    122, 186n13

Ehrenreich, Barbara, 155, 156
England, Robert, 38, 42-43
entitlement
    and bureaucracy, 39-42
    vs charity, 36
    and citizenship, 43
    gendered nature of, 30-31, 51
    hierarchy of, 30
    idealization of, 38
    and manliness, 22, 33, 36, 37, 38,
        40, 50
    paradox of, 39-40
    and psychiatrists, 46, 50
    rights-based, 37
    and risk, 35-36
    and the threatened man, 39-49
    of veterans, 15, 22, 30-51
ethnicity. *See* race
expertise
    of engineers, 66, 67-68
    and excitement, 88-99
    interfering, 123
    of ironworkers, 68
    of psychiatrists, 48-49
    and rationality, 90-91
    safety, 141
    socially constructed nature of, 68
    technological, 134
experts
    bureaucrats, 77, 122, 152
        at City Hall, 146-47
        contempt for, 146
        government, 40
        middle-class, 39
        rebellion against, 157

and criminal justice system, 23-24
and death penalty debate, 121
and development, 146
and family life, 151-52
and governance, 148
and masculinity, 102
medical, 24
mental health
    and behavioural explanations,
        104, 108-9
    and capital cases, 106
    and environmental explana-
        tions, 109-10
    focus of, 109
    language of, 23
    privileged status of, 48-49
    professionalization of, 104-5,
        122
    respect for, 106-7
    and veterans' entitlement, 45-
        49, 122-23
middle-class men as, 23-24
on murder, 107-8
and postwar generations, 3
and rational investigation, 70
respect for, 106-7
safety, 132, 141
and safety consensus, 145
and truth, 75
types of, 3
urban planners, 9

Faludi, Susan, 19-20, 168n47
family
    breadwinner-homemaker, 5, 51, 62
    and breadwinning, 33-34, 37
    and car culture, 128, 129, 130
    and discipline, 91
    idealized, 4
    and male authority, 151, 152
    men and, 156
    and middle-class men, 89
    and murderers, 108-9
    and patriarchal control, 2
    and psychological discourse, 110-
        13, 121
    and violence, 108
Farris, John Jr., 66, 67, 68
Fisher, Ferne Blanche, 116-18

Fordist compromise. *See* postwar,
  compromise
Freud, Sigmund (Freudian), 20, 29,
  47, 174n52, 184n59

Gaglardi, Philip, 10, 55, 145
gender
  and antimodernist fears, 18-19
  anxiety, 4, 18-19
  and class, 190n4
  contradictions of, 88-89
  definition of, 15-17
  different notions of, 160-61
  and disaster, 61
  distinctions, 4-5
  divisions, 4, 89-90, 183n46
  and driving, 127
  and economics, 37
  and entitlement, 30
  history, 17, 159, 167n42
  ideals, 5, 64
  medicalization of, 103
  of men, 17-18
  politics of, 16
  and politics of masculinity, 15-21
  and rationality, 2-3
  relations, 3-4, 149
  and risk, 54
  and sex-role theory, 195n3
  social construction of, 16-17,
    195n3
  and social organization, 16
  and state assistance, 36
  threat, 74
  and traffic safety discourse, 140-41
General Motors, 128, 143, 144
Gordon, Joseph, 114-15
Graham, Roger, 110-11
Greater Vancouver. *See* Vancouver
Grouse Mountain, 84, 88

Haig-Brown, Roderick, 14-15, 142
Henderson, Bill, 113-14
high modernism
  authoritarianism of, 147
  automobile-centred, 127
  bureaucracy of, 40-42, 49
  and discipline, 42-43
  as dominant ideology, 9

and expertise, 45-49
and infrastructure development,
  56
optimism of, 60
response to, 14-15
and workers, 1
highway accidents. *See* traffic
  accidents
Hobsbawm, Eric, 53, 174n1

ideal
  breadwinner, 62
  breadwinner/homemaker, 5
  disciplined modern man, 108-9
  driver, 126-27
  family, 4-5
  hyper-rational individual, 149
  liberal self-sufficiency, 43-44
  manly modern, 50, 78
  of masculinity, 43
  middle-class male, 127
  of postwar manhood, 116
  of the reasonable man, 5, 126, 127,
    157
  soldier, 42-43
identity
  categories of, 15-16
  gendered, 17, 24, 160
  masculine, 16, 17, 79, 98, 160
  and security, 29
  of veterans, 39
  and work, 67
ideology
  and gender, 127
  of high modernism, 9, 56
  of male breadwinning, 29
  of manly modernism
    and Kirchner commission, 22
    and men's privilege, 154
    and modern subjectivity, 135
    postwar, 17, 71
    and risk management, 24-26
    and risk taking, 61
    as social glue, 56
  of modernist project, 74
  of raw growth, 10
ironworkers, 54-55, 66, 68, 70, 72-74
Ironworkers' Local 97, 66-67, 69-70,
    72, 179nn48-49

Jacobs, Jane, 24, 127, 147, 148, 157
Jervis, John, 12, 13

Kafer, Esther, 90, 183n32
Keynesian economic policy, 3, 44
Kimmel, Michael, 19, 20, 89, 97,
    164n11
Kirchner, Walter H., 31-33, 40-41, 48
    See also Royal Commission to
    Investigate Complaints Made
    by Walter H. Kirchner;
    veterans

language
    of gendered citizenship, 39, 91
    of gendered crisis, 62
    of immaturity, 119
    of male deviance, 158
    of male entitlement, 31
    of masculinity, 149, 160
    of maturity, 108
    medicalized, 119
    of mental health experts, 23,
        106-7, 109, 117
    of modern manliness, 98
    of modernity, 92
    of participatory democracy, 148
    of partnership, 59, 63
    of postwar life, 154
    of psychiatrists, 118, 121, 122-23
    of public discourse, 116
    racialized, 119
    of risk management, 127
    of self-discipline, 154
    of sexuality, 116
    See also discourse
Lasserre, Fred, 11, 98
Lett, Sherwood, 66, 67, 68, 70,
    178n34
liberal
    bias, 7
    capitalism, 42
    everyman, 40, 45
    individualism, 42-43
    "new liberalism," 9
    self-sufficiency, 44-45
    values, 9, 42, 44
Liberal government, 32-33, 43

Mackenzie King, William Lyon,
    32-33, 34-35
manhood
    and alcohol, 139
    and breadwinning, 148
    medicalization of, 106-23
    and problem drivers, 140
    racialized, 119
    and responsibility, 138
    and suburban life, 78, 144
manliness, 112, 121, 144
manly modern(ism)
    ambiguities of, 154-56
    and American Cool, 65
    and anxiety, 142
    consequences of, 5
    contradictions of, 26, 74-75, 78
    critique of, 141-50
    defined, 1-7
    gendered authority of, 151-53, 157
    in hindsight, 151-61
    inequalities of, 154
    logic of, 65
    and men's privilege, 154
    and safe driving, 127
    and self-discipline, 60
    turn away from, 160
    and voice of authority, 151-52
    working-class, 64, 69
Manson, A.M. (Justice), 71, 72, 106-7,
    110, 114, 118
Marsh, Leonard, 147, 148
masculinity
    and aggressiveness, 114-15
    and authority, 74
    and breadwinner norm, 112-13
    and character, 111
    and competitiveness, 79
    debates about, 160
    and discipline, 43, 91, 109, 114
    dominant features of, 33
    double nature of, 7, 20-21
    and entitlement, 36, 50
    and expertise, 92, 152
    heroic, 61
    as heterosexual, 116
    and historical crisis, 169n48
    historical narratives of, 17-19

idealized, 128
ideals of, 33-34, 121, 127
medicalization of, 23-24, 102, 119-
 20
and men's movement, 159
and men's violence, 17
and military service, 33-34
and modernist project, 131
and modernist traits, 3
and modernity, 5, 19
and murderers, 121
and the nation, 30
and postwar reconstruction, 50-51
of risk, 54, 56
and risk management, 102
and sacrifice, 36
threatened, 40-42, 160
and violence, 114
and war, 171n13
and wilderness, 82
working-class, 64-65
See also manhood; manliness;
 rationality
Matthews, Charles, 118-20, 122,
 186n13, 189n70
McKenna, Joseph, 107-8, 186n13
McKinley Driving School, 133, 137
Medos, Harry, 111, 113-14
mental illness
 behavioural explanations, 104,
  108-9
 and capital cases, 106, 117
 classification of, 105
 environmental explanations, 109-
  10, 122
 and Freudian psychoanalysis, 47
 and manliness, 48, 112
 and psychiatric profession, 105
 treatment of, 105
 wartime, 46-48, 122-23
 See also experts, mental health;
  murderers
Minshall, Harold, 67, 69-70, 77
modern
 age, 125, 126
 critique of, 144
 defining, 166n34
 dilemmas, 97

experience, 13-14, 18
explanations of murder, 107
subjectivity, 135
technological determinism, 126
modernism/modernity
 anxiety about, 142
 apex of, 3
 attitudes toward, 148
 consequences of, 14, 156
 contradictions of, 12, 25, 94-95
 and control, 13
 dark potential of, 61
 definitions of, 12-13, 164n16
 and democracy, 146-47
 and discipline, 54-60
 double nature of, 7-15, 98
 downside of, 149
 and experts, 3
 and gender, 15, 92
 ghosts of, 14
 irony of, 15
 key tensions of, 98
 meaning, 18
 vs postmodernity, 159, 195n11
 and privilege, 3
 promise of, 55
 theoretical underpinnings of,
  11-12
 and vigilance, 134
 See also high modernism
modernist project
 and anxiety, 141
 and control, 153-54
 and counterculture, 142
 criticism of, 14-15, 128
 dynamics of, 12-13
 gendered support for, 153-54
 masculinity of, 61
 and middle-class men, 77-78
 negative attributes of, 143
 one-dimensionality of, 13
 vs postmodernism, 159
 rebellion against, 142-43
 responses to, 13-14
 and risk, 12-13
 task of, 51
 tensions within, 159
 values of, 157

and workplace deaths, 58
See also development;
    suburbanization; urban
    planning
modernization
    and bridge building, 56-57
    in British Columbia, 10, 22, 57
    critics of, 143
    as dominant concern, 8
    economic, 22
    manhood's, 18
    and masculinity, 156
    and middle class, 23
    risks of, 53, 70
Mount McKinley expedition, 92, 94
Mount Seymour, 82, 84, 86
mountaineering
    and civilization vs wilderness, 81-
        88
    and control, 96
    dilemma of, 85-86
    etiquette, 87
    and gender, 89-90
    and Goldilocks dilemma, 89, 97
    and imperial ambitions, 84-85
    importance of, 95
    and leadership, 88
    as military undertaking, 91
    as modern activity, 180n1
    and naming, 85
    organizations, 79-80
    and risk management, 77, 88, 91-
        92
    and suburban life, 78, 96
    and wilderness protection, 86
    wilderness vs specialized, 97
    See also British Columbia Moun-
        taineering Club (BCMC)
murderers
    as aggressive psychopaths, 109
    and commutation, 102, 112
    and experts, 102, 105, 108, 111,
        112, 122
    family life of, 110-11
    gendered ideology of, 24
    and manhood, 23, 108
    and manliness, 114, 115, 121
    and race, 119
    and rehabilitation, 105

    and risk management, 23
    sexuality of, 116-18
    work records of, 112-13

Nader, Ralph
    on automobile technology, 144,
        145
    and car culture, 157
    Corvair exposé, 137, 143-44
    and experts, 148
    influence of, 24, 143-44
    on traffic-safety approach, 127
    and US Senate subcommittee,
        194n47
nationalism, 37, 38, 79-80
Nye, David, 57, 175n7

Oakalla Prison Farm, 104, 105, 109
Organization Man, 5-6, 89, 96, 148
Owram, Doug, 29, 169n2, 184n51

Pacific Great Eastern Railway, 10, 81
Painters' Local 98, 66
Pendakur, Setty, 146, 148
Pilkington, R.A.M., 84, 85, 93
postwar
    anxieties, 157-58
    boom, 58
    cars, 130
    compromise, 73
    conservatism, 29
    criminal justice system, 103-4
    culture, 108
    economic expansion, 53, 73
    experts, 152
    family life, 129-30
    gender relations, 95-96
    "good life," 53, 82
    history, 29
    ideals, 109
    manhood, 61, 121-22
    mother-bashing, 110
    mythology, 22-23
    New Woman, 18
    optimism, 128
    popular culture, 34
    psychological discourse, 113-14
    psychology, 104-5
    safety debate, 138

urbanization, 8
power
 of the automobile, 130
 of manly modernism, 153-54
 and masculinity, 89
 masculinity as, 17
 of mass consumer culture, 8
 and mountaineering, 79
 of psychology, 101
 relations, 16-17
Pratley, J.B., 66, 178n34
progress
 and automobiles, 128, 130-31, 138
 belief in, 98, 159
 and bridge building, 57, 71, 72
 double-edged, 15
 gendered nature of, 54
 and highway development, 84
 and manly modernism, 157
 and men, 1-2
 modern, 1-2, 6
 and modernist project, 12-13
 mythology of, 22, 23, 97
 and risk, 53
 and veterans, 34
 and violence, 56
propaganda, 34, 42-43, 44
psychiatrists. *See* experts, mental
  health
psychologists. *See* experts, mental
  health

race
 and alienation, 6-7
 and income, 73
 and manhood, 33
 and modernity, 164n16
 and primitivism, 119
 and racist assumptions, 118-19
 and sexuality, 189n70
rationality
 and capital punishment, 121
 and discipline, 60
 and driving, 135, 137-38
 vs emotionalism, 65-66, 145
 of mountaineering, 91-92
 and risk management, 64-73
 valorization of, 102
 of WCB experts, 64

regulation
 and bureaucracy, 40
 of climbers, 87
 consequences of, 155
 of drivers, 134, 136, 138
 of the environment, 78-79, 86
 of men, 7, 156, 158
 of social life, 15, 51
 of violence, 33
 of workers, 60, 63-64, 72, 74
Richmond, R.G.E., 104, 109, 111, 120
rights, 22, 33, 36, 37, 59
risk
 calculated, 70
 vs danger, 1, 13, 94
 and disaster, 53
 and entitlement, 35-36
 and gender, 97-98
 and male authority, 74
 as a managerial process, 59
 and men's violence, 102
 and middle-class men, 95
 military, 33
 as positive, 180n1
 and reason, 92
 technological, 137
 and traffic accidents, 126
 and wages, 72
risk management
 and alcohol, 139
 and automobiles, 131-41
 and balance, 141
 and discipline, 59-60
 discourse of, 24
 and expertise, 59
 and modernist planning, 13
 and risk taking, 23
 social significance of, 3
 technocratic, 127
 and traffic accidents, 132
Royal Commission on Second
  Narrows bridge collapse
 and engineers, 66
 findings, 70-71
 government's goal, 170n11
 and labour organizations, 66
 proceedings, 67-70
 questioning of engineers, 67-68
 questioning of workers, 67

role of engineers, 67
role of workers, 67
and social mixing, 68
See also Second Narrows Bridge,
  collapse
Royal Commission to Investigate
  Complaints Made by Walter
  H. Kirchner
and entitlement, 30-31
establishment of, 31-33
findings of, 50
legacy of, 49-51
and the manly modern, 22
proceedings of, 39-49
vitriol of, 47-48
See also veterans

sacrifice
and entitlement, 21, 30, 38
heroic, 61
hierarchy of, 30
and manhood, 61-64
of nonwhite men, 33
and pension claims, 35
and rationality, 65
and Veterans Charter, 21
work as, 63
of workers, 63
safety
advocates, 134
and automobile makers, 143-44
vs compensation, 179n49
debate, 138-40
and disciplined character, 126
and education, 133, 137-38
establishment, 143
experts, 125-26
features, 136
inspection, 136
and risk management, 92
standards, 192n24
and the "Three Es," 135-40
workplace, 63-64
Scott, James, 12, 147
Second Narrows Bridge
collapse, 22, 53, 61-64 (*see also*
  Royal Commission on Second
  Narrows bridge collapse)

deaths, 61, 69, 178n35, 179n48
enquiry into, 66-73
explanation of, 69
narrative of, 54-56
response to, 54
responsibility for, 69-70
firsts, 57
and prosperity, 72
and Workmen's Compensation
  Board (WCB), 58
worksite, 63
Shaughnessy Hospital, 32, 48
Social Credit government, 57, 129
Social Credit Party, 10-11, 81
soldiers
and conscription, 34-35
and entitlement, 30, 38-39
and gender, 21, 30, 34-35
honour of, 35
idealization of, 38, 42-43
mental illness of, 46-47
and National Resources Mobilization Act (NRMA), 35
and sacrifice, 38-39
Spock, Benjamin, 140-41, 193n42
state planning, 9, 51
Stearns, Peter, 65, 178n30
stoicism, 20, 39, 61, 64, 69, 71, 95
suburbanization, 57, 81, 82, 128, 129
See also urban planning

technological sublime, 57, 175n7
traffic accidents
acceptance of, 132-33
and alcohol, 139
and deaths, 131-32
as events, 132
and injuries, 144
and masculinity, 126
and modernism, 141
and politicians, 144
prevalence of, 131-32
public policy on, 138
and responsibility, 134, 143
role of drivers, 136
role of vehicle, 136
and traffic-safety discourse, 125,
  127

and US Senate Subcommittee,
194n47

urban planning
and activists, 146-47
alternative vision of, 147
automobile-centred, 127, 145-46
and counterculture, 146
gendered nature of, 147
and redevelopment, 146-47
See also development; suburbanization; Vancouver

values
of capitalism, 9
cultural, 130
of individual self-sufficiency,
43-45
laissez-innover, 128
of liberal individualism, 42-43
modernist, 2-3, 14
of "new liberalism," 9
patriarchal, 4
shift in, 155, 157
Vancouver
Board of Trade, 134
Chinatown, 127, 146, 148
City Council, 146
Council of Women, 113, 134
freeway plan, 24, 127, 146-47, 157,
194n55
Housing Research Committee, 148
infrastructure development, 56-57
mountaineering, 79-81
Non-Partisan Association (NPA),
146
Official Traffic Commission (OTC),
133, 135-36
in postwar era, 7-8
School of Architecture (UBC), 11,
98
suburbanization, 11, 129
traffic accidents, 131-32
Traffic and Safety Council (VTSC),
125, 133, 137, 141
urban renewal scheme, 148
Vancouver and District Labour
Council, 62

Vancouver–New Westminster
Building Trades Council, 66
Vancouver Province, 54, 61, 62, 65-66,
93, 115, 140
Vancouver Sun, 54, 55, 62, 93, 112,
128
veterans
complaints of, 31-32
deservedness of, 34
disabled, 44
entitlement, 32, 41, 51
and gender, 30, 33-39, 173n38
individual cases
John B., 37, 48, 49
John M., 41
John T., 36
Sholto M., 45
and pension policy, 46-47
and pensions vs treatment, 46-47
vs psychiatrists, 48, 49
and psycho-neurotic injuries, 46-47
Second World War vs Great War,
32
war veterans' allowance (WVA), 36
See also Canadian Pension
Commission (CPC); Royal
Commission to Investigate
Complaints Made by Walter
H. Kirchner; soldiers; Veterans
Charter
Veterans Charter, 21-22, 30, 32, 38,
43-45

Wallberg, Jocelyn, 118, 119, 189n70
welfare state
and assistance plans, 34
and fear of alternatives, 43
and Keynesian economics, 9
and modern masculinity, 40
and "new liberalism," 9
postwar, 30
and postwar reconstruction, 147-48
and veterans, 34, 50-51
Wilson, Fraser, 1, 2, 26
Winters, R.H., 32, 36
women
anxiety of, 19
as bad mother, 113

and cars, 130
cheap labour of, 18
and driving, 131, 137
and entitlement, 36
and gender, 15-16
and gender history, 159-60
and gender relations, 153-54, 157
and male breadwinning, 29
medicalization of, 103
and modernity, 2, 18
mountaineers, 89-90
and patriarchal family, 4-5
and suburbanization, 82
as threat, 74
and veterans, 30
workers, 4
Woodfield, Jim, 94, 95
Workmen's Compensation Board
    (WCB)

compensation schedules of, 59
context of, 59
creation of, 58
purpose of, 58
and regulation, 60
safety inspectors, 60
safety regulations, 63
and welfare capitalism, 60
and workplace violence, 56
workplace
danger, 179n49
deaths, 57-58, 176n1, 178n35,
    179n48 (*see also* deaths under
    Second Narrows Bridge,
    collapse)
discipline, 63
mortality, 57-58
safety, 58, 71-72, 177n18
violence, 56